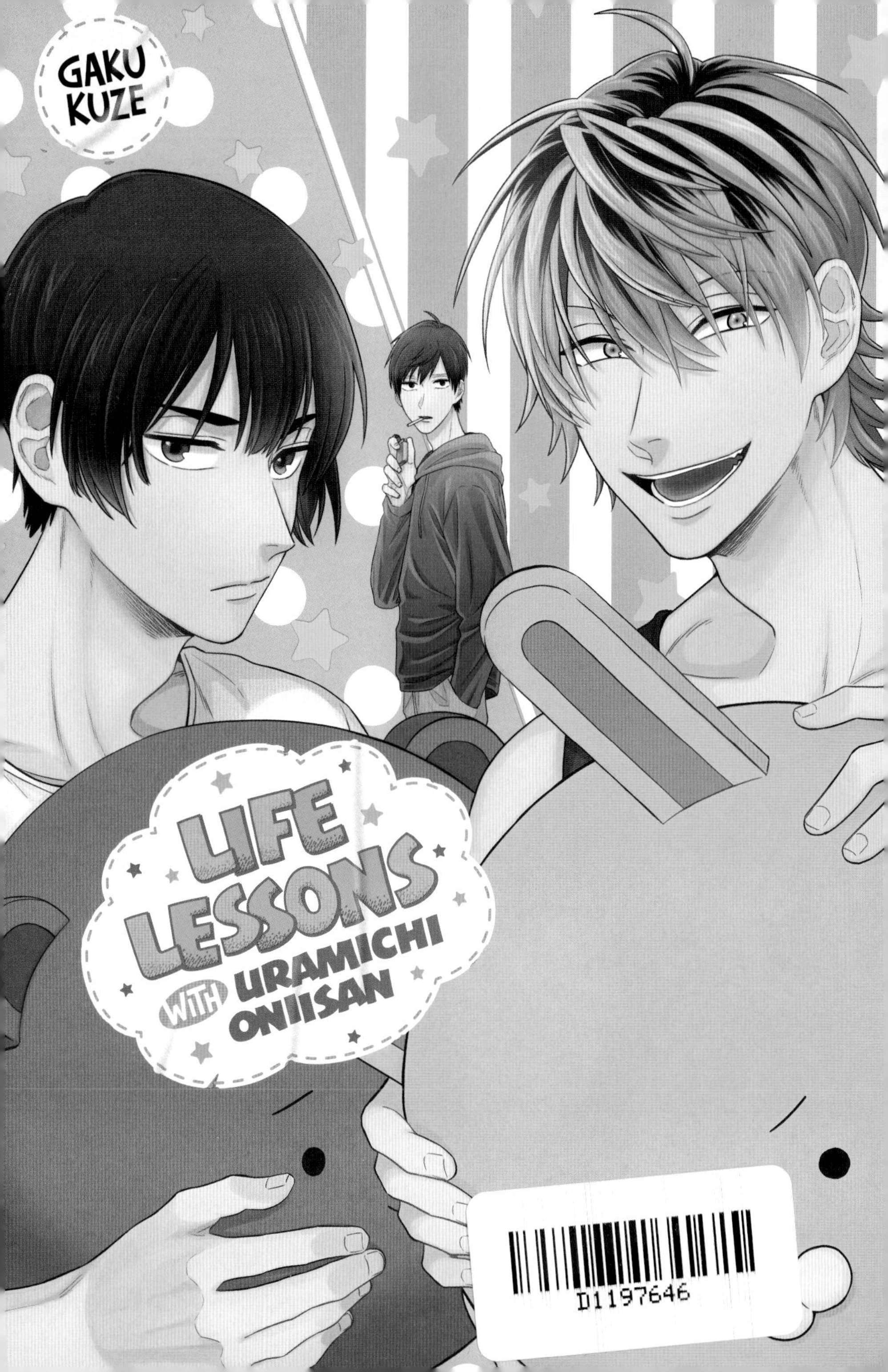
GAKU KUZE
LIFE LESSONS WITH URAMICHI ONIISAN

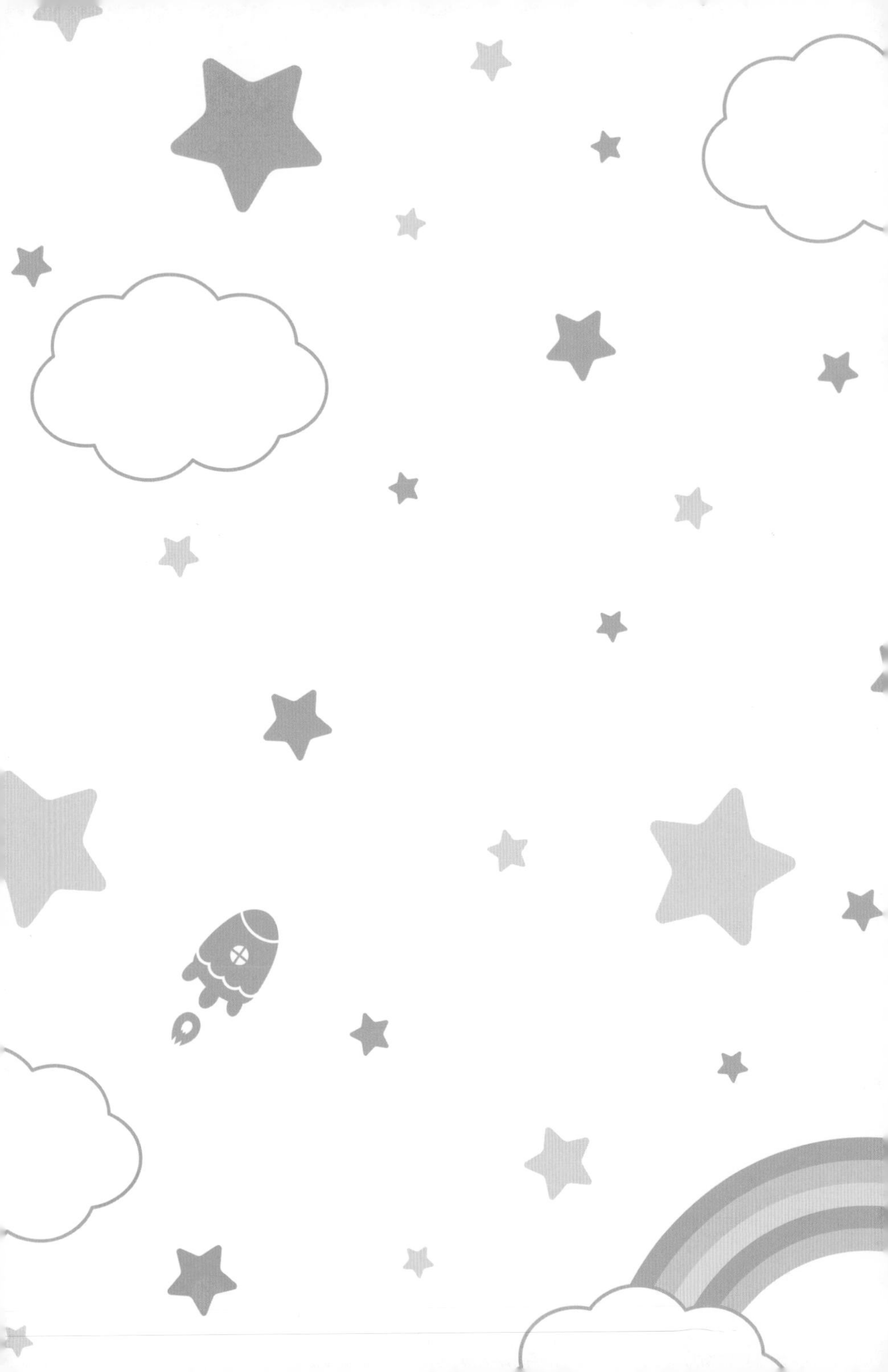

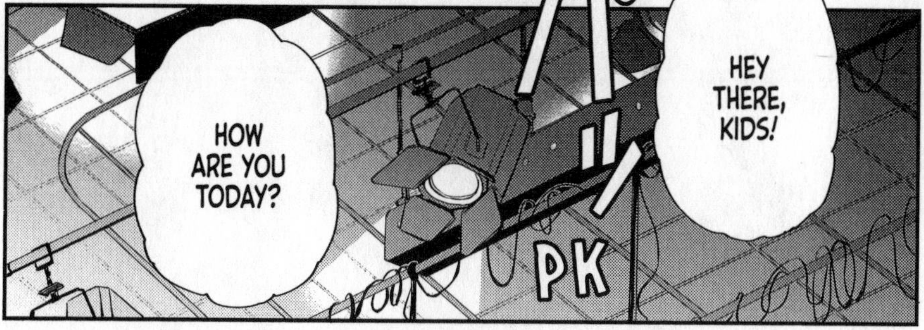
HEY THERE, KIDS!
PK
HOW ARE YOU TODAY?

URAMICHI OMOTA.
31 YEARS OLD.
SINGLE.

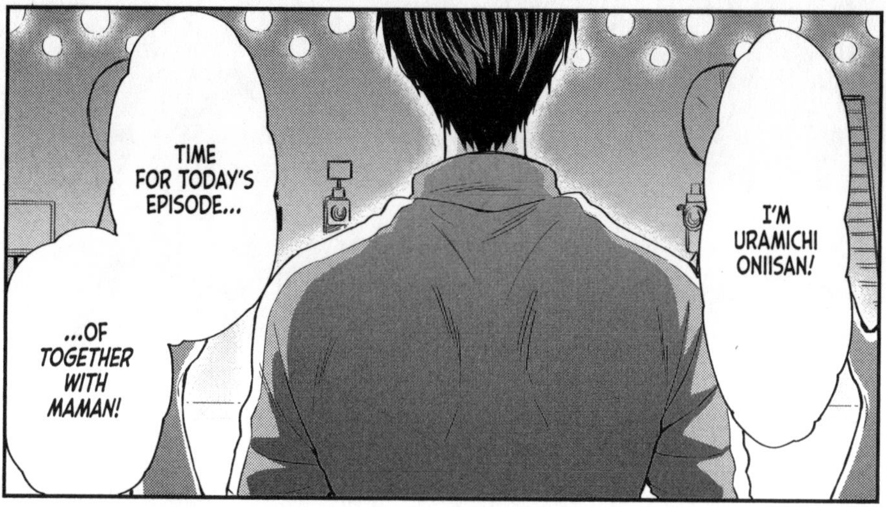
I'M URAMICHI ONIISAN!
TIME FOR TODAY'S EPISODE...
...OF TOGETHER WITH MAMAN!

FORMER PROFESSIONAL GYMNAST.

CORE STABILITY: ROCK-SOLID.

EMOTIONAL STABILITY: ALL BUT NONEXISTENT.

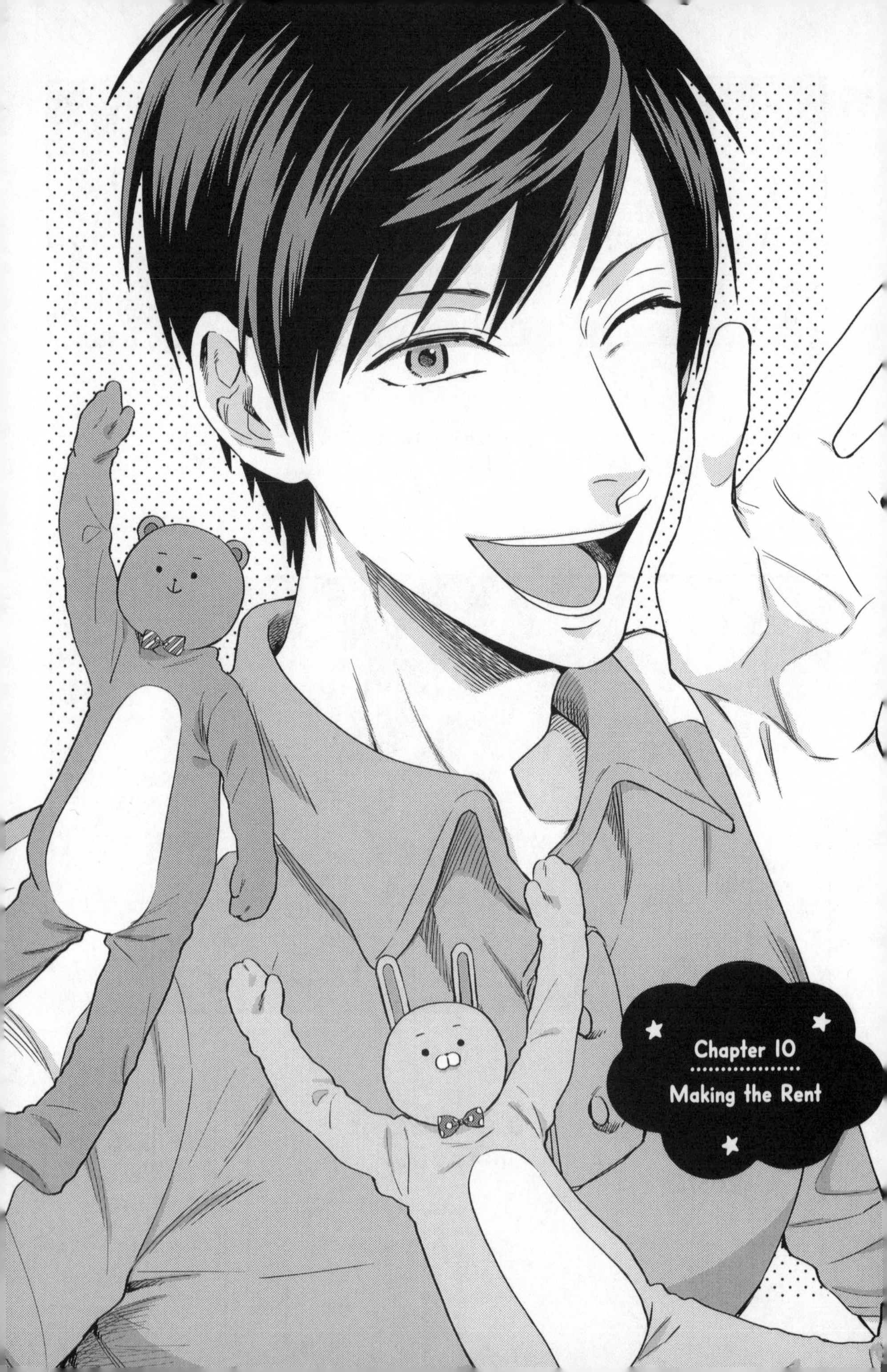
Chapter 10
Making the Rent

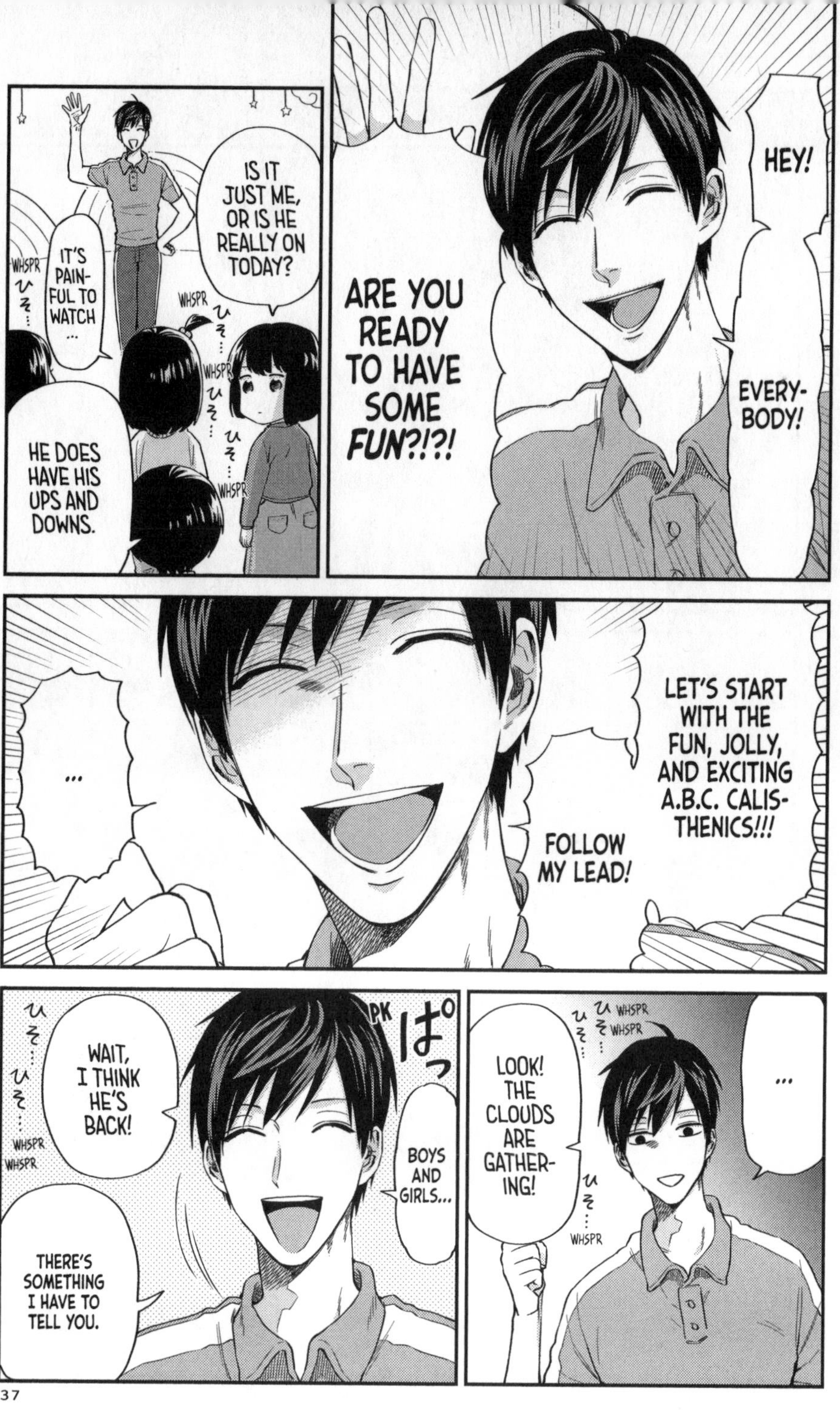
HEY!
EVERY-BODY!
ARE YOU READY TO HAVE SOME FUN?!?!
IS IT JUST ME, OR IS HE REALLY ON TODAY?
WHSPR ひそ…
WHSPR ひそ…
ひそ… WHSPR
IT'S PAIN-FUL TO WATCH…
WHSPR ひそ…
HE DOES HAVE HIS UPS AND DOWNS.
LET'S START WITH THE FUN, JOLLY, AND EXCITING A.B.C. CALIS-THENICS!!!
FOLLOW MY LEAD!
…
…
ひそ WHSPR ひそ WHSPR
LOOK! THE CLOUDS ARE GATHER-ING!
ひそ… WHSPR
PK ぱっ
BOYS AND GIRLS…
ひそ… ひそ… WHSPR WHSPR
WAIT, I THINK HE'S BACK!
THERE'S SOMETHING I HAVE TO TELL YOU.

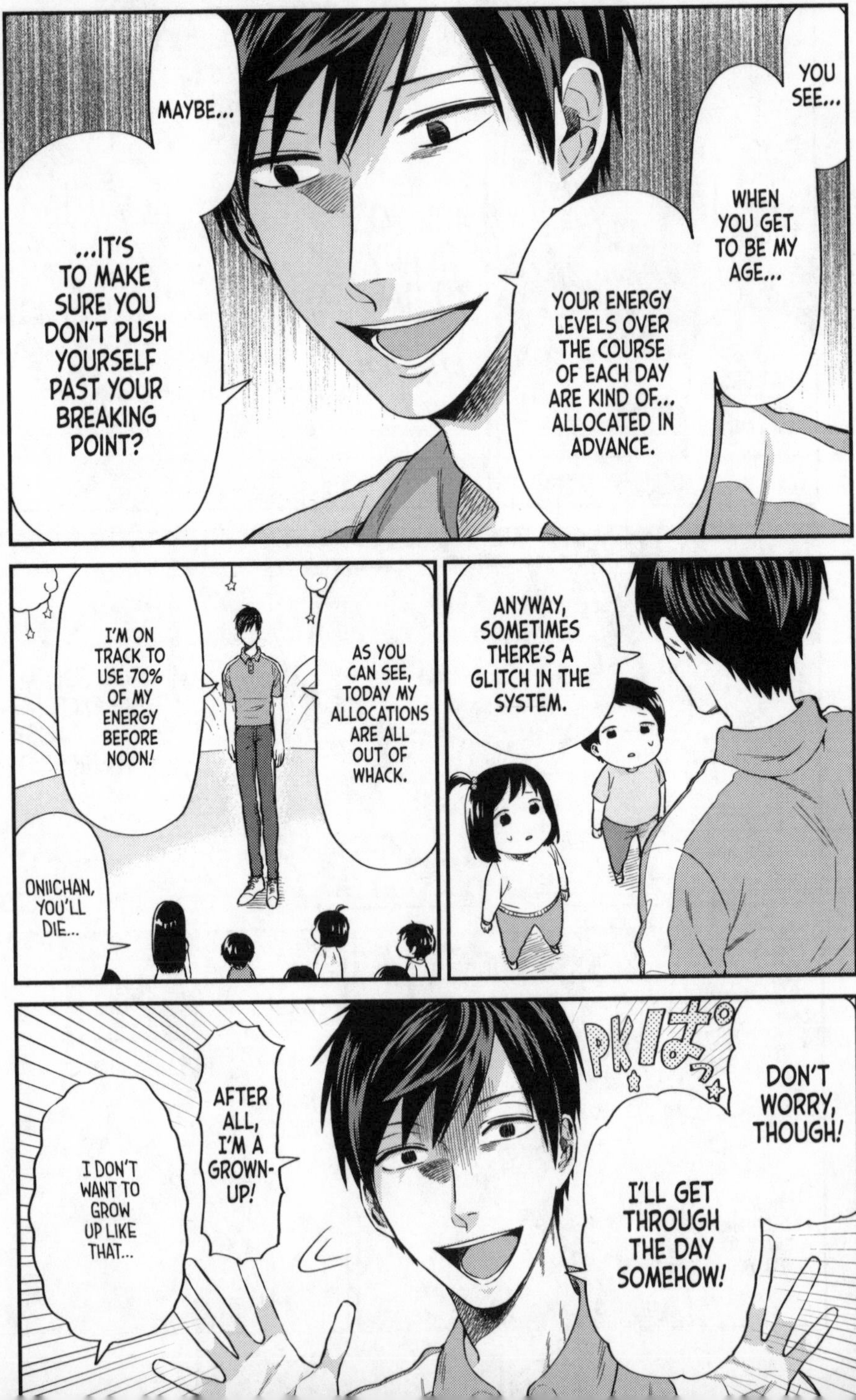
YOU SEE...
WHEN YOU GET TO BE MY AGE...
YOUR ENERGY LEVELS OVER THE COURSE OF EACH DAY ARE KIND OF... ALLOCATED IN ADVANCE.
MAYBE...
...IT'S TO MAKE SURE YOU DON'T PUSH YOURSELF PAST YOUR BREAKING POINT?
ANYWAY, SOMETIMES THERE'S A GLITCH IN THE SYSTEM.
AS YOU CAN SEE, TODAY MY ALLOCATIONS ARE ALL OUT OF WHACK.
I'M ON TRACK TO USE 70% OF MY ENERGY BEFORE NOON!
ONIICHAN, YOU'LL DIE...
DON'T WORRY, THOUGH!
PK はっ
I'LL GET THROUGH THE DAY SOMEHOW!
AFTER ALL, I'M A GROWN-UP!
I DON'T WANT TO GROW UP LIKE THAT...

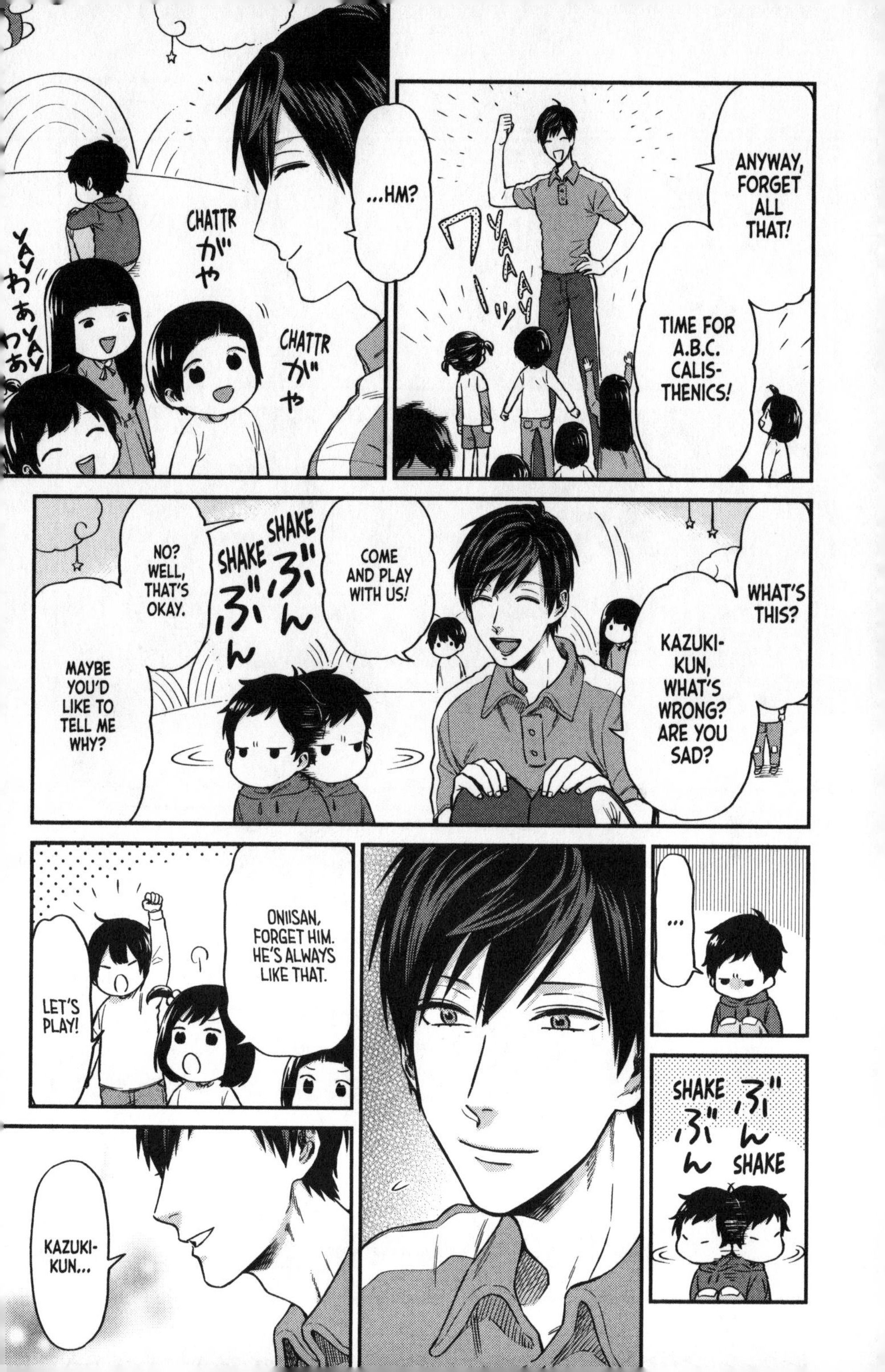
ANYWAY, FORGET ALL THAT!
TIME FOR A.B.C. CALIS-THENICS!
YAAAAY
ワァーッ
...HM?
CHATTR
がや
CHATTR
がや
YAY
わぁ
YAY
わぁ
WHAT'S THIS?
KAZUKI-KUN, WHAT'S WRONG? ARE YOU SAD?
COME AND PLAY WITH US!
SHAKE
ぶん
SHAKE
ぶん
NO? WELL, THAT'S OKAY.
MAYBE YOU'D LIKE TO TELL ME WHY?
...
SHAKE
ぶん
ぶん
SHAKE
ONIISAN, FORGET HIM. HE'S ALWAYS LIKE THAT.
LET'S PLAY!
KAZUKI-KUN...

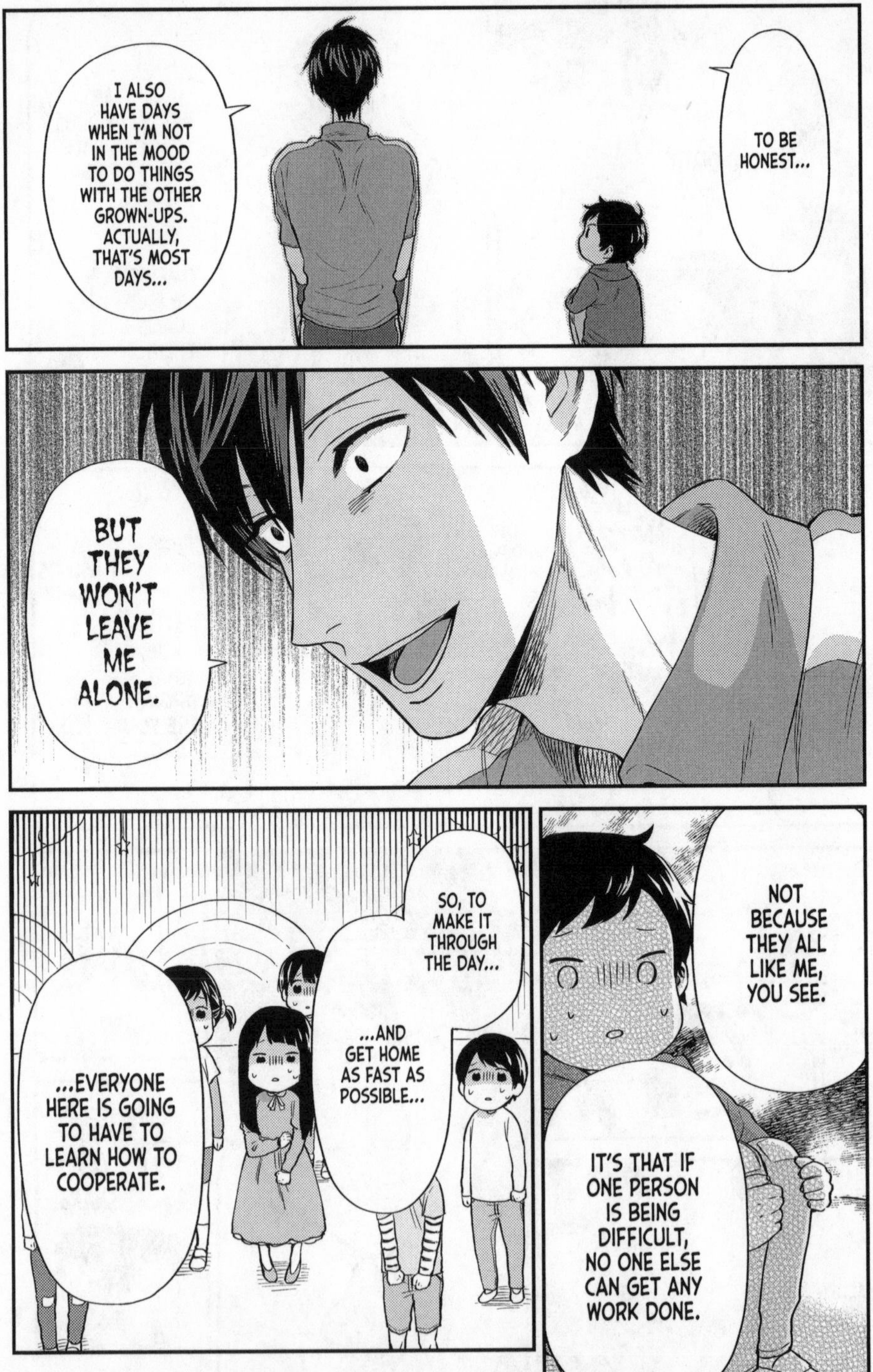
TO BE HONEST...
I ALSO HAVE DAYS WHEN I'M NOT IN THE MOOD TO DO THINGS WITH THE OTHER GROWN-UPS. ACTUALLY, THAT'S MOST DAYS...
BUT THEY WON'T LEAVE ME ALONE.
NOT BECAUSE THEY ALL LIKE ME, YOU SEE.
IT'S THAT IF ONE PERSON IS BEING DIFFICULT, NO ONE ELSE CAN GET ANY WORK DONE.
SO, TO MAKE IT THROUGH THE DAY...
...AND GET HOME AS FAST AS POSSIBLE...
...EVERYONE HERE IS GOING TO HAVE TO LEARN HOW TO COOPERATE.

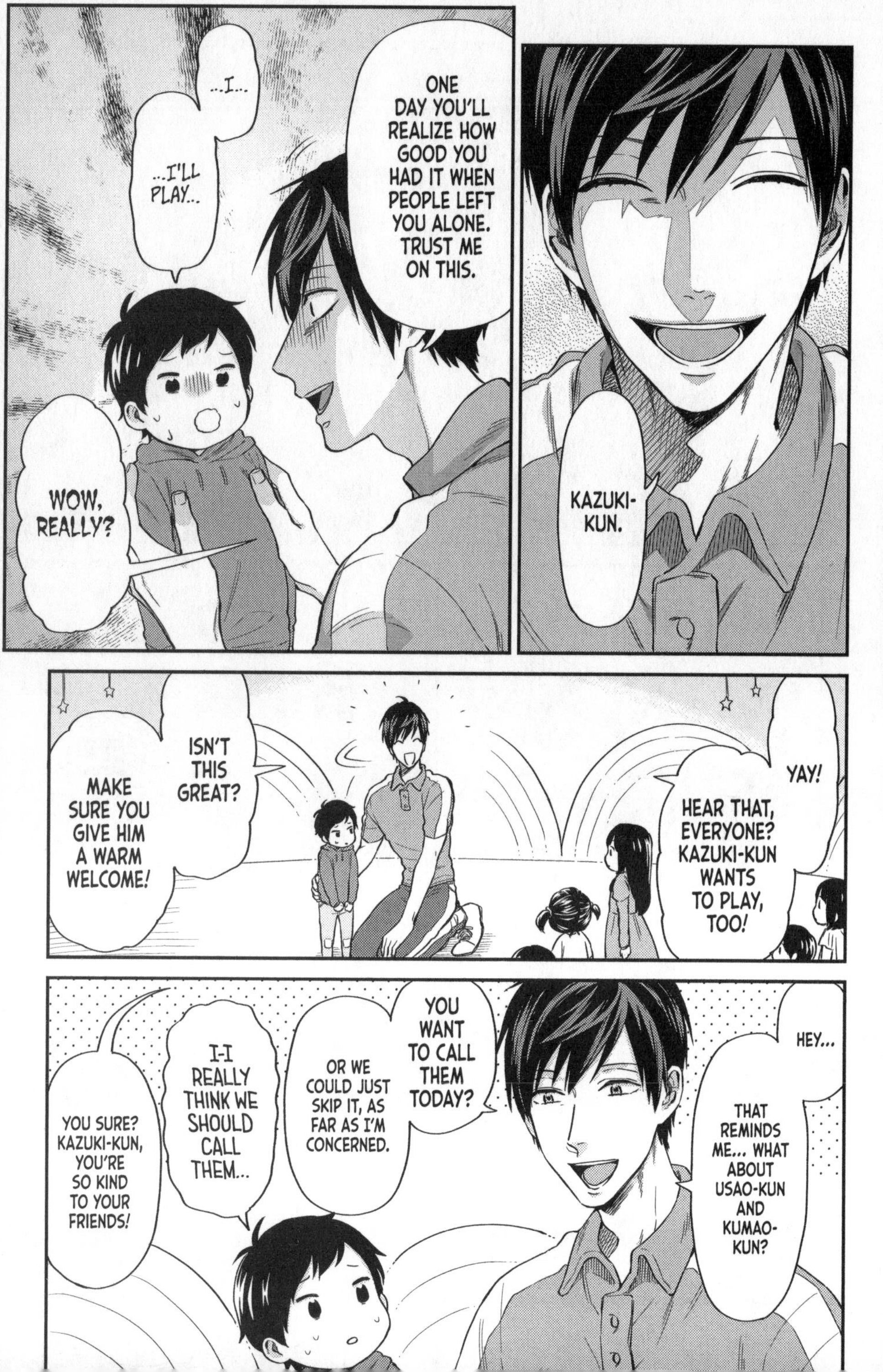
KAZUKI-KUN.
ONE DAY YOU'LL REALIZE HOW GOOD YOU HAD IT WHEN PEOPLE LEFT YOU ALONE. TRUST ME ON THIS.
...I...
...I'LL PLAY...
WOW, REALLY?
YAY!
HEAR THAT, EVERYONE? KAZUKI-KUN WANTS TO PLAY, TOO!
ISN'T THIS GREAT?
MAKE SURE YOU GIVE HIM A WARM WELCOME!
HEY...
THAT REMINDS ME... WHAT ABOUT USAO-KUN AND KUMAO-KUN?
YOU WANT TO CALL THEM TODAY?
OR WE COULD JUST SKIP IT, AS FAR AS I'M CONCERNED.
I-I REALLY THINK WE SHOULD CALL THEM...
YOU SURE? KAZUKI-KUN, YOU'RE SO KIND TO YOUR FRIENDS!

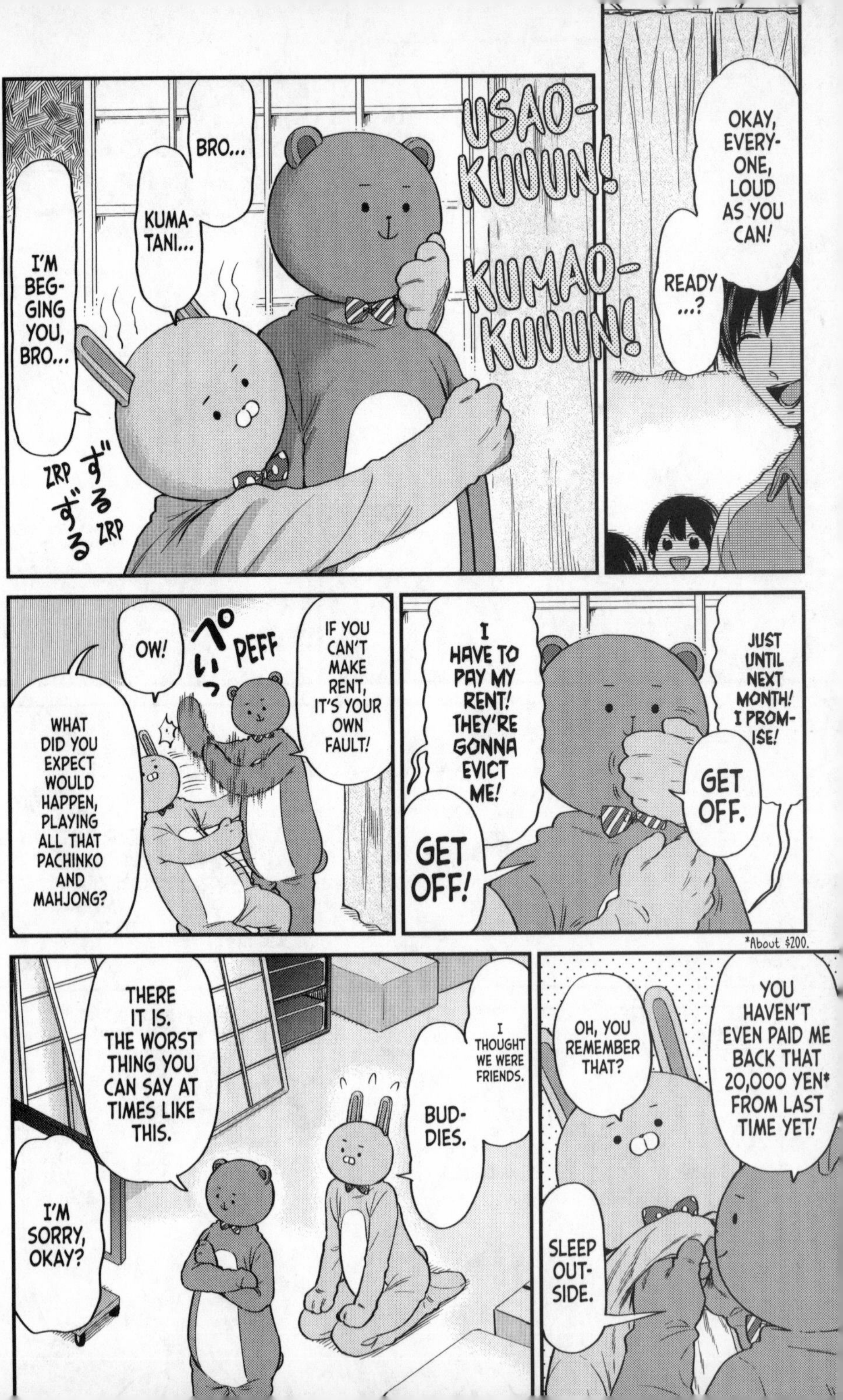
OKAY, EVERYONE, LOUD AS YOU CAN!
READY ...?
USAO-KUUUN!
KUMAO-KUUUN!
BRO...
KUMATANI...
I'M BEGGING YOU, BRO...
ZRP ずるずる ZRP
JUST UNTIL NEXT MONTH! I PROMISE!
GET OFF.
I HAVE TO PAY MY RENT! THEY'RE GONNA EVICT ME!
GET OFF!
IF YOU CAN'T MAKE RENT, IT'S YOUR OWN FAULT!
ぺいっ PEFF
OW!
WHAT DID YOU EXPECT WOULD HAPPEN, PLAYING ALL THAT PACHINKO AND MAHJONG?
YOU HAVEN'T EVEN PAID ME BACK THAT 20,000 YEN* FROM LAST TIME YET!
OH, YOU REMEMBER THAT?
SLEEP OUTSIDE.
I THOUGHT WE WERE FRIENDS.
BUDDIES.
THERE IT IS. THE WORST THING YOU CAN SAY AT TIMES LIKE THIS.
I'M SORRY, OKAY?

*About $200.

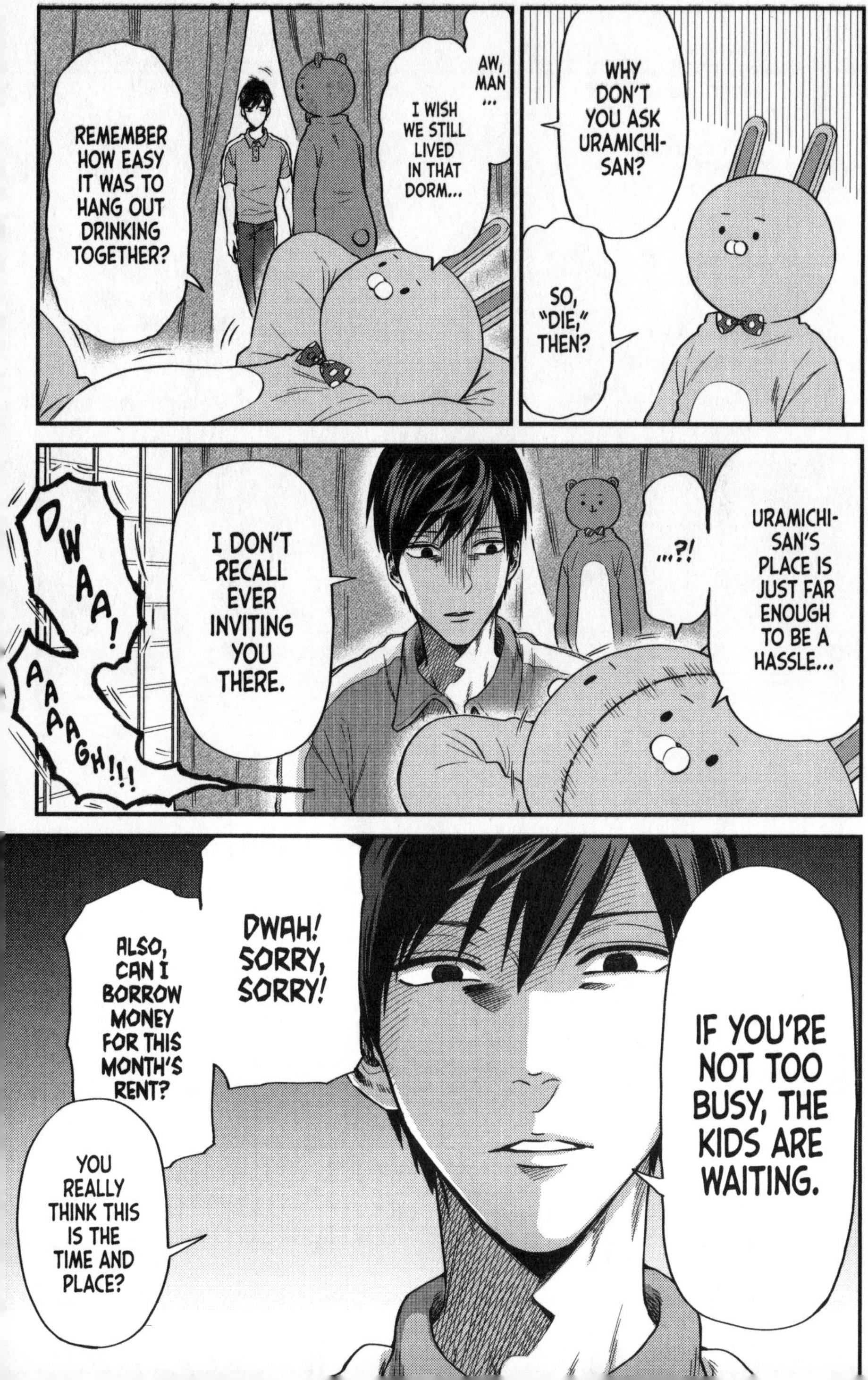
WHY DON'T YOU ASK URAMICHI-SAN?
SO, "DIE," THEN?
AW, MAN ...
I WISH WE STILL LIVED IN THAT DORM...
REMEMBER HOW EASY IT WAS TO HANG OUT DRINKING TOGETHER?
URAMICHI-SAN'S PLACE IS JUST FAR ENOUGH TO BE A HASSLE...
...?!
I DON'T RECALL EVER INVITING YOU THERE.
DWAA! AAAAGH!!!
IF YOU'RE NOT TOO BUSY, THE KIDS ARE WAITING.
DWAH! SORRY, SORRY!
ALSO, CAN I BORROW MONEY FOR THIS MONTH'S RENT?
YOU REALLY THINK THIS IS THE TIME AND PLACE?

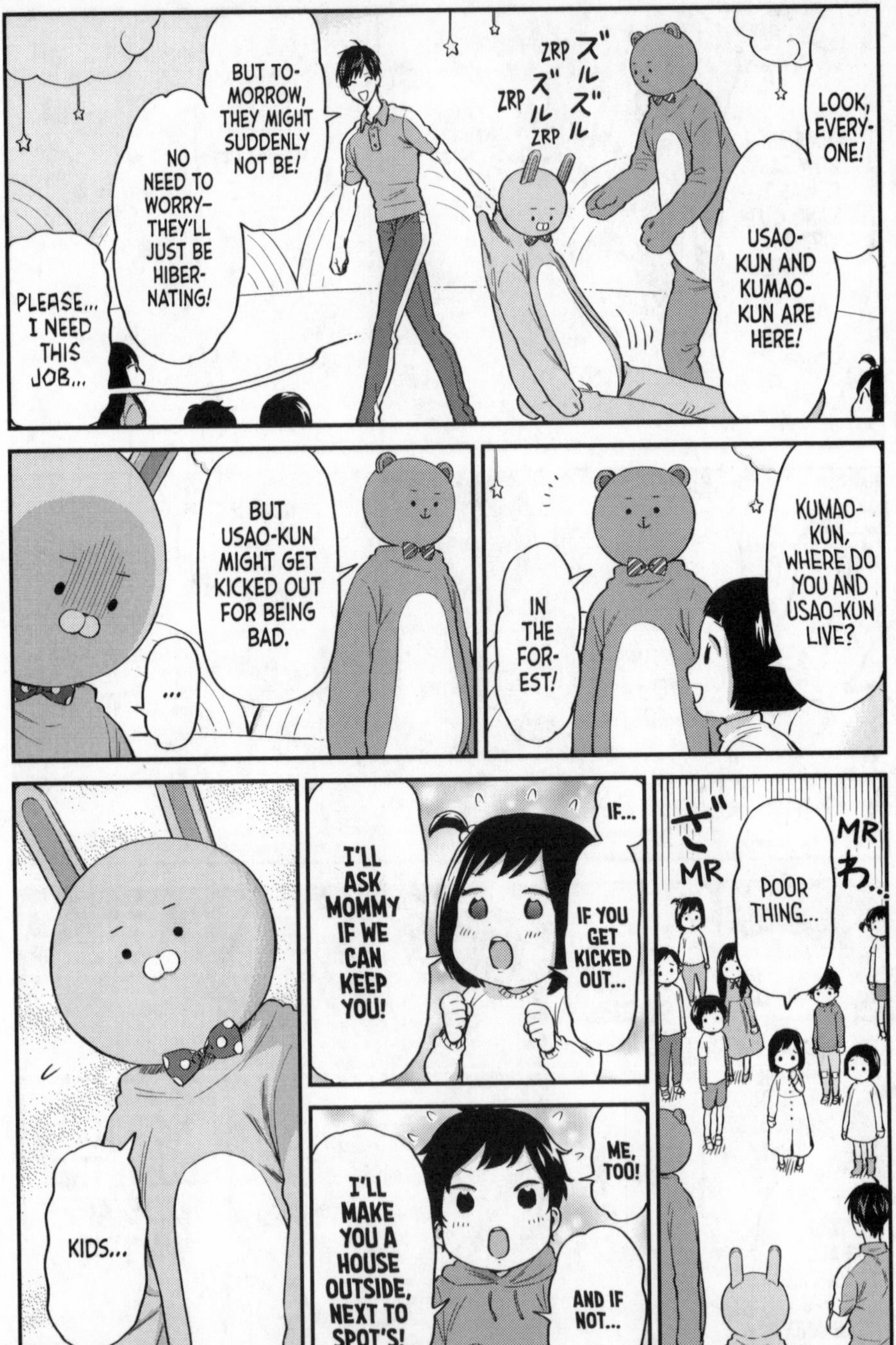
LOOK, EVERYONE!
USAO-KUN AND KUMAO-KUN ARE HERE!
ズルズル ZRP ZRP
ズルズル ZRP ZRP
BUT TO-MORROW, THEY MIGHT SUDDENLY NOT BE!
NO NEED TO WORRY—THEY'LL JUST BE HIBER-NATING!
PLEASE... I NEED THIS JOB...
KUMAO-KUN, WHERE DO YOU AND USAO-KUN LIVE?
IN THE FOR-EST!
BUT USAO-KUN MIGHT GET KICKED OUT FOR BEING BAD.
...
ざわ MR MR
POOR THING...
IF...
IF YOU GET KICKED OUT...
I'LL ASK MOMMY IF WE CAN KEEP YOU!
ME, TOO!
AND IF NOT...
I'LL MAKE YOU A HOUSE OUTSIDE, NEXT TO SPOT'S!
KIDS...

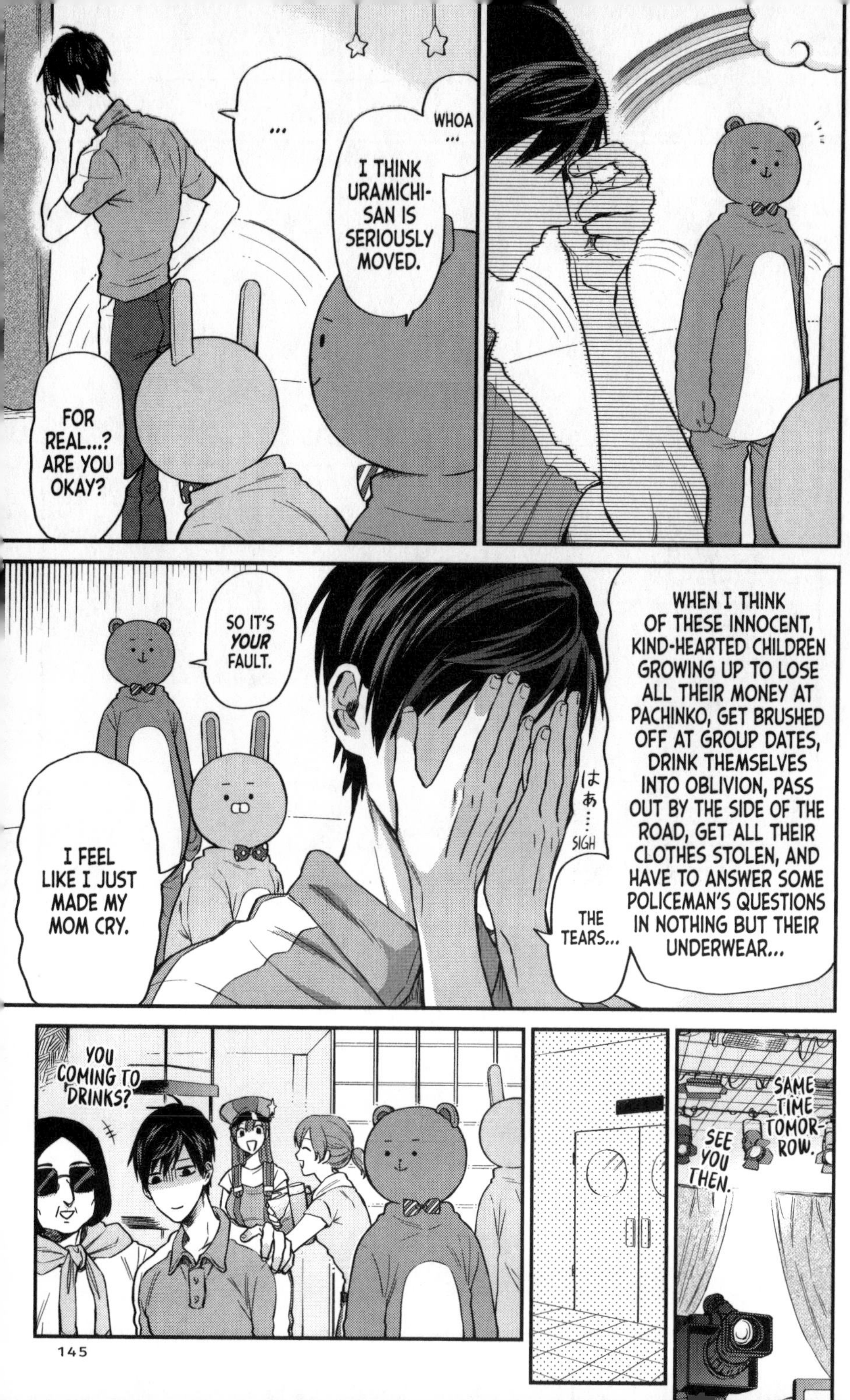
...
WHOA ...
I THINK URAMICHI-SAN IS SERIOUSLY MOVED.
FOR REAL...? ARE YOU OKAY?
WHEN I THINK OF THESE INNOCENT, KIND-HEARTED CHILDREN GROWING UP TO LOSE ALL THEIR MONEY AT PACHINKO, GET BRUSHED OFF AT GROUP DATES, DRINK THEMSELVES INTO OBLIVION, PASS OUT BY THE SIDE OF THE ROAD, GET ALL THEIR CLOTHES STOLEN, AND HAVE TO ANSWER SOME POLICEMAN'S QUESTIONS IN NOTHING BUT THEIR UNDERWEAR...
はぁ…
SIGH
THE TEARS...
SO IT'S *YOUR* FAULT.
I FEEL LIKE I JUST MADE MY MOM CRY.
SAME TIME TOMORROW.
SEE YOU THEN.
YOU COMING TO DRINKS?

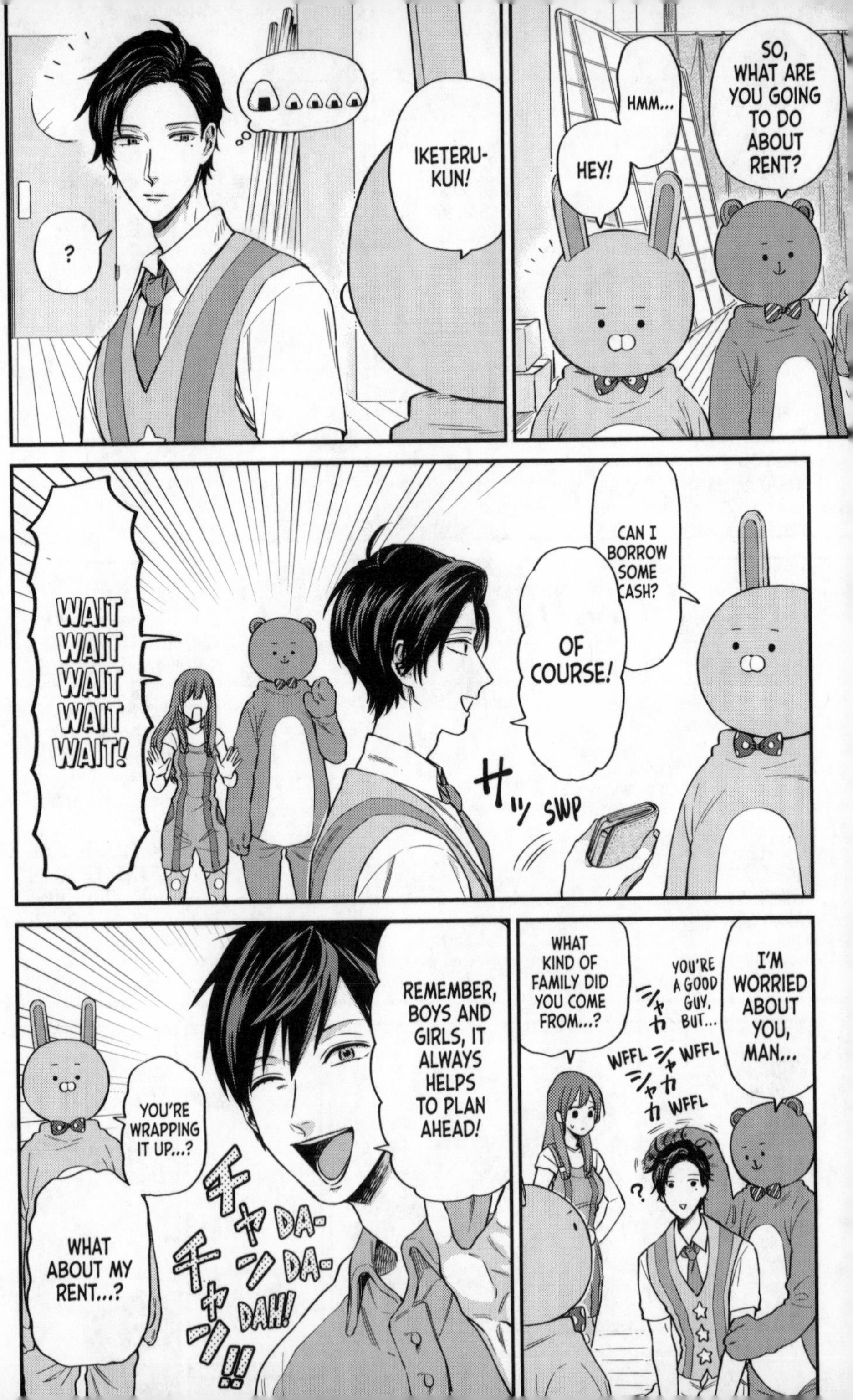
SO, WHAT ARE YOU GOING TO DO ABOUT RENT?
HMM...
HEY!
IKETERU-KUN!
?
CAN I BORROW SOME CASH?
OF COURSE!
サッ SWP
WAIT WAIT WAIT WAIT WAIT WAIT!
I'M WORRIED ABOUT YOU, MAN...
YOU'RE A GOOD GUY, BUT...
WHAT KIND OF FAMILY DID YOU COME FROM...?
シャカ WFFL シャカ WFFL シャカ WFFL
?
REMEMBER, BOYS AND GIRLS, IT ALWAYS HELPS TO PLAN AHEAD!
YOU'RE WRAPPING IT UP...?
WHAT ABOUT MY RENT...?
チャン DA- チャン DA- チャーン!! DAH!

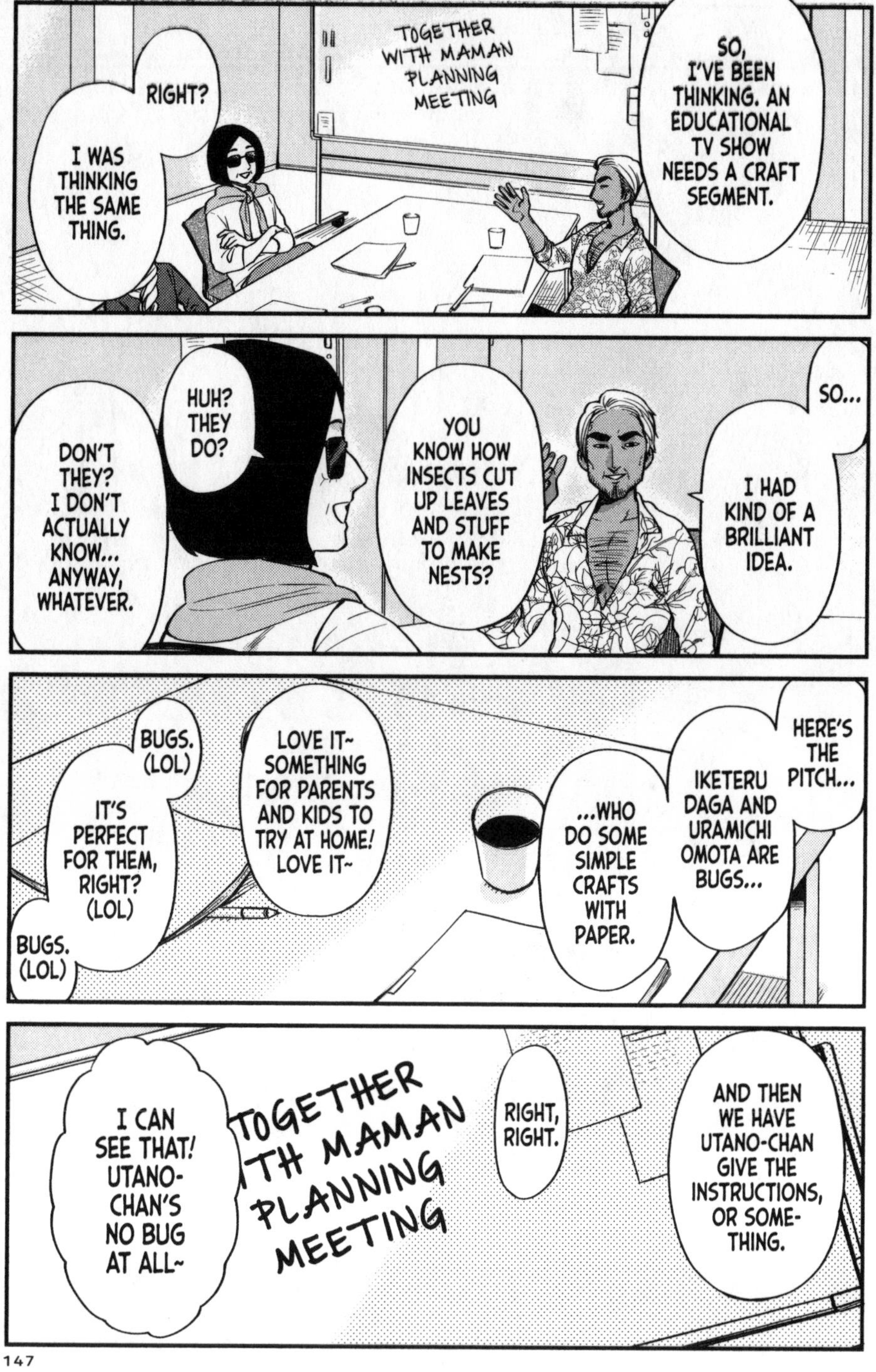
SO, I'VE BEEN THINKING. AN EDUCATIONAL TV SHOW NEEDS A CRAFT SEGMENT.
TOGETHER WITH MAMAN PLANNING MEETING
RIGHT? I WAS THINKING THE SAME THING.
SO...
I HAD KIND OF A BRILLIANT IDEA.
YOU KNOW HOW INSECTS CUT UP LEAVES AND STUFF TO MAKE NESTS?
HUH? THEY DO?
DON'T THEY? I DON'T ACTUALLY KNOW... ANYWAY, WHATEVER.
HERE'S THE PITCH...
IKETERU DAGA AND URAMICHI OMOTA ARE BUGS...
...WHO DO SOME SIMPLE CRAFTS WITH PAPER.
LOVE IT~ SOMETHING FOR PARENTS AND KIDS TO TRY AT HOME! LOVE IT~
BUGS. (LOL)
IT'S PERFECT FOR THEM, RIGHT? (LOL)
BUGS. (LOL)
AND THEN WE HAVE UTANO-CHAN GIVE THE INSTRUCTIONS, OR SOME-THING.
RIGHT, RIGHT.
TOGETHER TH MAMAN PLANNING MEETING
I CAN SEE THAT! UTANO-CHAN'S NO BUG AT ALL~

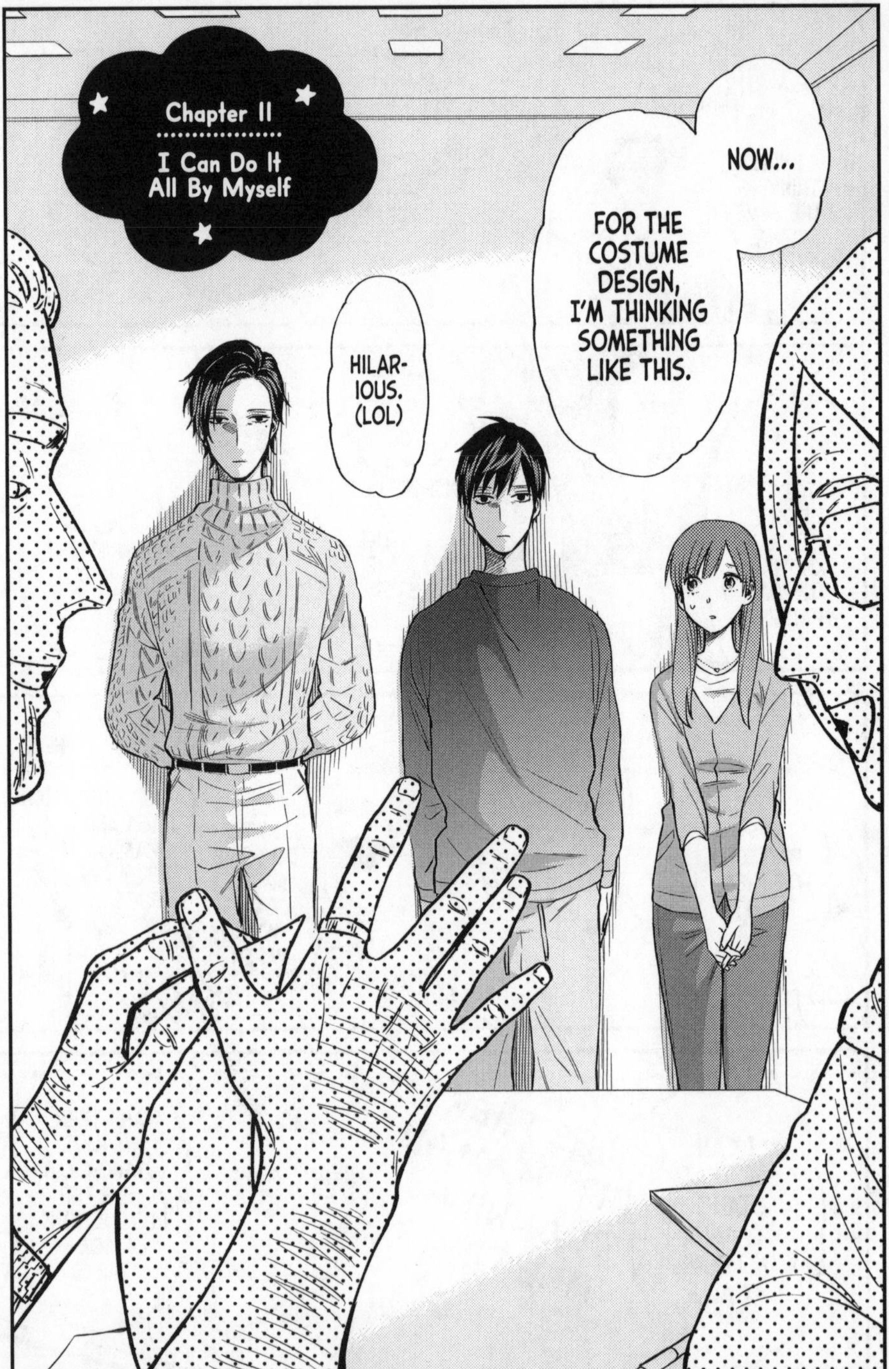
Chapter 11
I Can Do It All By Myself
NOW... FOR THE COSTUME DESIGN, I'M THINKING SOMETHING LIKE THIS.
HILAR-IOUS. (LOL)

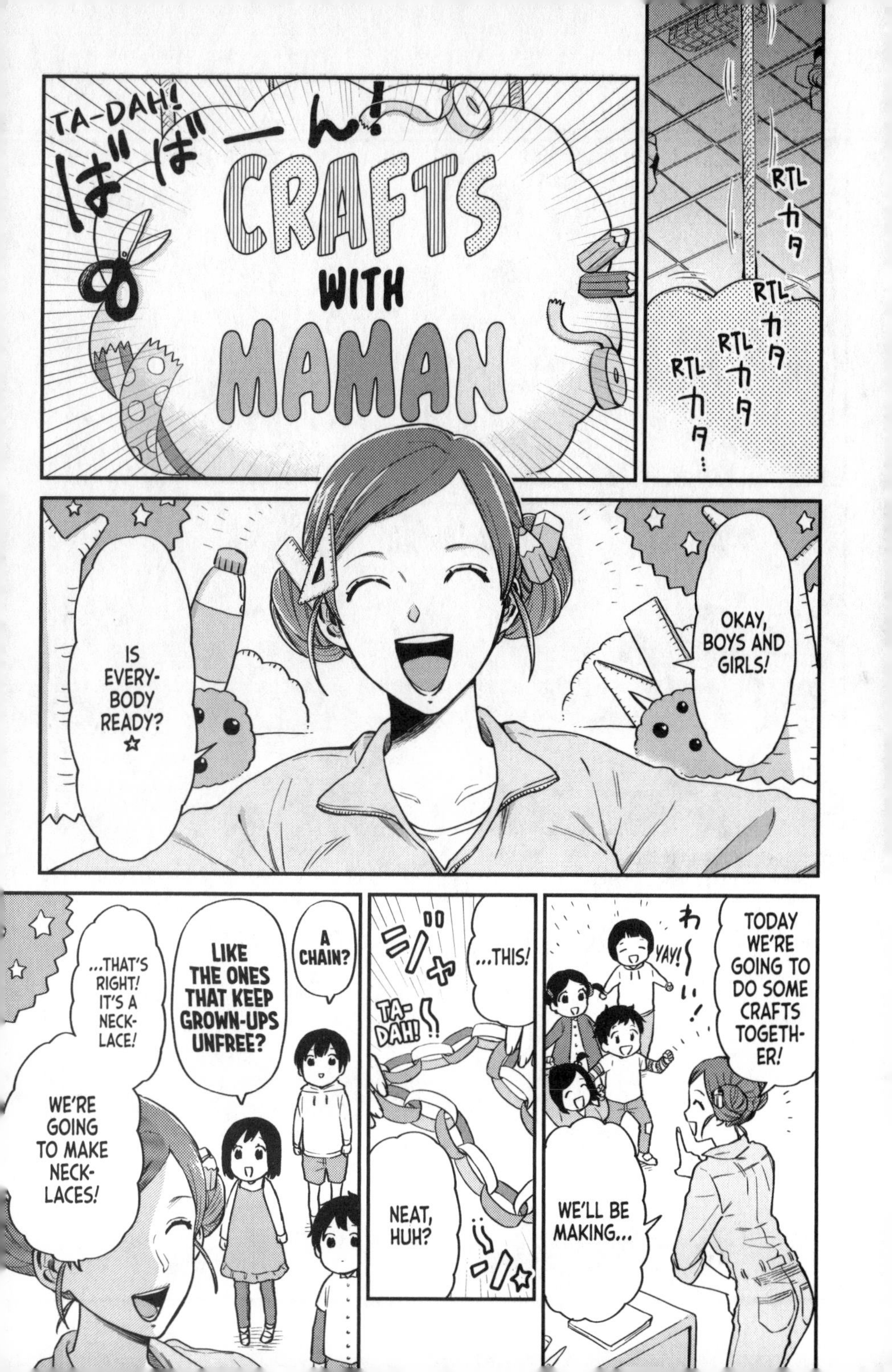

RTL カタ
RTL カタ
RTL カタ
RTL カタ…
TA-DAH!
ばばーん!
CRAFTS WITH MAMAN
OKAY, BOYS AND GIRLS!
IS EVERY-BODY READY? ☆
TODAY WE'RE GOING TO DO SOME CRAFTS TOGETH-ER!
YAY!
WE'LL BE MAKING...
...THIS!
TA-DAH!
NEAT, HUH?
A CHAIN?
LIKE THE ONES THAT KEEP GROWN-UPS UNFREE?
...THAT'S RIGHT! IT'S A NECK-LACE!
WE'RE GOING TO MAKE NECK-LACES!

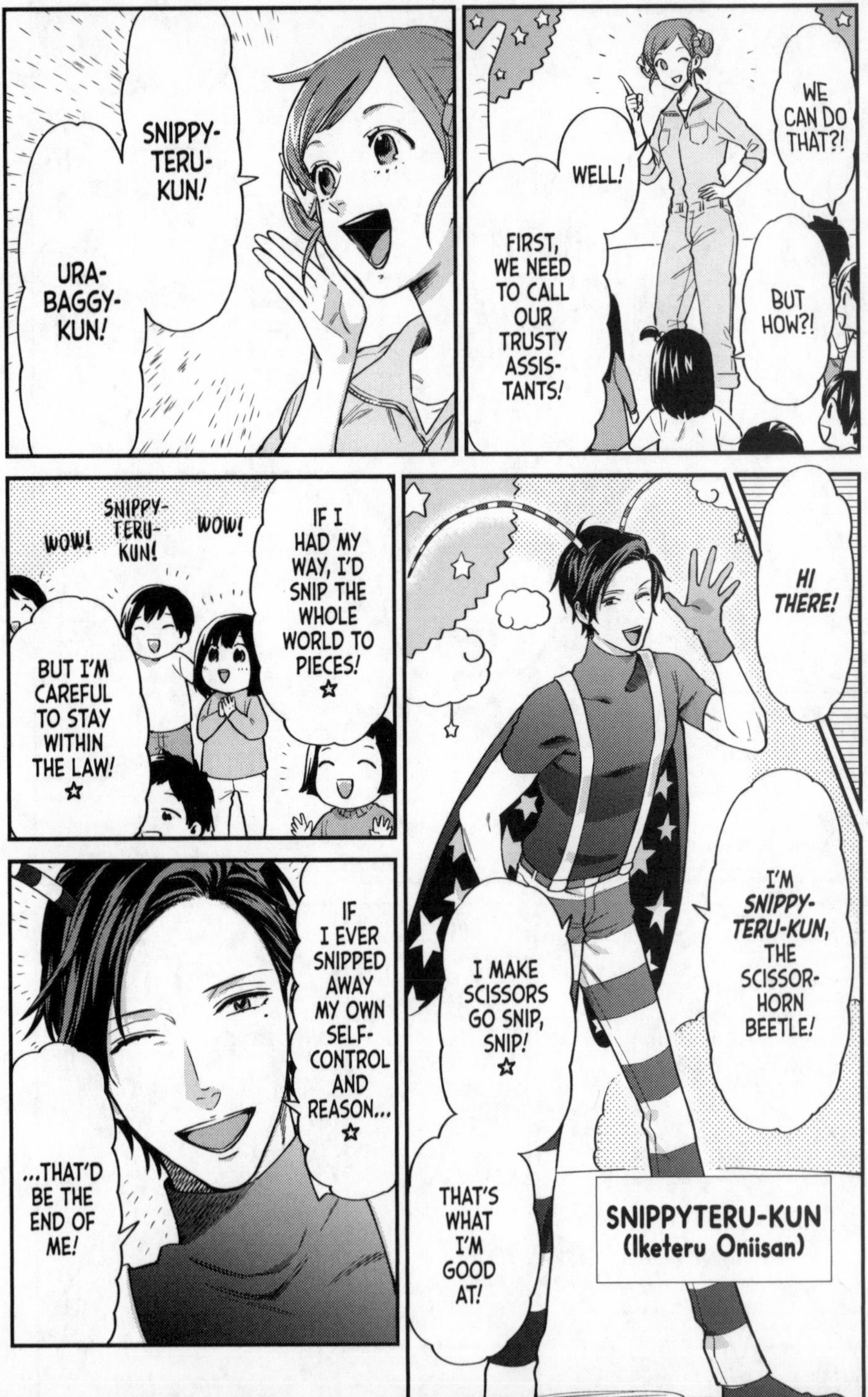
WE CAN DO THAT?!
BUT HOW?!
WELL!
FIRST, WE NEED TO CALL OUR TRUSTY ASSIS-TANTS!
SNIPPY-TERU-KUN!
URA-BAGGY-KUN!
HI THERE!
I'M SNIPPY-TERU-KUN, THE SCISSOR-HORN BEETLE!
I MAKE SCISSORS GO SNIP, SNIP! ☆
THAT'S WHAT I'M GOOD AT!
SNIPPYTERU-KUN
(Iketeru Oniisan)
IF I HAD MY WAY, I'D SNIP THE WHOLE WORLD TO PIECES! ☆
BUT I'M CAREFUL TO STAY WITHIN THE LAW! ☆
WOW!
SNIPPY-TERU-KUN!
WOW!
IF I EVER SNIPPED AWAY MY OWN SELF-CONTROL AND REASON... ☆
...THAT'D BE THE END OF ME!

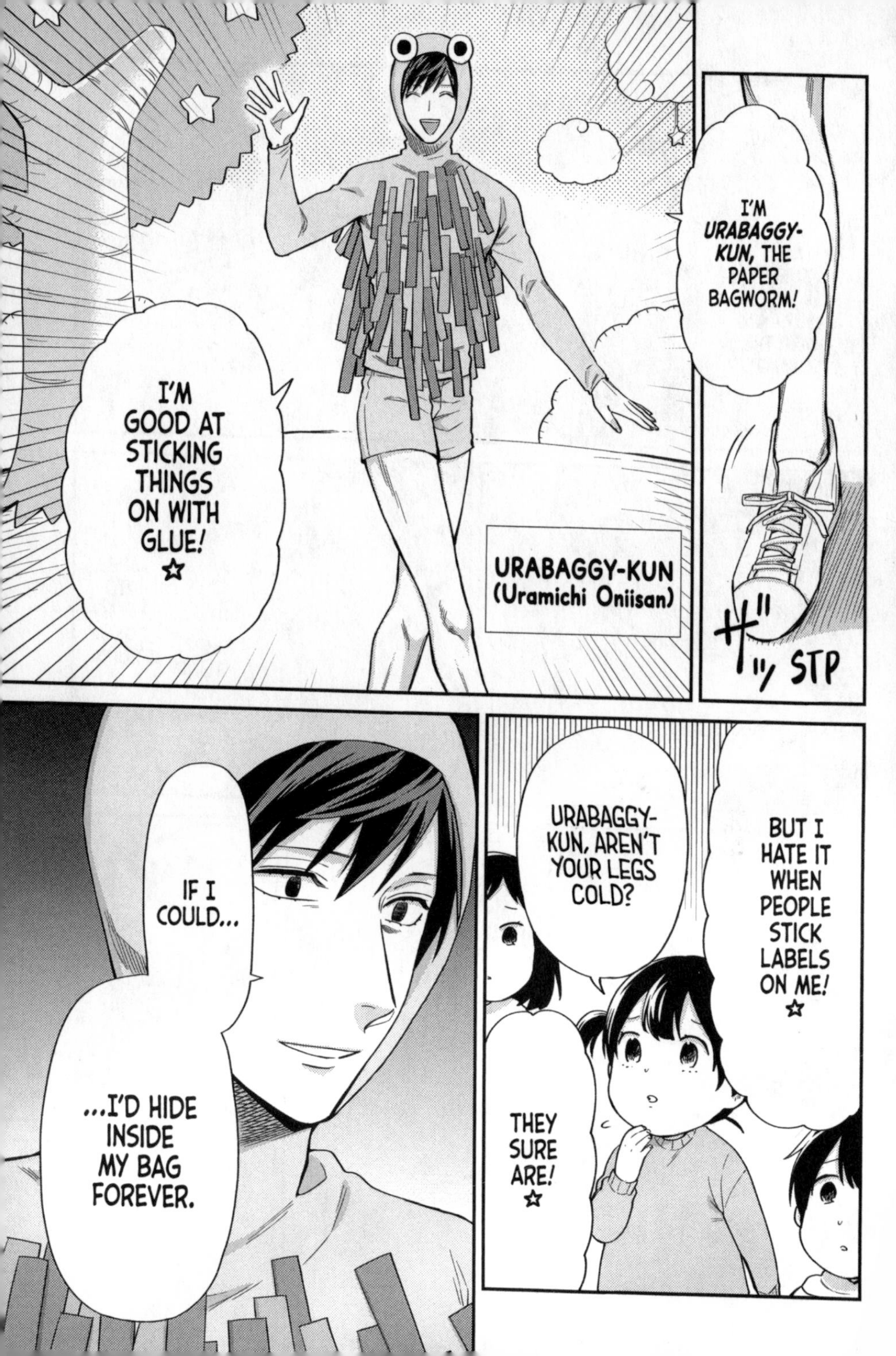
I'M URABAGGY-KUN, THE PAPER BAGWORM!
STP
I'M GOOD AT STICKING THINGS ON WITH GLUE! ☆
URABAGGY-KUN (Uramichi Oniisan)
BUT I HATE IT WHEN PEOPLE STICK LABELS ON ME! ☆
URABAGGY-KUN, AREN'T YOUR LEGS COLD?
THEY SURE ARE! ☆
IF I COULD...
...I'D HIDE INSIDE MY BAG FOREVER.

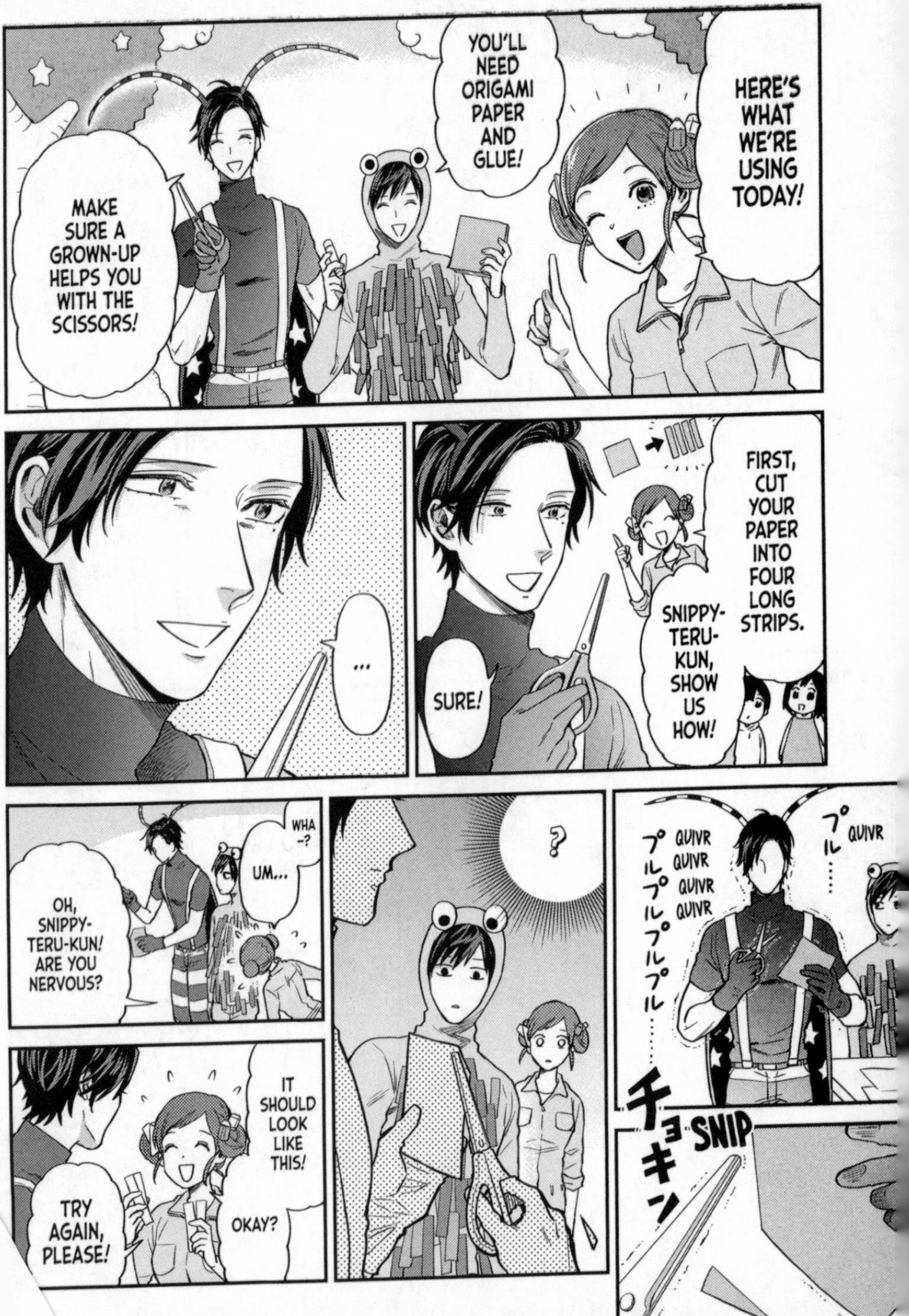
HERE'S WHAT WE'RE USING TODAY!
YOU'LL NEED ORIGAMI PAPER AND GLUE!
MAKE SURE A GROWN-UP HELPS YOU WITH THE SCISSORS!
FIRST, CUT YOUR PAPER INTO FOUR LONG STRIPS.
SNIPPY-TERU-KUN, SHOW US HOW!
SURE!
...
プル……
QUIVR
プルプルプルプル……
QUIVR QUIVR QUIVR QUIVR
チョキン
SNIP
?
WHA—?
UM...
OH, SNIPPY-TERU-KUN! ARE YOU NERVOUS?
IT SHOULD LOOK LIKE THIS!
OKAY?
TRY AGAIN, PLEASE!

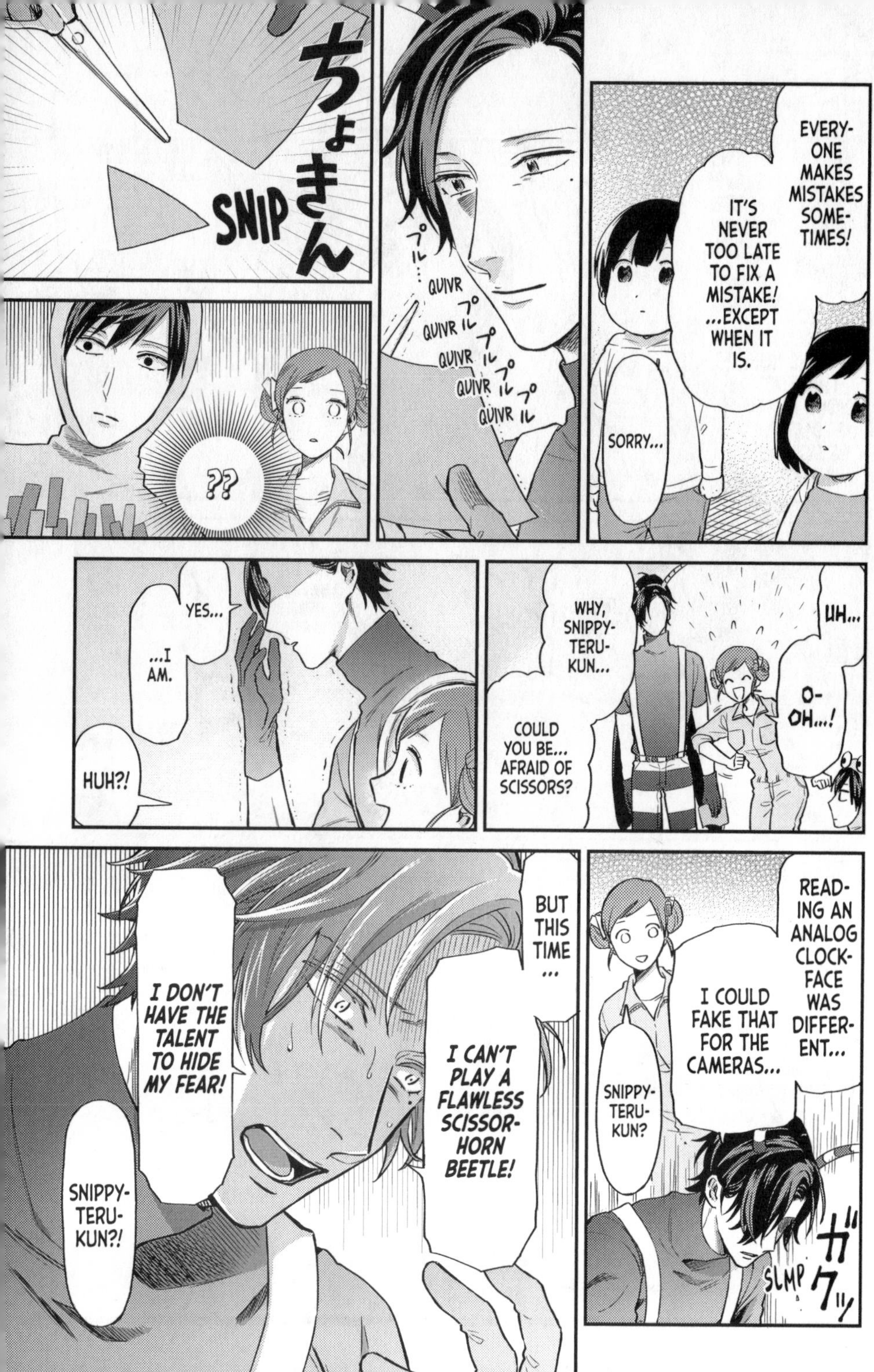
EVERY-ONE MAKES MISTAKES SOME-TIMES!
IT'S NEVER TOO LATE TO FIX A MISTAKE! ...EXCEPT WHEN IT IS.
SORRY...
プル…
QUIVR
プル
QUIVR
プル
QUIVR
プル
QUIVR
プル
QUIVR
ちょきん
SNIP
??
UH...
O-OH...!
WHY, SNIPPY-TERU-KUN...
COULD YOU BE... AFRAID OF SCISSORS?
YES...
...I AM.
HUH?!
READING AN ANALOG CLOCK-FACE WAS DIFFERENT...
I COULD FAKE THAT FOR THE CAMERAS...
SNIPPY-TERU-KUN?
ガクッ
SLMP
BUT THIS TIME...
I CAN'T PLAY A FLAWLESS SCISSOR-HORN BEETLE!
I DON'T HAVE THE TALENT TO HIDE MY FEAR!
SNIPPY-TERU-KUN?!

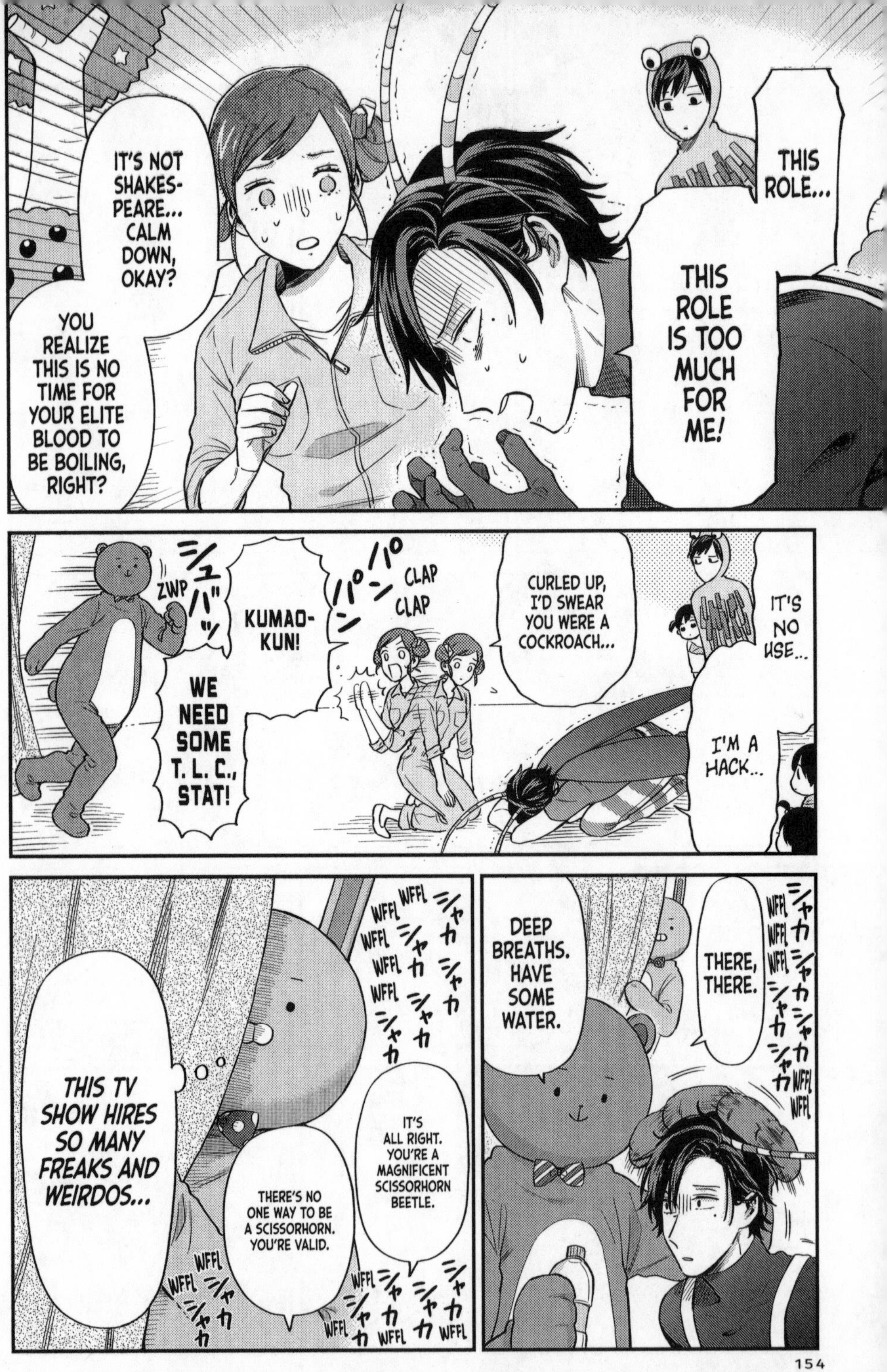
THIS ROLE...
THIS ROLE IS TOO MUCH FOR ME!
IT'S NOT SHAKES-PEARE... CALM DOWN, OKAY?
YOU REALIZE THIS IS NO TIME FOR YOUR ELITE BLOOD TO BE BOILING, RIGHT?
IT'S NO USE...
I'M A HACK...
CURLED UP, I'D SWEAR YOU WERE A COCKROACH...
パンパン
CLAP CLAP
KUMAO-KUN!
WE NEED SOME T. L. C., STAT!
シュバッ
ZWP
シャカシャカ
WFFL WFFL
THERE, THERE.
DEEP BREATHS. HAVE SOME WATER.
シャカシャカ
WFFL WFFL
IT'S ALL RIGHT. YOU'RE A MAGNIFICENT SCISSORHORN BEETLE.
THERE'S NO ONE WAY TO BE A SCISSORHORN. YOU'RE VALID.
THIS TV SHOW HIRES SO MANY FREAKS AND WEIRDOS...

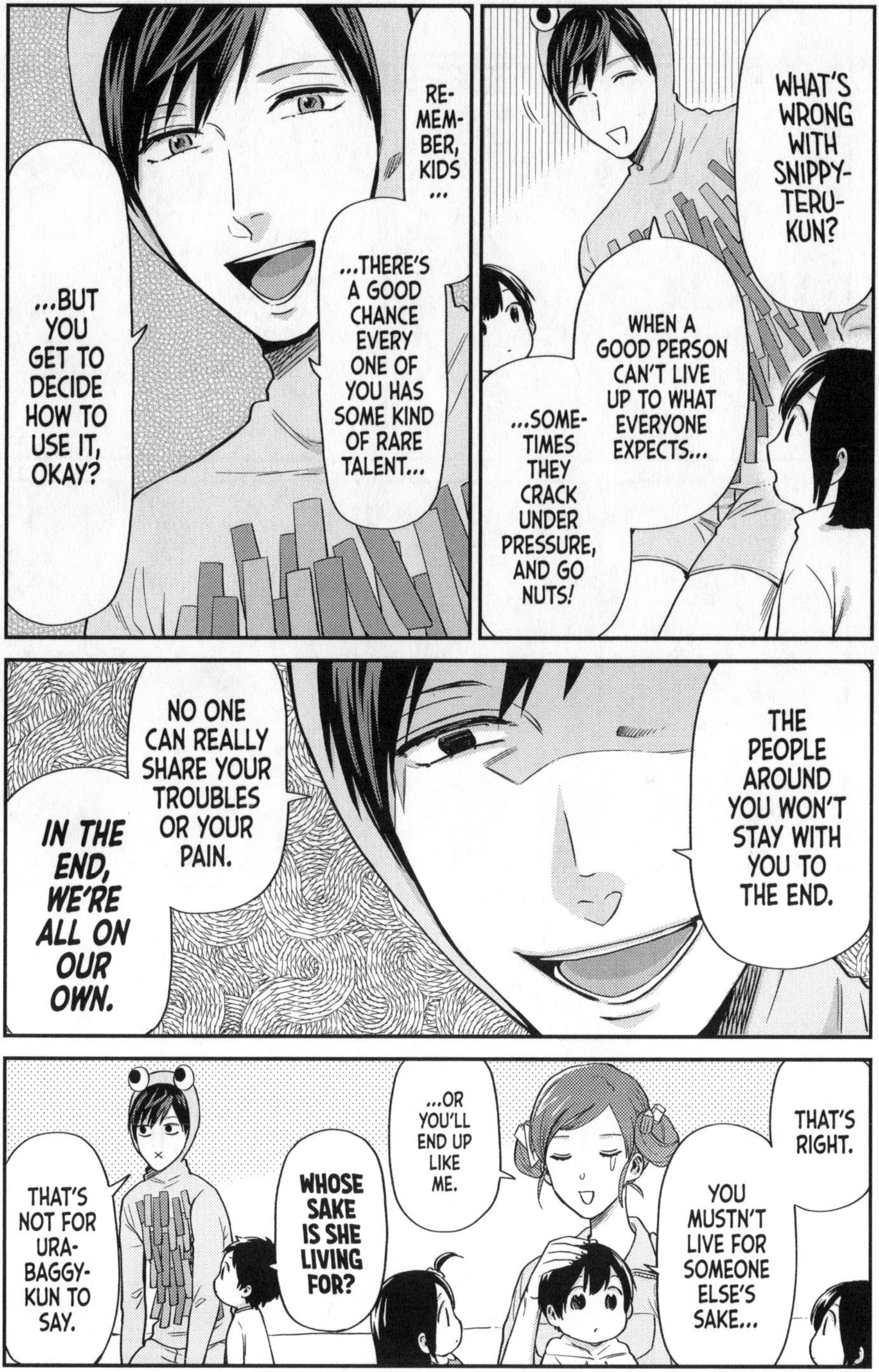
WHAT'S WRONG WITH SNIPPY-TERU-KUN?
WHEN A GOOD PERSON CAN'T LIVE UP TO WHAT EVERYONE EXPECTS...
...SOMETIMES THEY CRACK UNDER PRESSURE, AND GO NUTS!
RE-MEMBER, KIDS...
...THERE'S A GOOD CHANCE EVERY ONE OF YOU HAS SOME KIND OF RARE TALENT...
...BUT YOU GET TO DECIDE HOW TO USE IT, OKAY?
THE PEOPLE AROUND YOU WON'T STAY WITH YOU TO THE END.
NO ONE CAN REALLY SHARE YOUR TROUBLES OR YOUR PAIN.
IN THE END, WE'RE ALL ON OUR OWN.
THAT'S RIGHT.
YOU MUSTN'T LIVE FOR SOMEONE ELSE'S SAKE...
...OR YOU'LL END UP LIKE ME.
WHOSE SAKE IS SHE LIVING FOR?
THAT'S NOT FOR URA-BAGGY-KUN TO SAY.

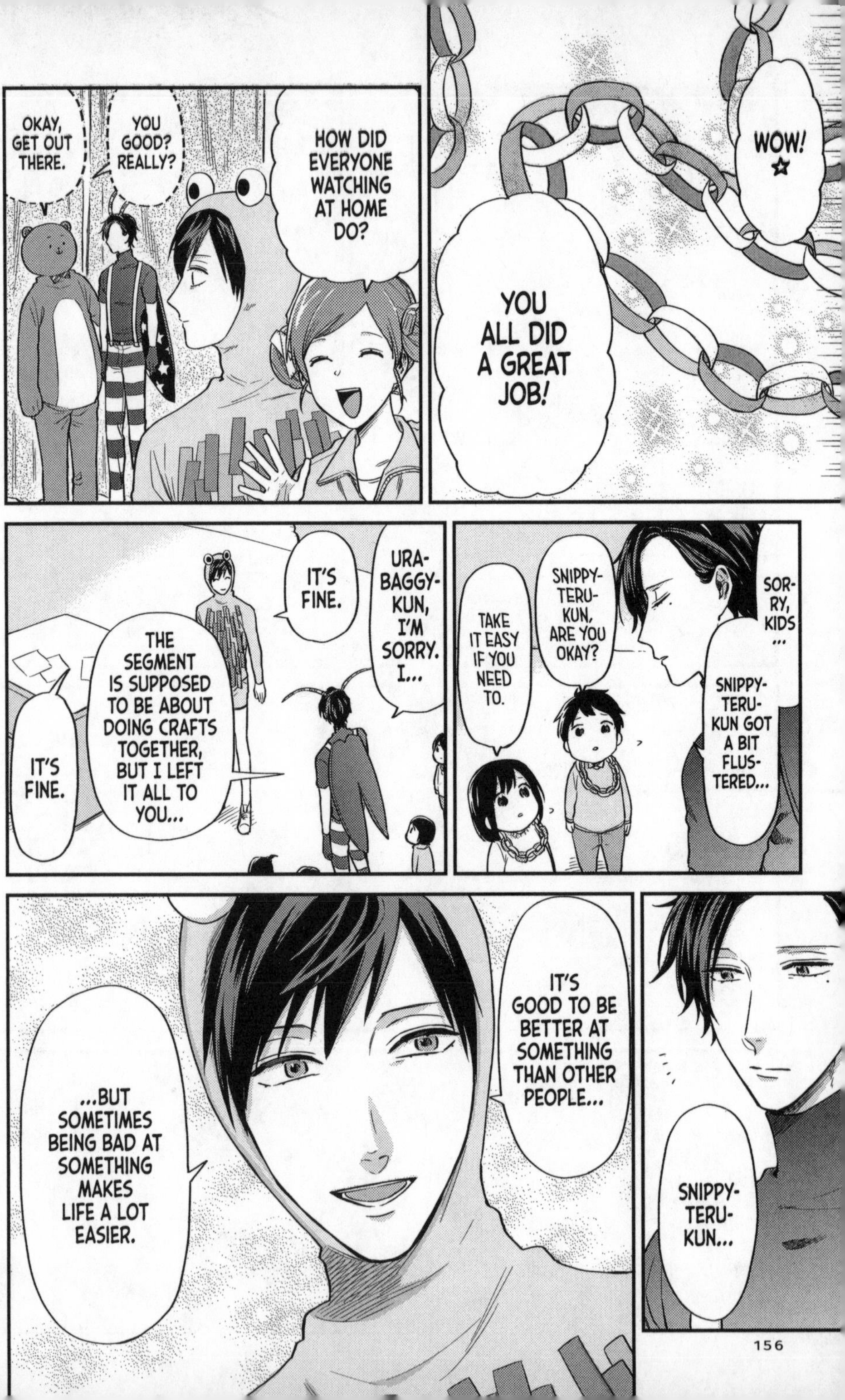
WOW! ☆
YOU ALL DID A GREAT JOB!
HOW DID EVERYONE WATCHING AT HOME DO?
YOU GOOD? REALLY?
OKAY, GET OUT THERE.
SOR-RY, KIDS...
SNIPPY-TERU-KUN GOT A BIT FLUS-TERED...
SNIPPY-TERU-KUN, ARE YOU OKAY?
TAKE IT EASY IF YOU NEED TO.
URA-BAGGY-KUN, I'M SORRY. I...
IT'S FINE.
THE SEGMENT IS SUPPOSED TO BE ABOUT DOING CRAFTS TOGETHER, BUT I LEFT IT ALL TO YOU...
IT'S FINE.
SNIPPY-TERU-KUN...
IT'S GOOD TO BE BETTER AT SOMETHING THAN OTHER PEOPLE...
...BUT SOMETIMES BEING BAD AT SOMETHING MAKES LIFE A LOT EASIER.

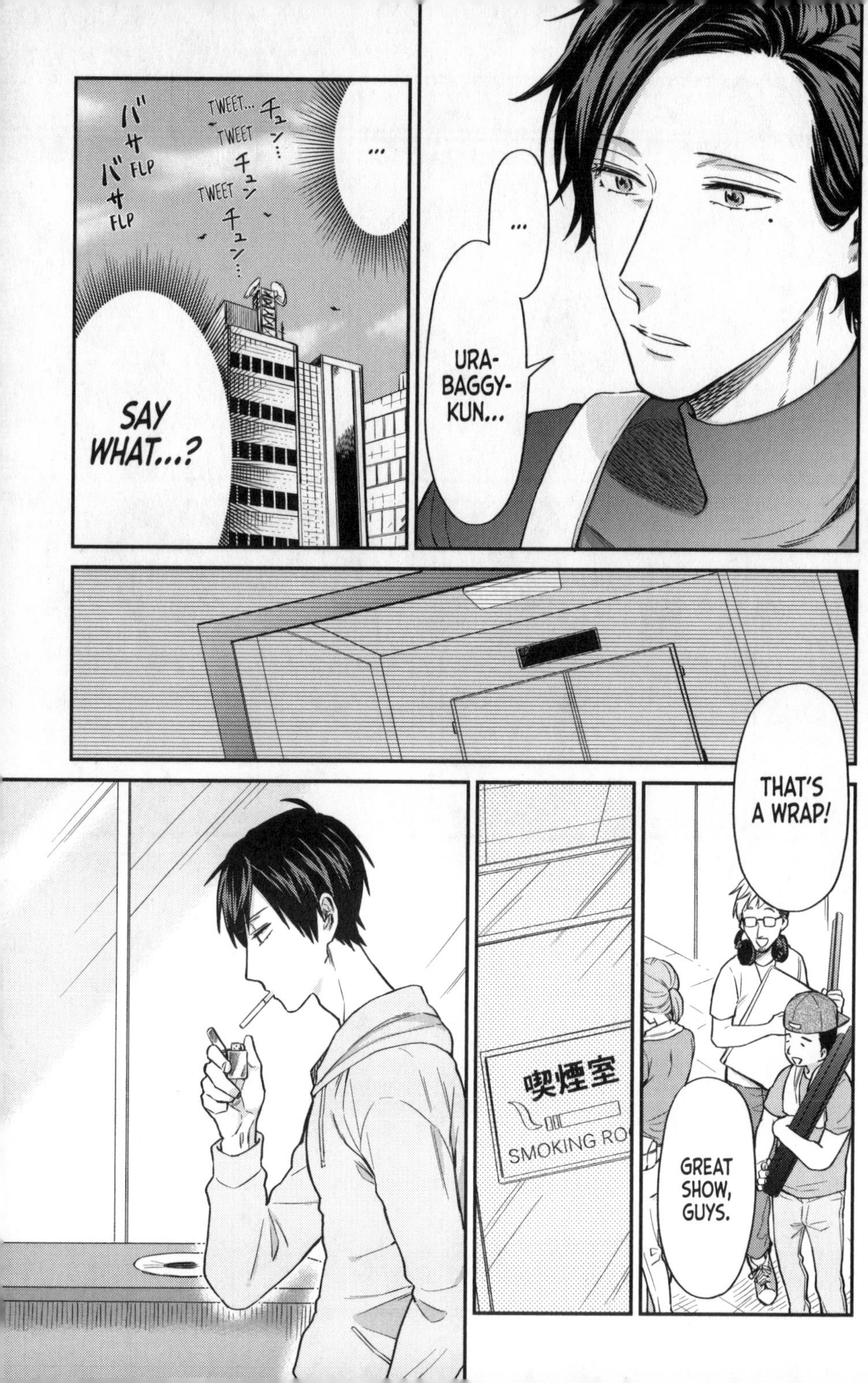
...
URA-BAGGY-KUN...
...
SAY WHAT...?
チュン… TWEET...
チュン TWEET
チュン… TWEET
バサ FLP
バサ FLP
THAT'S A WRAP!
GREAT SHOW, GUYS.
喫煙室
SMOKING RO

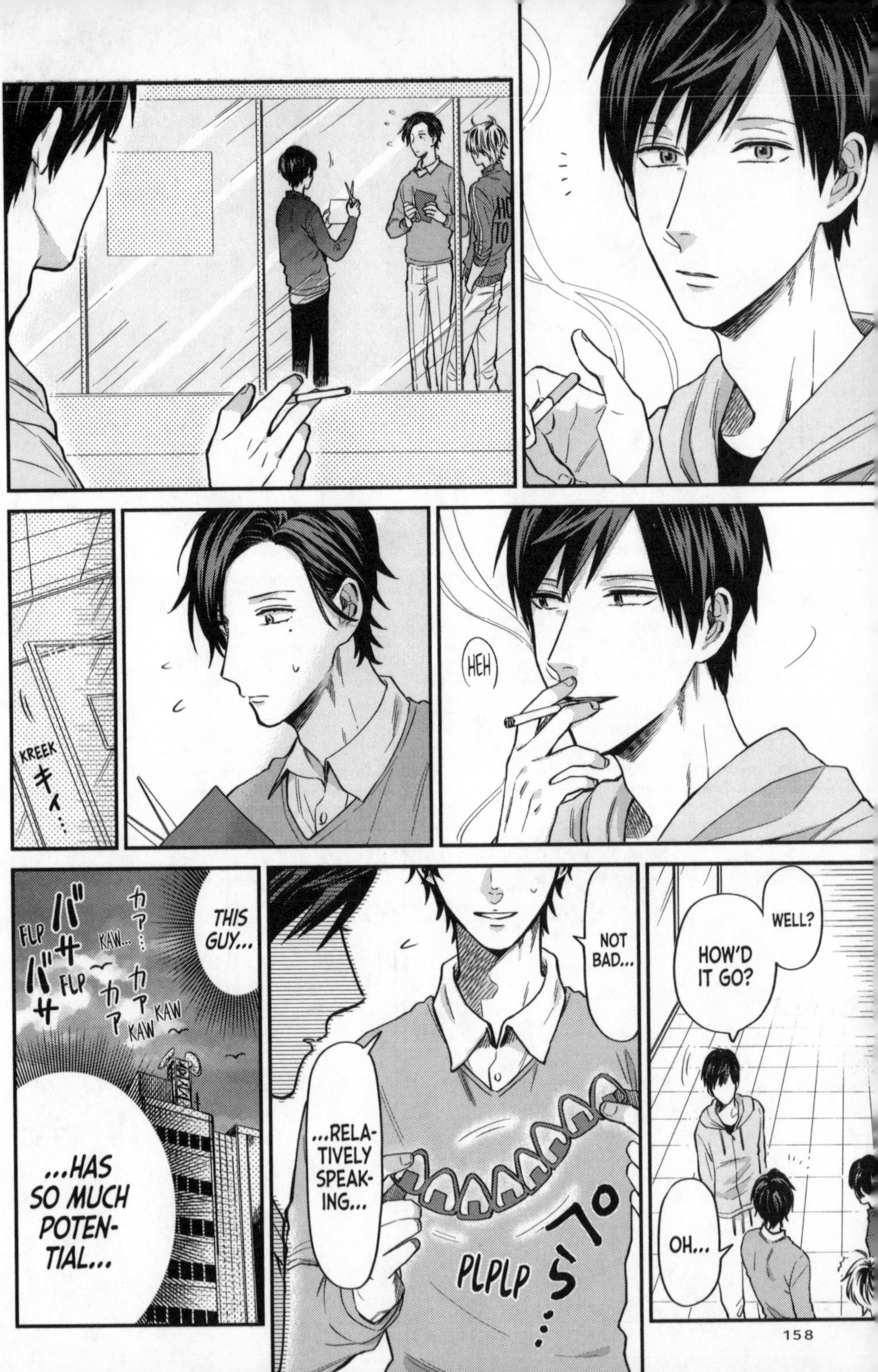
HEH
KREEK
キィ…
WELL?
HOW'D IT GO?
OH...
NOT BAD...
...RELATIVELY SPEAKING...
ぺら…
PLPLP
THIS GUY...
バサバサ
FLP FLP
カァ… カァ
KAW... KAW KAW
...HAS SO MUCH POTENTIAL...

Life Lessons with
Uramichi Oniisan

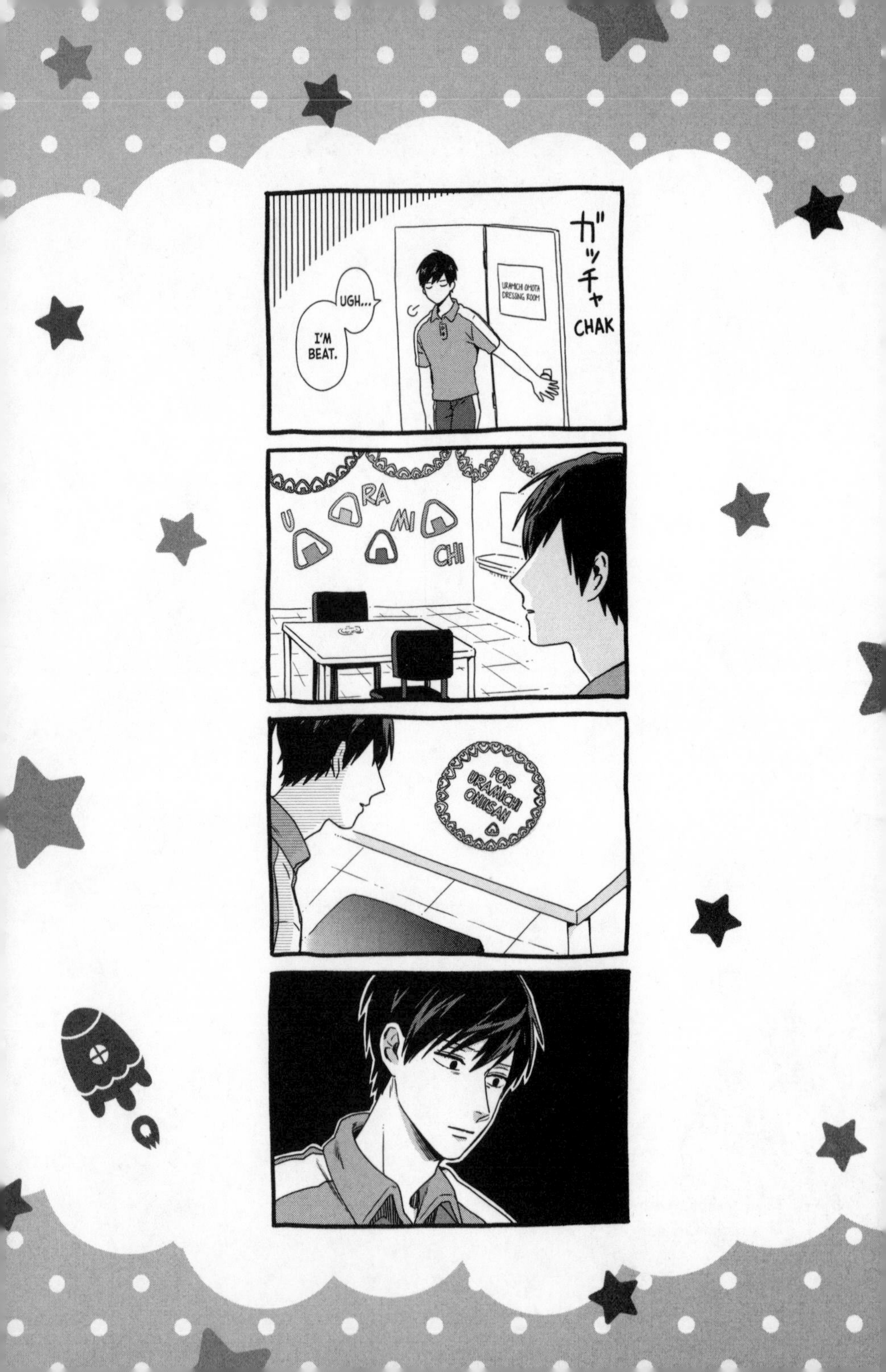
ガッチャ
CHAK
UGH...
I'M BEAT.
URAMICHI OMOTA DRESSING ROOM
U RA MI CHI
FOR URAMICHI ONIISAN

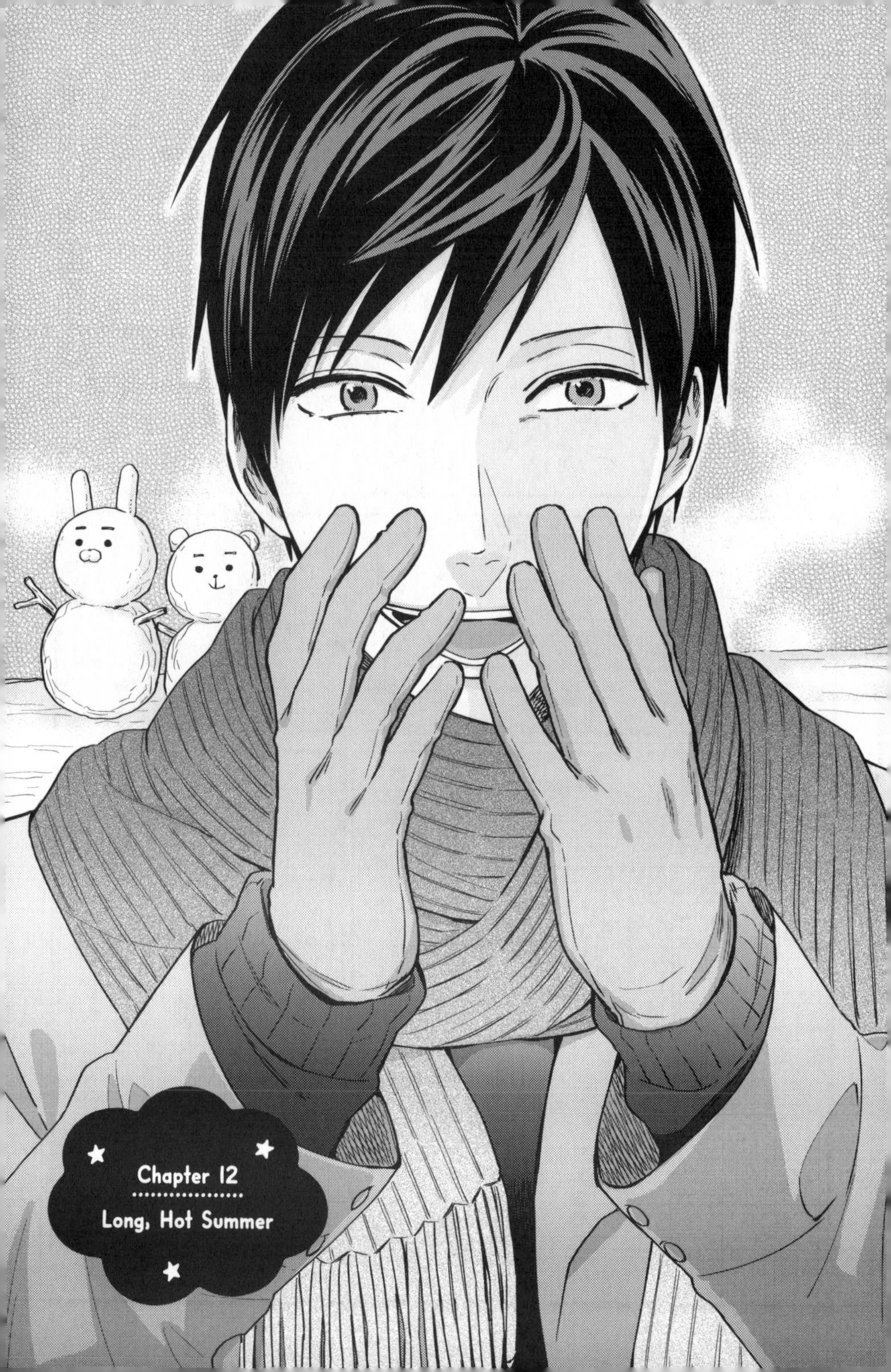
Chapter 12
Long, Hot Summer

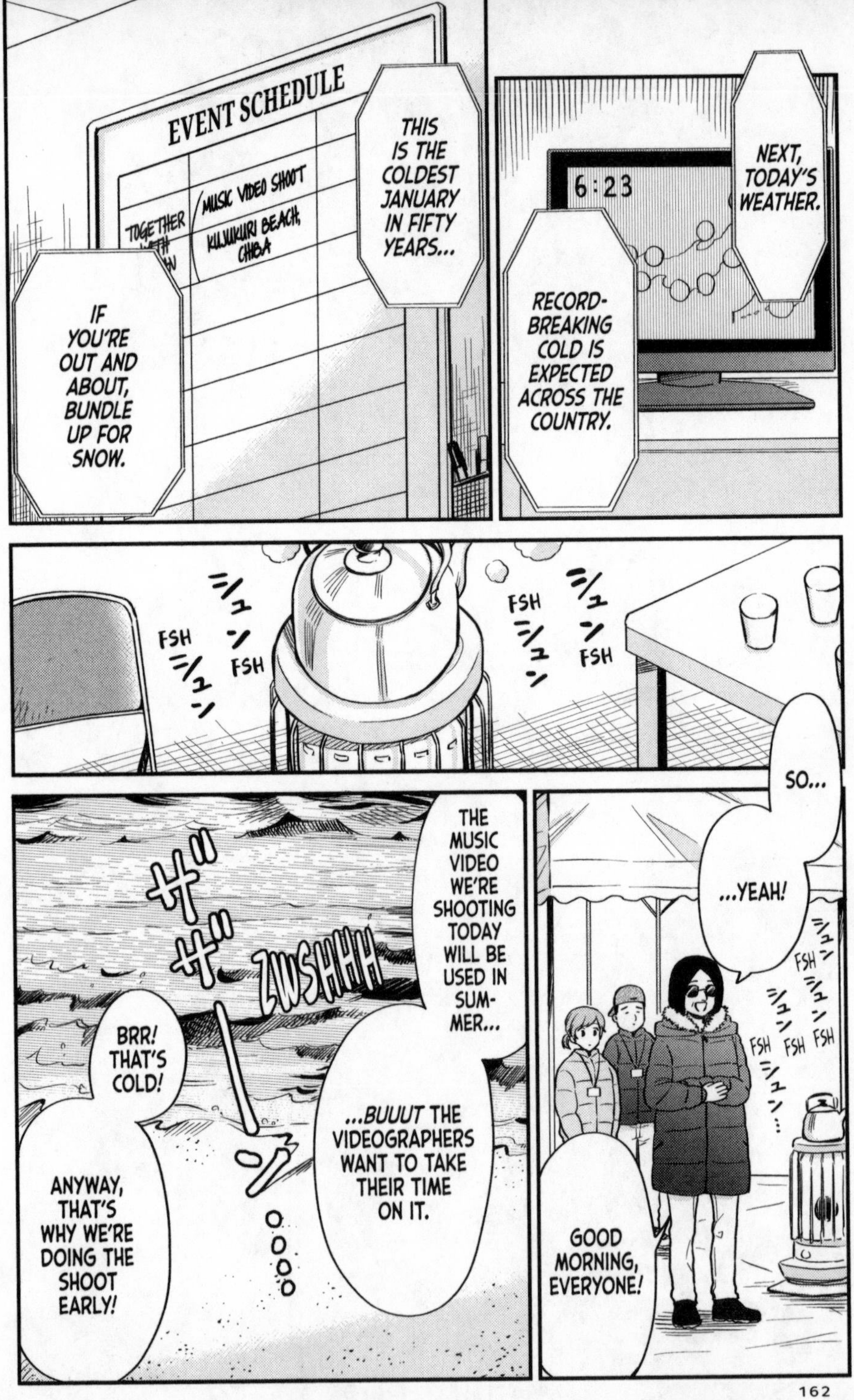
6:23
NEXT, TODAY'S WEATHER.
RECORD-BREAKING COLD IS EXPECTED ACROSS THE COUNTRY.
EVENT SCHEDULE
TOGETHER WITH
MUSIC VIDEO SHOOT
KUJUKURI BEACH, CHIBA
THIS IS THE COLDEST JANUARY IN FIFTY YEARS...
IF YOU'RE OUT AND ABOUT, BUNDLE UP FOR SNOW.
シュン FSH
シュン FSH
シュン FSH
シュン FSH
SO...
...YEAH!
シュン FSH
GOOD MORNING, EVERYONE!
THE MUSIC VIDEO WE'RE SHOOTING TODAY WILL BE USED IN SUM-MER...
...BUUUT THE VIDEOGRAPHERS WANT TO TAKE THEIR TIME ON IT.
ザザー
ZWSHHH
BRR! THAT'S COLD!
ANYWAY, THAT'S WHY WE'RE DOING THE SHOOT EARLY!

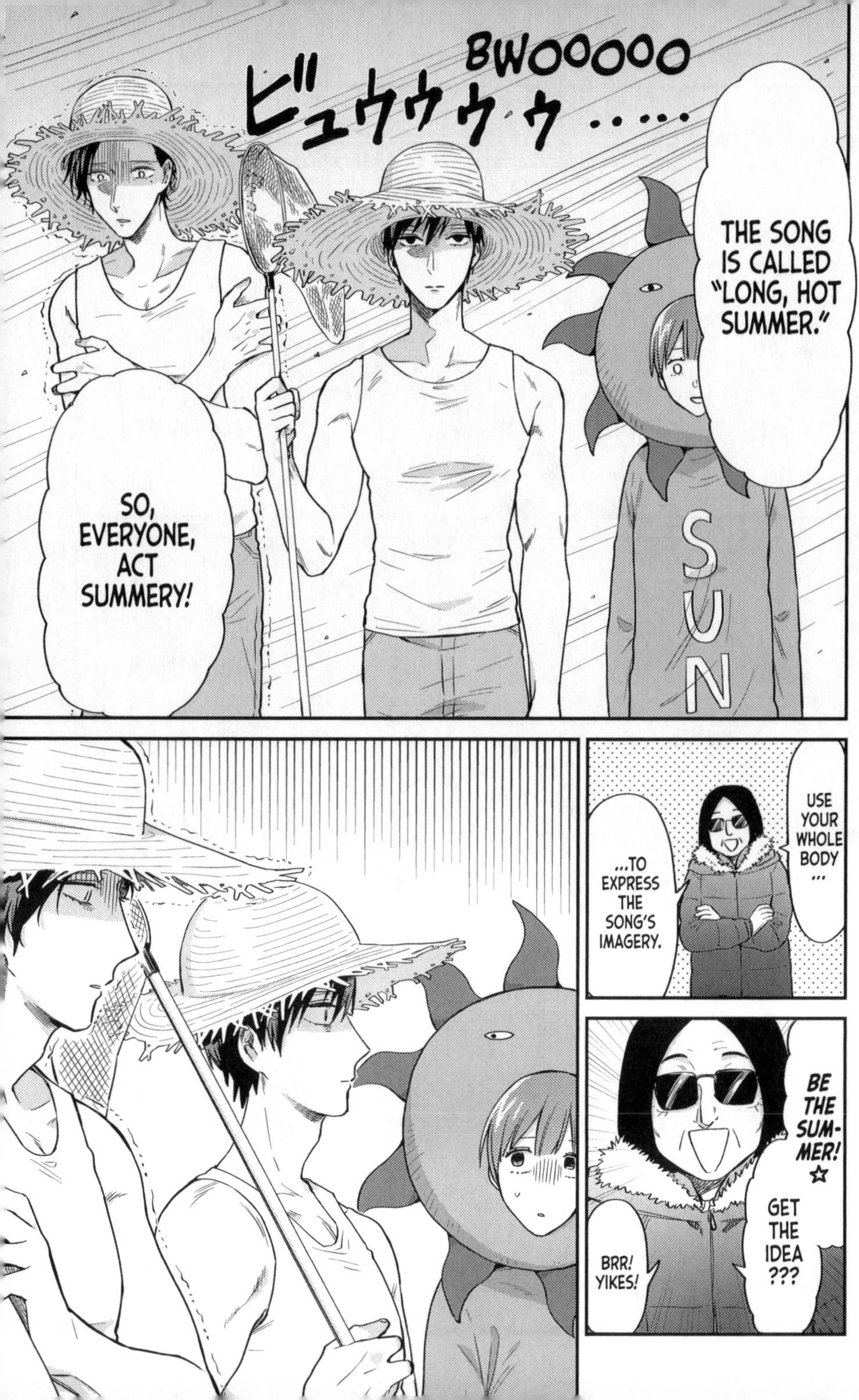
ビュウウウウ…
BWOOOOO
THE SONG IS CALLED "LONG, HOT SUMMER."
SO, EVERYONE, ACT SUMMERY!
USE YOUR WHOLE BODY...
...TO EXPRESS THE SONG'S IMAGERY.
BE THE SUMMER! ☆
GET THE IDEA???
BRR! YIKES!

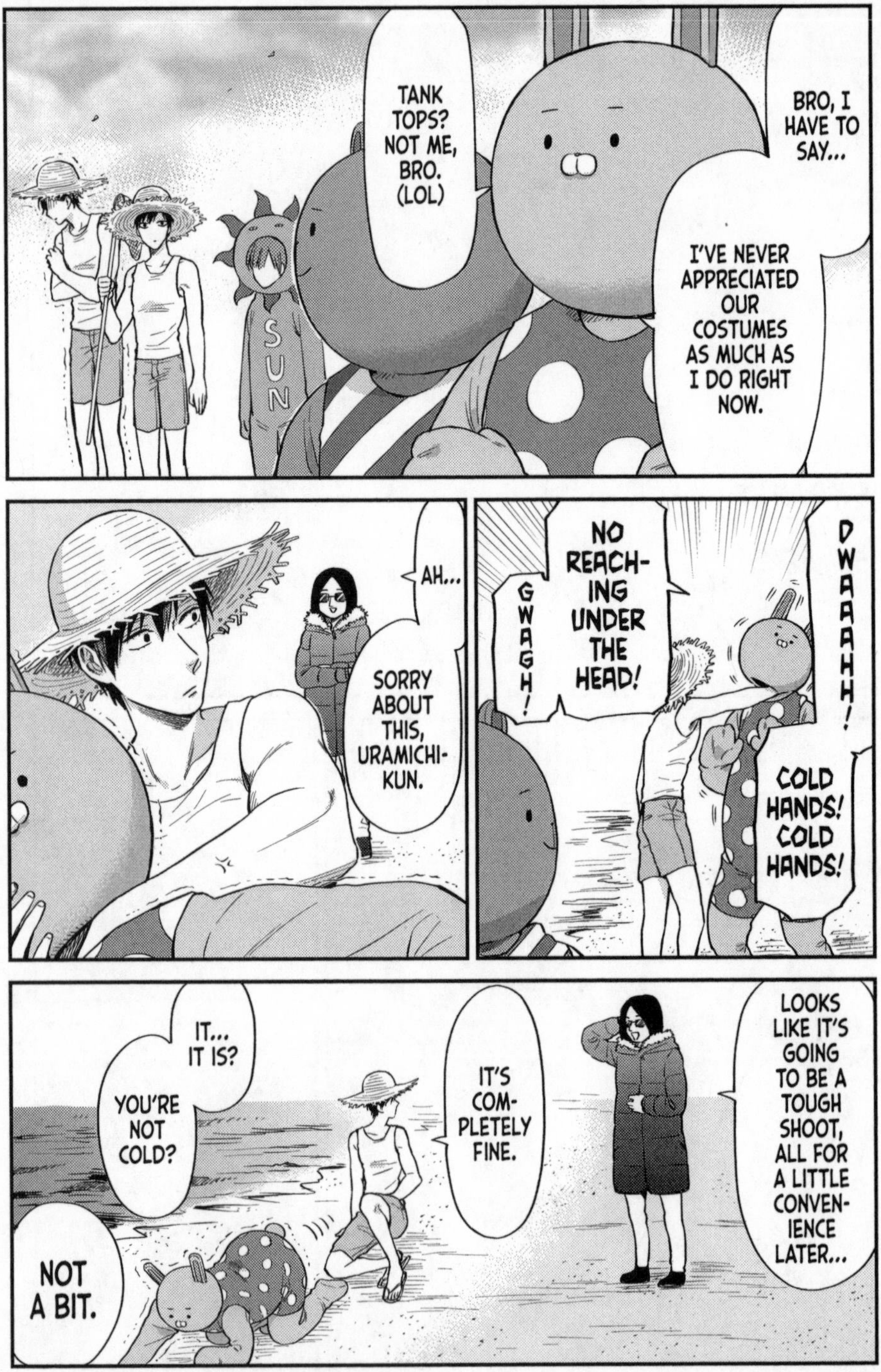

BRO, I HAVE TO SAY...
I'VE NEVER APPRECIATED OUR COSTUMES AS MUCH AS I DO RIGHT NOW.
TANK TOPS? NOT ME, BRO. (LOL)
SUN
DWAAAAHH!
NO REACHING UNDER THE HEAD!
GWAGH!
COLD HANDS! COLD HANDS!
AH...
SORRY ABOUT THIS, URAMICHI-KUN.
LOOKS LIKE IT'S GOING TO BE A TOUGH SHOOT, ALL FOR A LITTLE CONVENIENCE LATER...
IT'S COMPLETELY FINE.
IT... IT IS?
YOU'RE NOT COLD?
NOT A BIT.

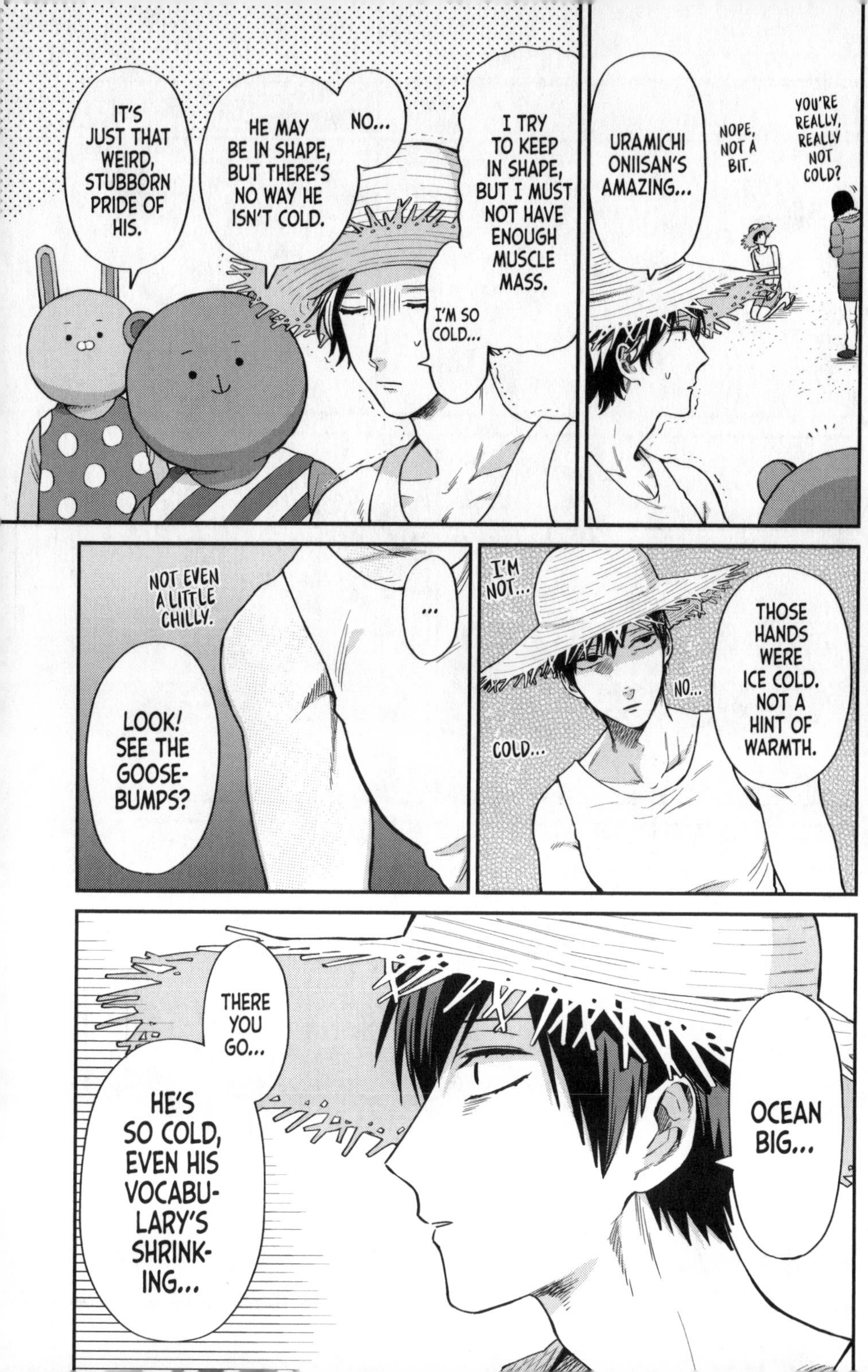
YOU'RE REALLY, REALLY NOT COLD?
NOPE, NOT A BIT.
URAMICHI ONIISAN'S AMAZING...
I TRY TO KEEP IN SHAPE, BUT I MUST NOT HAVE ENOUGH MUSCLE MASS.
I'M SO COLD...
NO...
HE MAY BE IN SHAPE, BUT THERE'S NO WAY HE ISN'T COLD.
IT'S JUST THAT WEIRD, STUBBORN PRIDE OF HIS.
THOSE HANDS WERE ICE COLD. NOT A HINT OF WARMTH.
I'M NOT...
NO...
COLD...
...
NOT EVEN A LITTLE CHILLY.
LOOK! SEE THE GOOSE-BUMPS?
OCEAN BIG...
THERE YOU GO...
HE'S SO COLD, EVEN HIS VOCABU-LARY'S SHRINK-ING...

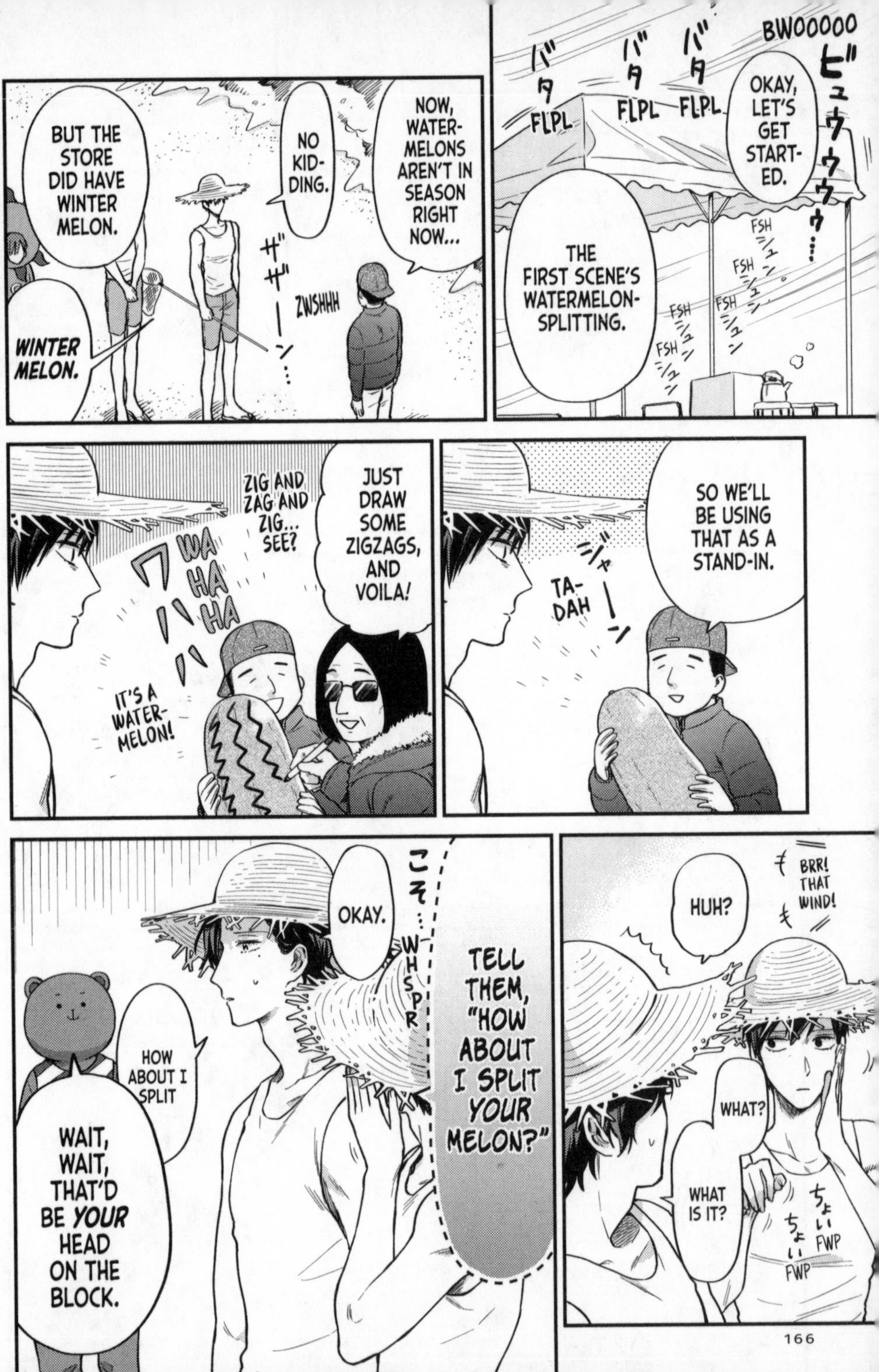
BWOOOOO
ビュウウウウ…
OKAY, LET'S GET START-ED.
バタ FLPL
バタ FLPL
バタ FLPL
THE FIRST SCENE'S WATERMELON-SPLITTING.
FSH
FSH
FSH
FSH
NOW, WATER-MELONS AREN'T IN SEASON RIGHT NOW...
NO KID-DING.
ザザーン…
ZWSHHH
BUT THE STORE DID HAVE WINTER MELON.
WINTER MELON.
SO WE'LL BE USING THAT AS A STAND-IN.
ジャーン
TA-DAH
JUST DRAW SOME ZIGZAGS, AND VOILA!
ZIG AND ZAG AND ZIG... SEE?
WA HA HA
ワハハ
IT'S A WATER-MELON!
BRR! THAT WIND!
HUH?
WHAT?
WHAT IS IT?
ちょい FWP
ちょい FWP
OKAY.
こそ…
WHSPR
TELL THEM, "HOW ABOUT I SPLIT YOUR MELON?"
HOW ABOUT I SPLIT
WAIT, WAIT, THAT'D BE YOUR HEAD ON THE BLOCK.

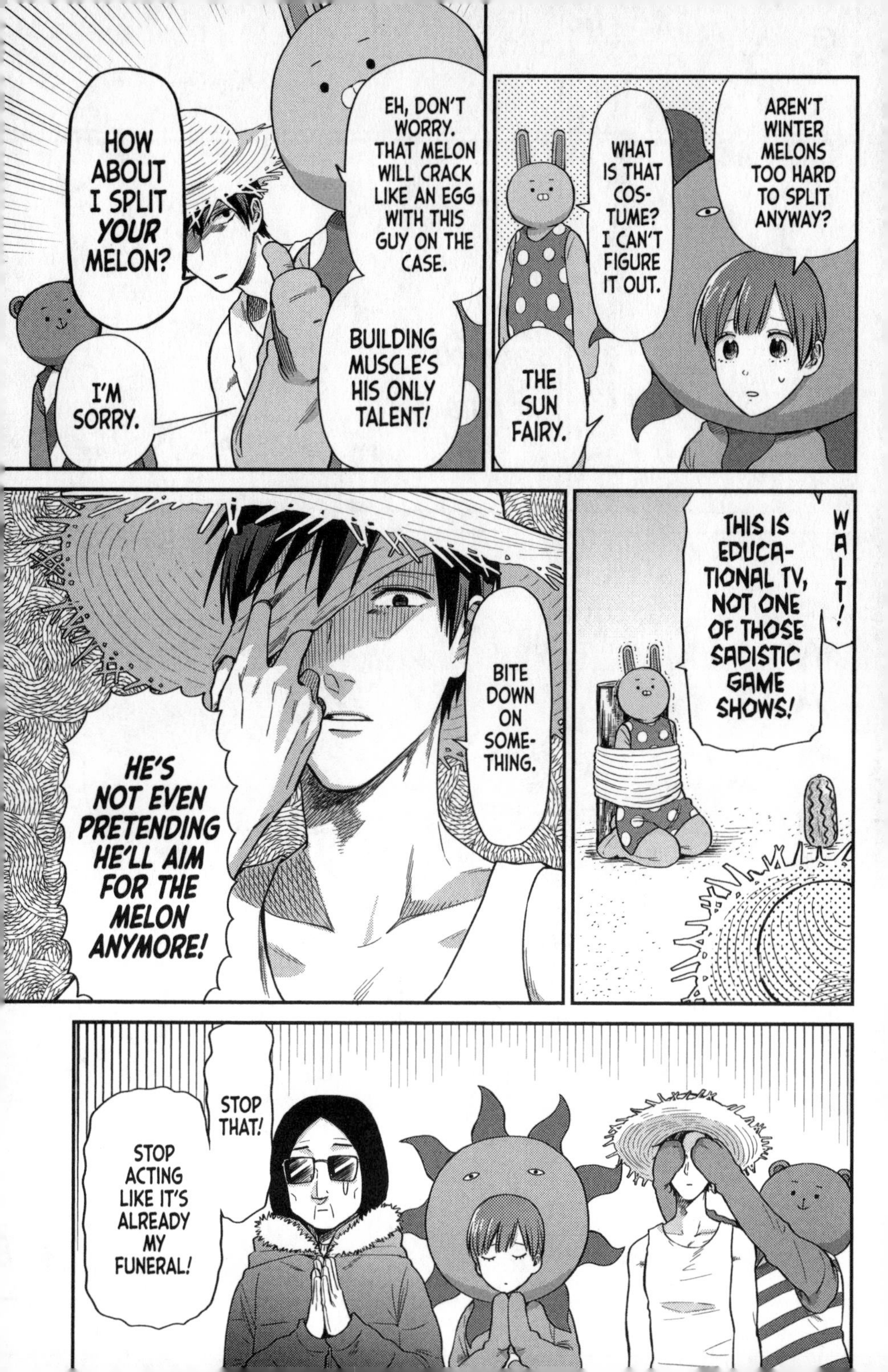
AREN'T WINTER MELONS TOO HARD TO SPLIT ANYWAY?
WHAT IS THAT COSTUME? I CAN'T FIGURE IT OUT.
THE SUN FAIRY.
EH, DON'T WORRY. THAT MELON WILL CRACK LIKE AN EGG WITH THIS GUY ON THE CASE.
HOW ABOUT I SPLIT *YOUR* MELON?
BUILDING MUSCLE'S HIS ONLY TALENT!
I'M SORRY.
WAIT!
THIS IS EDUCATIONAL TV, NOT ONE OF THOSE SADISTIC GAME SHOWS!
BITE DOWN ON SOMETHING.
HE'S NOT EVEN PRETENDING HE'LL AIM FOR THE MELON ANYMORE!
STOP THAT!
STOP ACTING LIKE IT'S ALREADY MY FUNERAL!

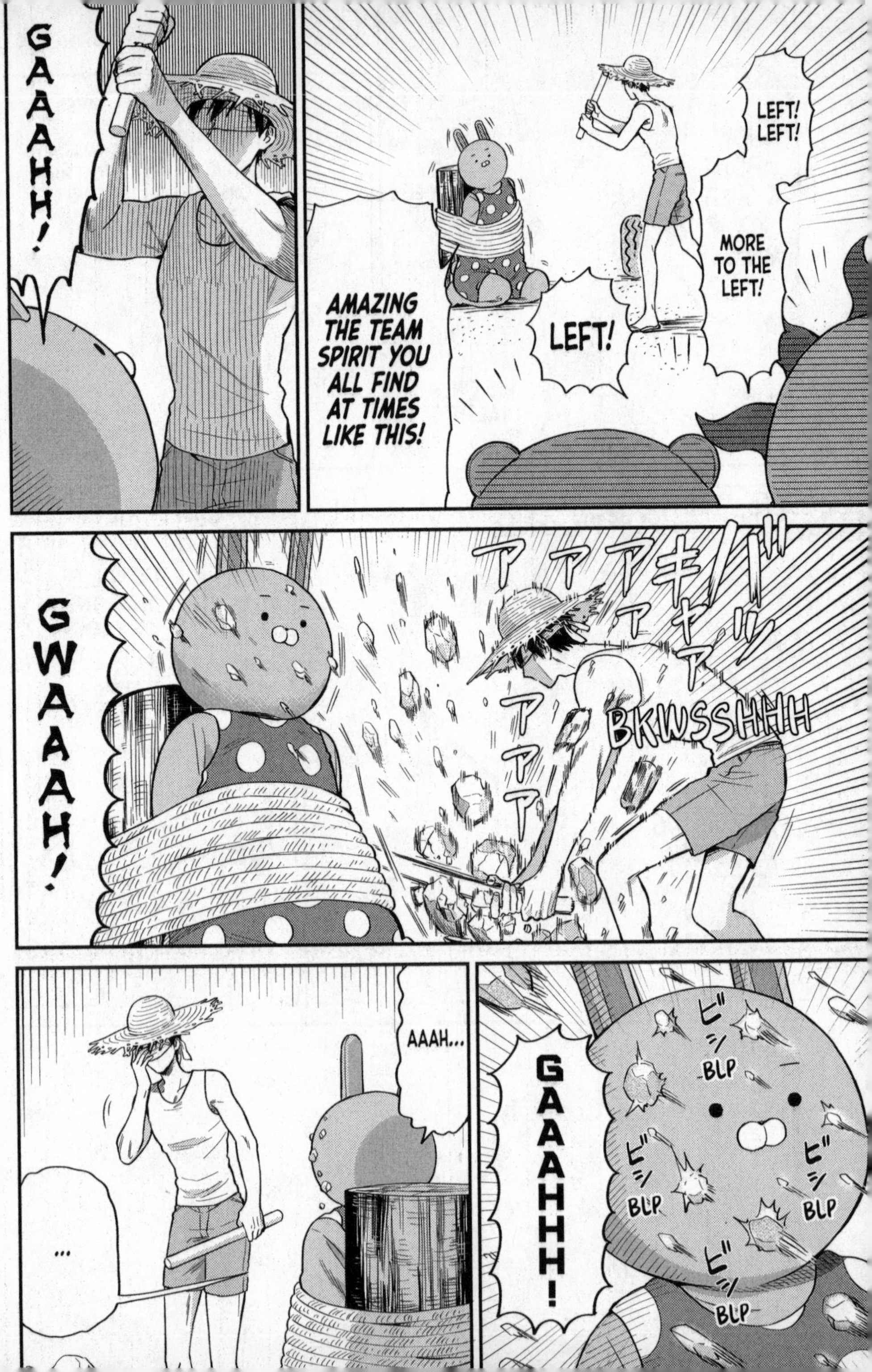
LEFT! LEFT!
MORE TO THE LEFT!
LEFT!
AMAZING THE TEAM SPIRIT YOU ALL FIND AT TIMES LIKE THIS!
GAAAHH!
BKWSSHHH
GWAAAAH!
GAAAHHH!
BLP
BLP
BLP
BLP
AAAH...
...

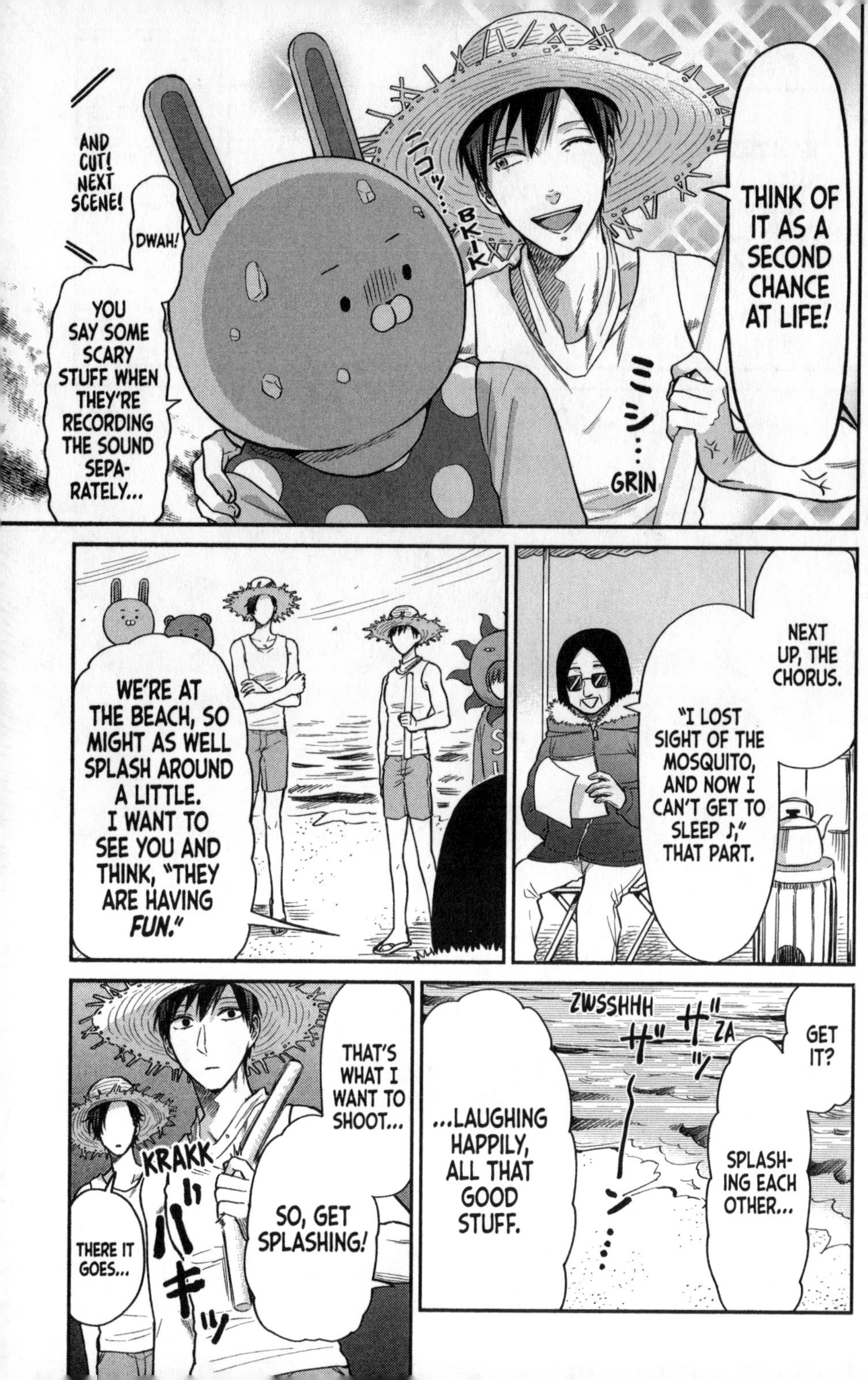
THINK OF IT AS A SECOND CHANCE AT LIFE!
BKIK
GRIN
DWAH!
AND CUT! NEXT SCENE!
YOU SAY SOME SCARY STUFF WHEN THEY'RE RECORDING THE SOUND SEPA-RATELY...
NEXT UP, THE CHORUS.
"I LOST SIGHT OF THE MOSQUITO, AND NOW I CAN'T GET TO SLEEP ♪," THAT PART.
WE'RE AT THE BEACH, SO MIGHT AS WELL SPLASH AROUND A LITTLE. I WANT TO SEE YOU AND THINK, "THEY ARE HAVING *FUN.*"
GET IT?
SPLASH-ING EACH OTHER...
...LAUGHING HAPPILY, ALL THAT GOOD STUFF.
ZWSSHHH
ZA
THAT'S WHAT I WANT TO SHOOT...
SO, GET SPLASHING!
KRAKK
THERE IT GOES...

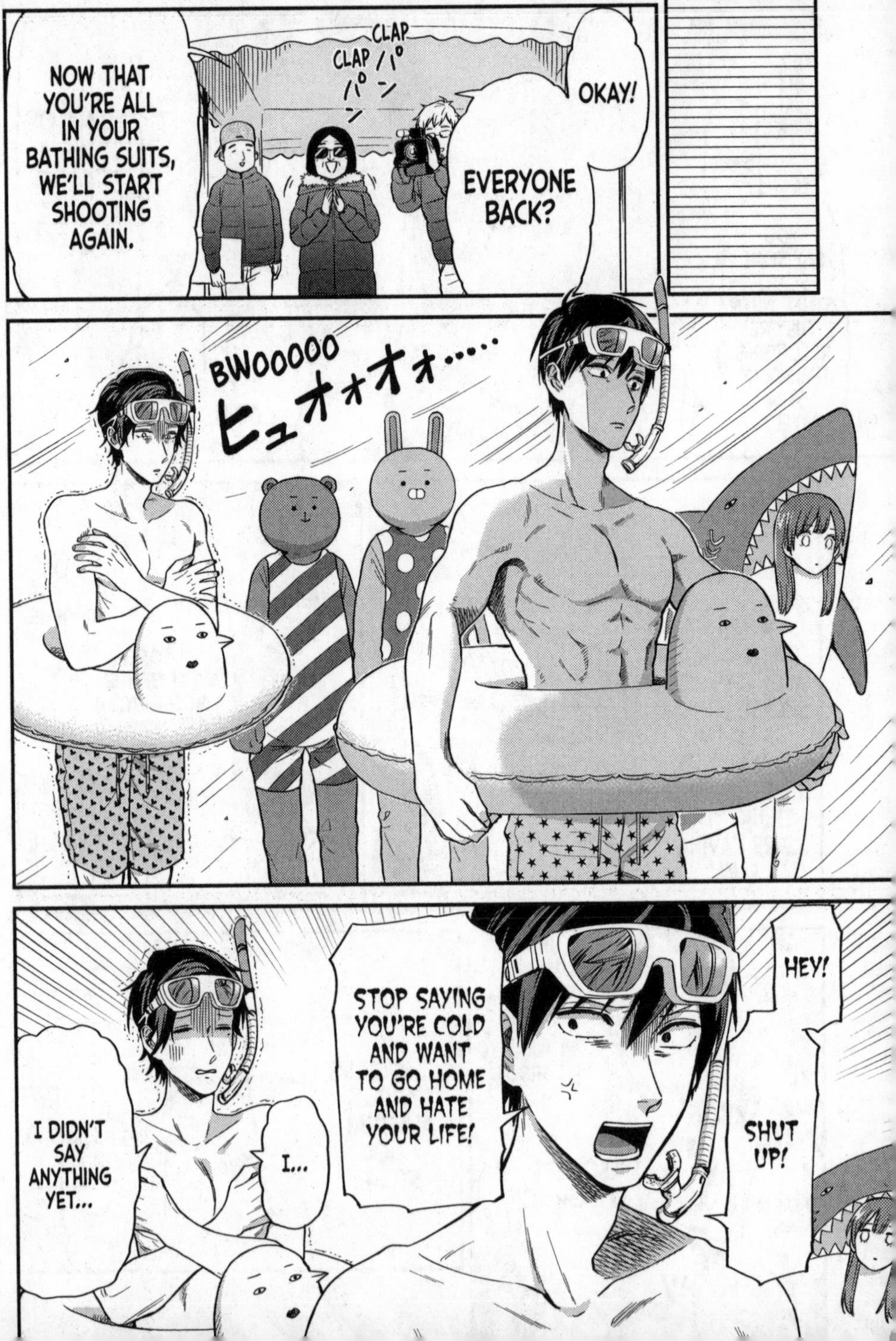
OKAY!
EVERYONE BACK?
CLAP CLAP パ パ ン ン
NOW THAT YOU'RE ALL IN YOUR BATHING SUITS, WE'LL START SHOOTING AGAIN.
BWOOOOO ヒュオォオォ……
HEY!
SHUT UP!
STOP SAYING YOU'RE COLD AND WANT TO GO HOME AND HATE YOUR LIFE!
I...
I DIDN'T SAY ANYTHING YET...

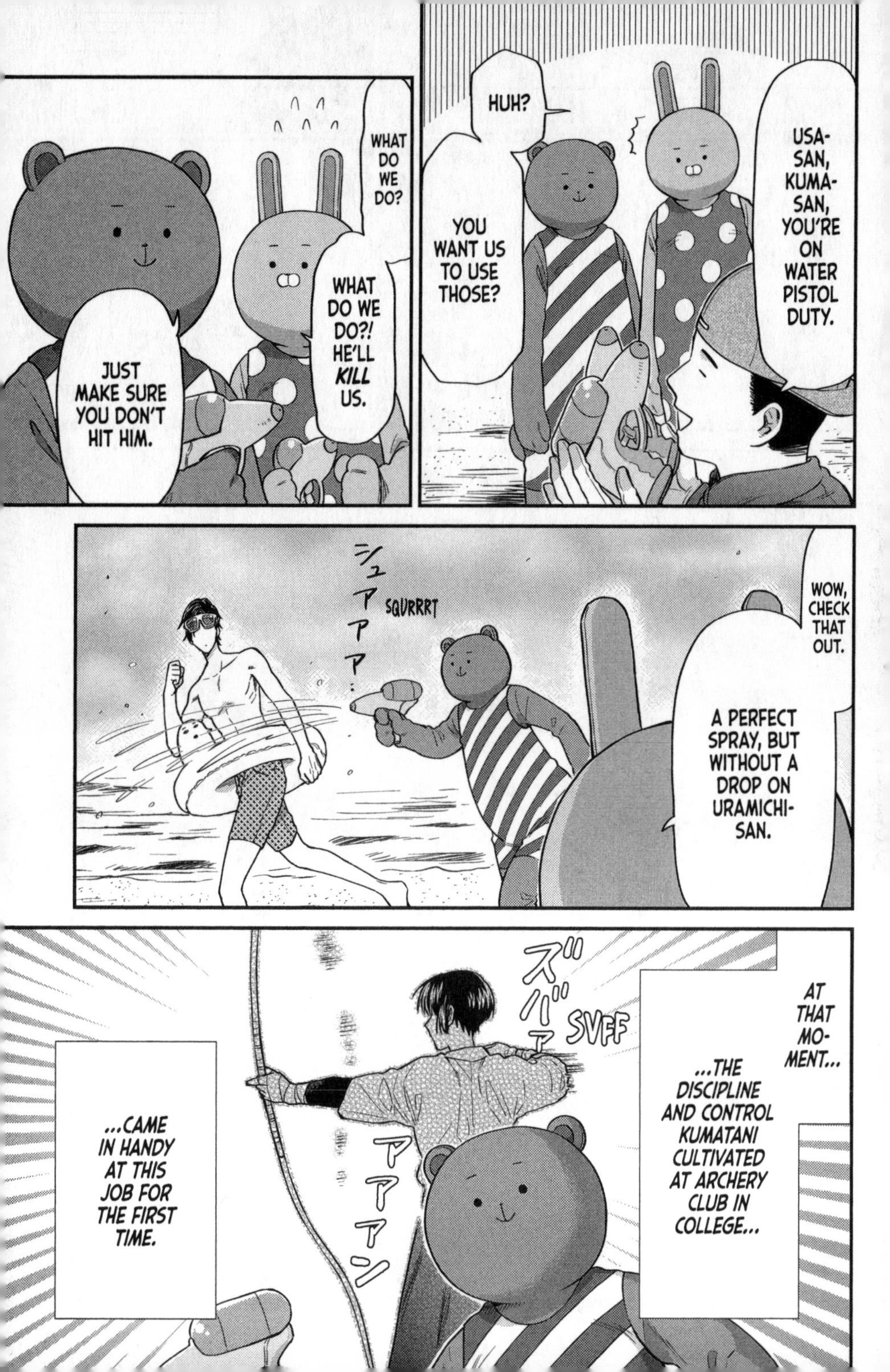
USA-SAN, KUMA-SAN, YOU'RE ON WATER PISTOL DUTY.
HUH?
YOU WANT US TO USE THOSE?
WHAT DO WE DO?
WHAT DO WE DO?! HE'LL *KILL* US.
JUST MAKE SURE YOU DON'T HIT HIM.
WOW, CHECK THAT OUT.
A PERFECT SPRAY, BUT WITHOUT A DROP ON URAMICHI-SAN.
シュアアア
SQURRRT
AT THAT MOMENT...
...THE DISCIPLINE AND CONTROL KUMATANI CULTIVATED AT ARCHERY CLUB IN COLLEGE...
ズバァ
SVFF
アアアン
...CAME IN HANDY AT THIS JOB FOR THE FIRST TIME.

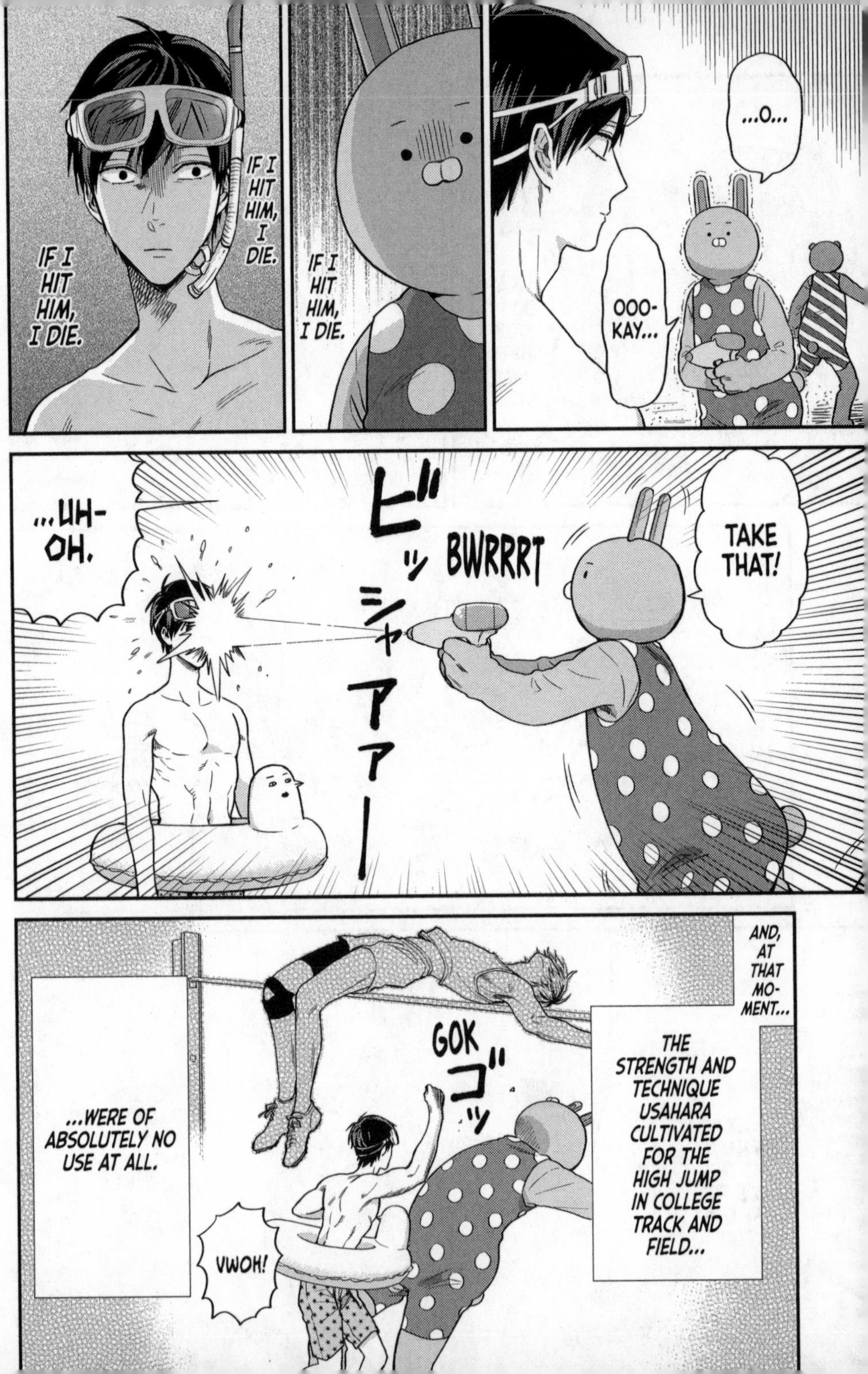
...O...
OOO-KAY...
IF I HIT HIM, I DIE.
IF I HIT HIM, I DIE.
IF I HIT HIM, I DIE.
TAKE THAT!
BWRRRT
ビッシャアー
...UH-OH.
AND, AT THAT MO-MENT...
THE STRENGTH AND TECHNIQUE USAHARA CULTIVATED FOR THE HIGH JUMP IN COLLEGE TRACK AND FIELD...
GOK
ゴッ
VWOH!
...WERE OF ABSOLUTELY NO USE AT ALL.

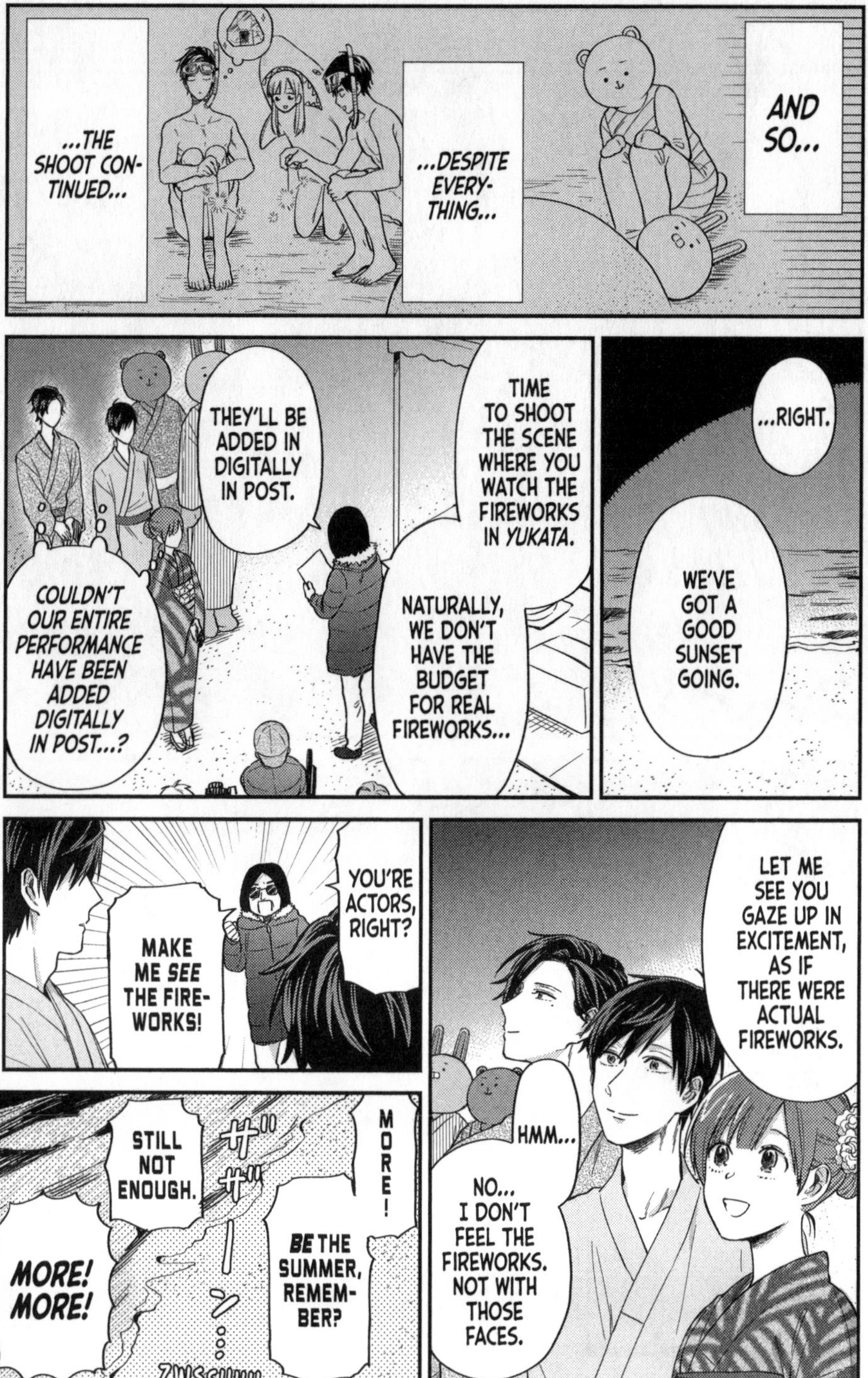
AND SO...
...DESPITE EVERYTHING...
...THE SHOOT CONTINUED...
...RIGHT.
WE'VE GOT A GOOD SUNSET GOING.
TIME TO SHOOT THE SCENE WHERE YOU WATCH THE FIREWORKS IN *YUKATA*.
NATURALLY, WE DON'T HAVE THE BUDGET FOR REAL FIREWORKS...
THEY'LL BE ADDED IN DIGITALLY IN POST.
COULDN'T OUR ENTIRE PERFORMANCE HAVE BEEN ADDED DIGITALLY IN POST...?
LET ME SEE YOU GAZE UP IN EXCITEMENT, AS IF THERE WERE ACTUAL FIREWORKS.
HMM...
NO... I DON'T FEEL THE FIREWORKS. NOT WITH THOSE FACES.
YOU'RE ACTORS, RIGHT?
MAKE ME *SEE* THE FIREWORKS!
MORE!
BE THE SUMMER, REMEMBER?
STILL NOT ENOUGH.
MORE! MORE!
ZWSSHHH

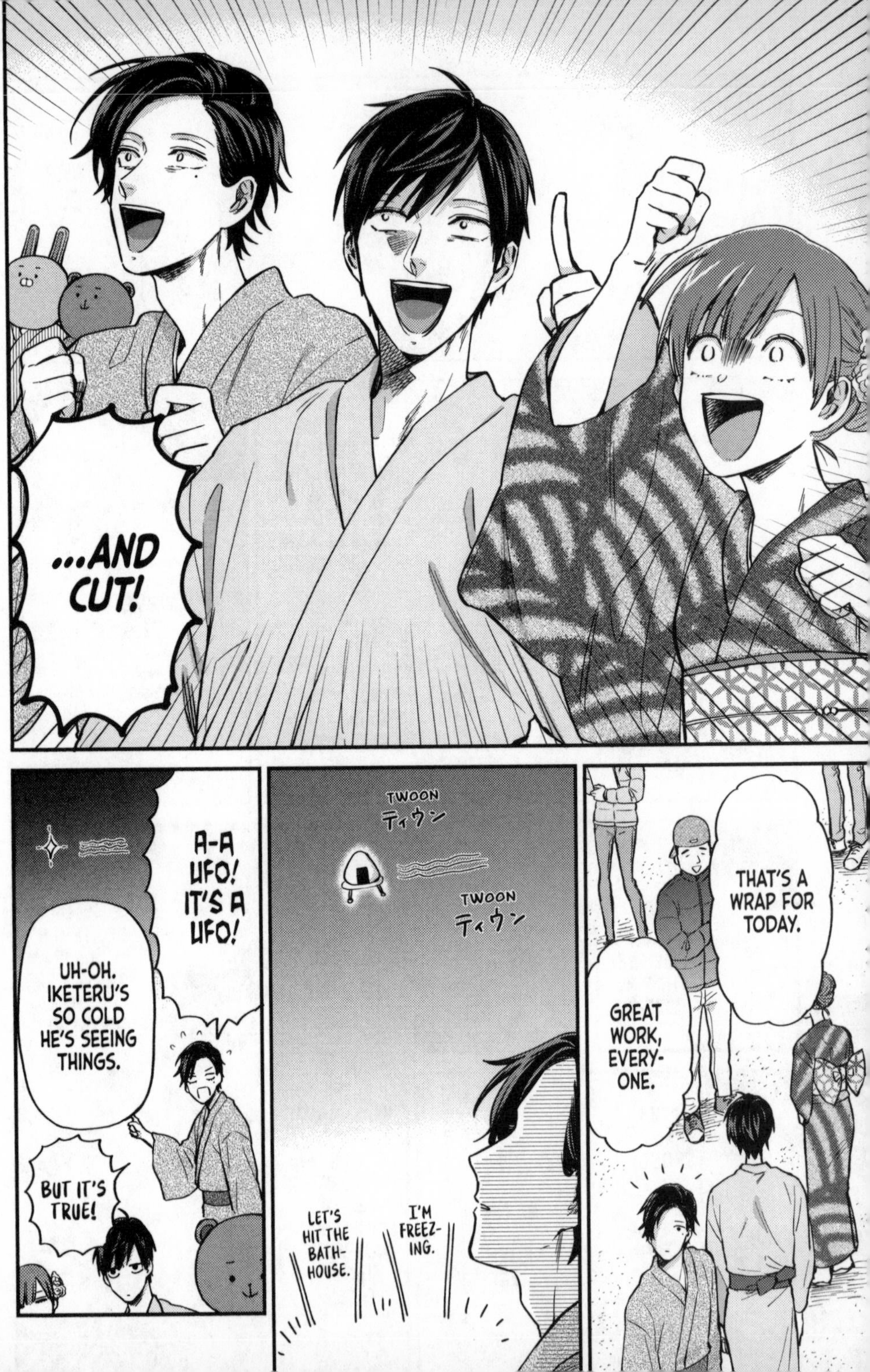
...AND CUT!
THAT'S A WRAP FOR TODAY.
GREAT WORK, EVERY-ONE.
TWOON ティウン
TWOON ティウン
I'M FREEZ-ING.
LET'S HIT THE BATH-HOUSE.
A-A UFO! IT'S A UFO!
UH-OH. IKETERU'S SO COLD HE'S SEEING THINGS.
BUT IT'S TRUE!

Life Lessons with
Uramichi Oniisan

Can and Can't

Sung by Iketeru Oniisan and
Utano Oneesan

Some things you can do, and others you can't
Don't try to do everything yourself

If someone can do what you can't
Say "Nice work!" and become their friend

Some people are good singers
Some people know how to draw
Some people tell funny stories
And some are great jumpers

We're all just people—ordinary people

There's more things you can't do than can
The things you can do aren't the things you want to

If someone can do what you can't

It's hard to be their friend
You can't get out the "Nice work!"

Saying "Nice work!" and becoming friends

That's the hardest thing of all

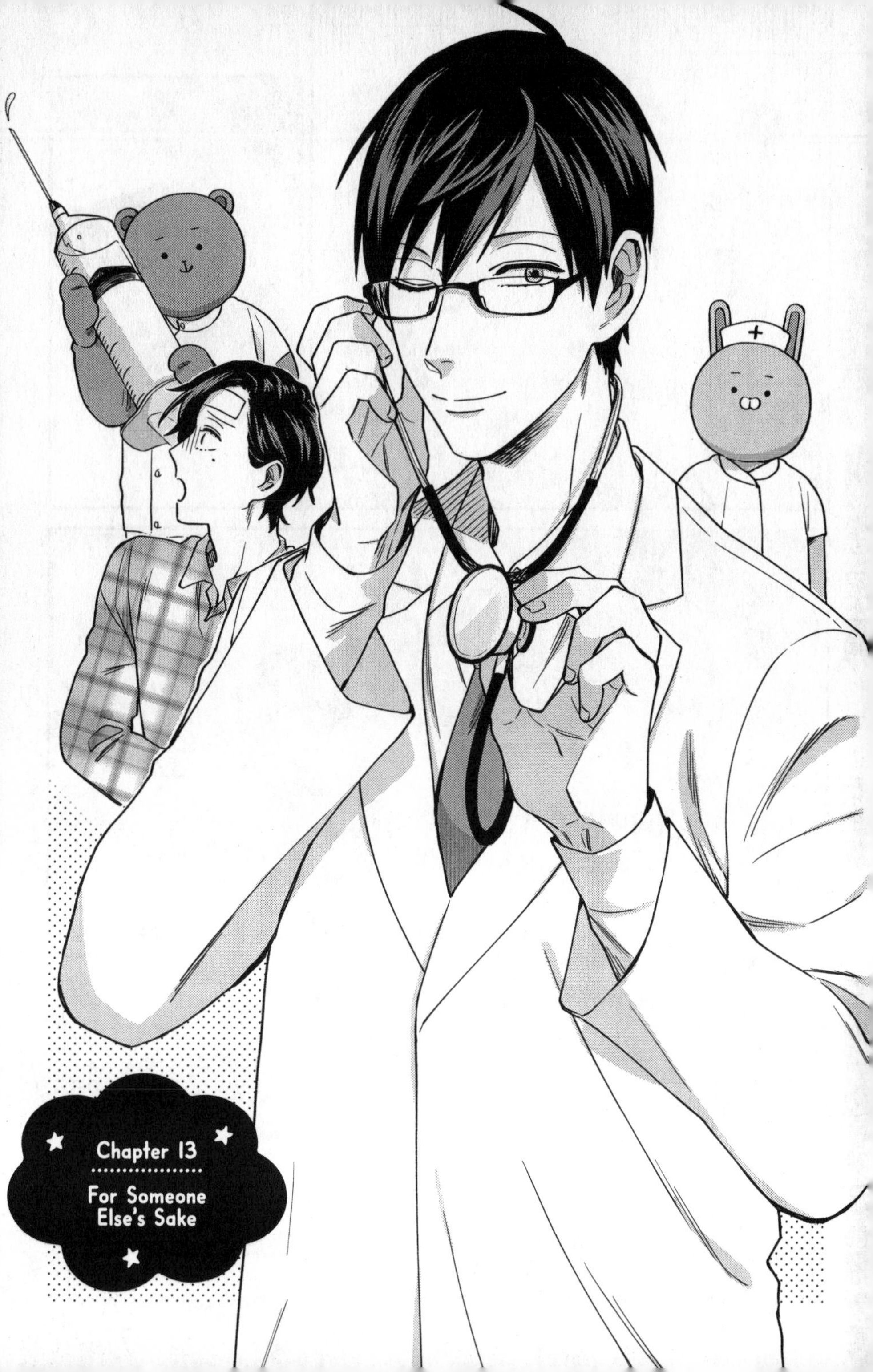
Chapter 13
For Someone Else's Sake

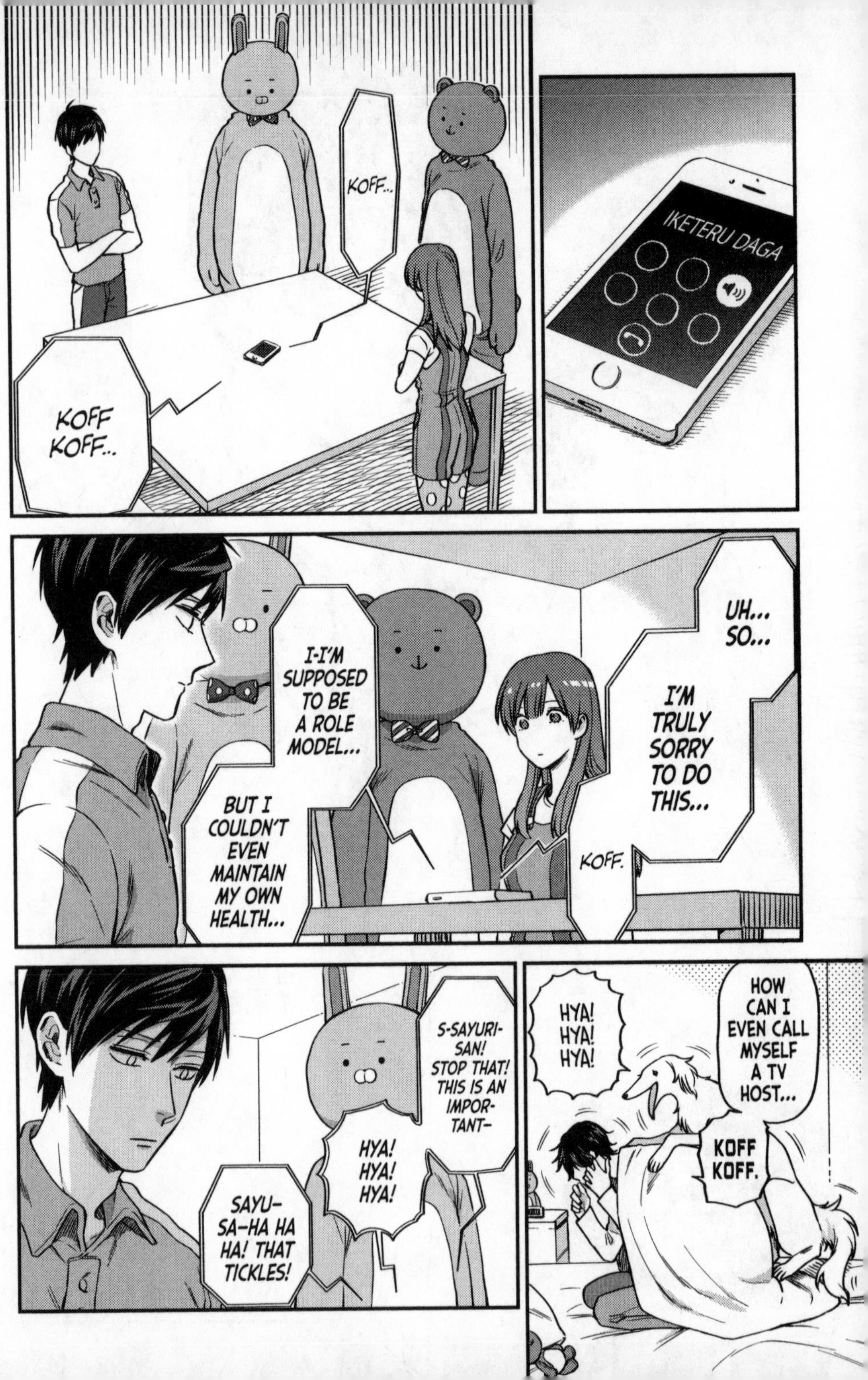
IKETERU DAGA
KOFF...
KOFF KOFF...
UH... SO...
I'M TRULY SORRY TO DO THIS...
KOFF.
I-I'M SUPPOSED TO BE A ROLE MODEL...
BUT I COULDN'T EVEN MAINTAIN MY OWN HEALTH...
HOW CAN I EVEN CALL MYSELF A TV HOST...
HYA! HYA! HYA!
KOFF KOFF.
S-SAYURI-SAN! STOP THAT! THIS IS AN IMPOR-TANT-
HYA! HYA! HYA!
SAYU-SA-HA HA HA! THAT TICKLES!

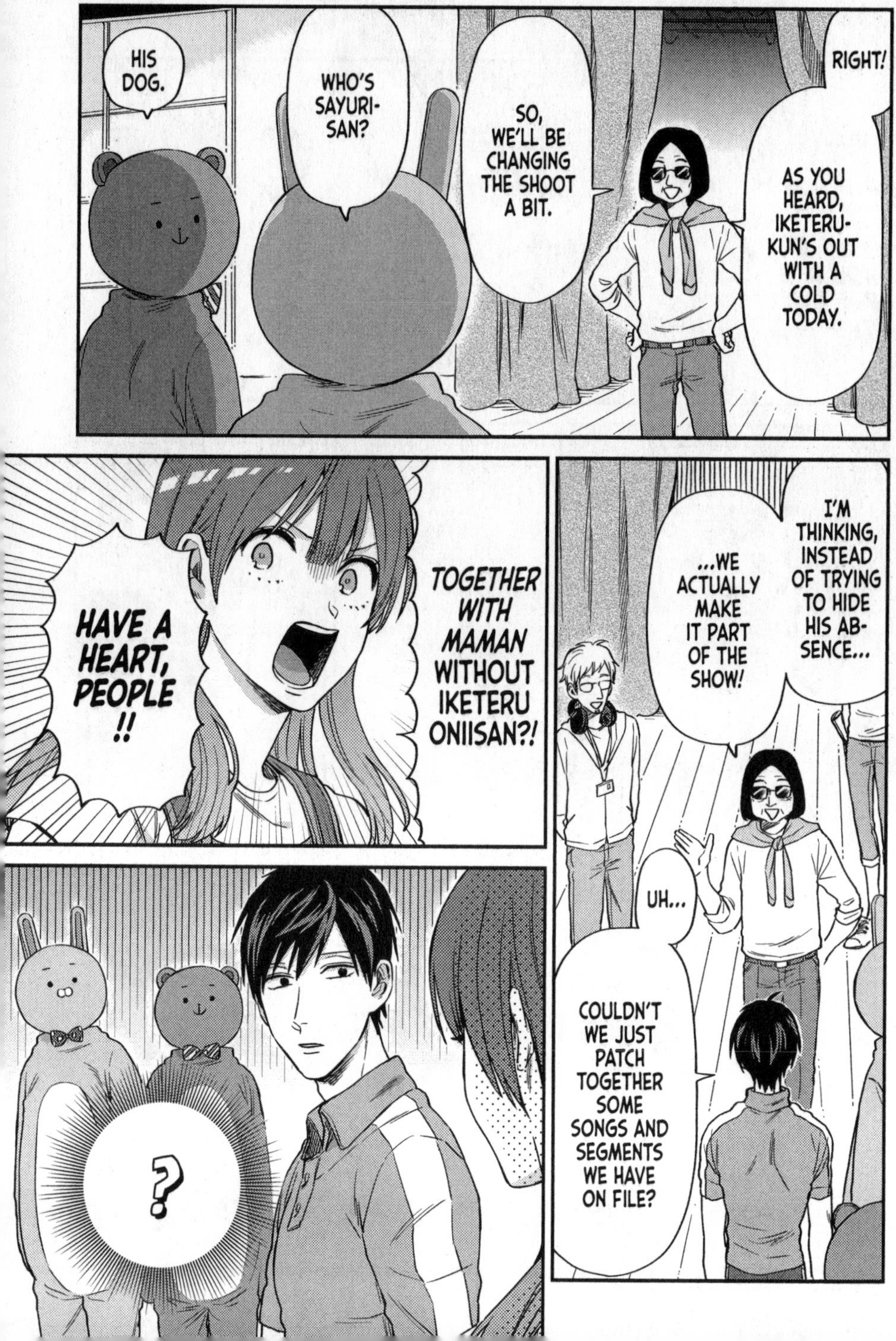
RIGHT!
AS YOU HEARD, IKETERU-KUN'S OUT WITH A COLD TODAY.
SO, WE'LL BE CHANGING THE SHOOT A BIT.
WHO'S SAYURI-SAN?
HIS DOG.
I'M THINKING, INSTEAD OF TRYING TO HIDE HIS ABSENCE...
...WE ACTUALLY MAKE IT PART OF THE SHOW!
UH...
COULDN'T WE JUST PATCH TOGETHER SOME SONGS AND SEGMENTS WE HAVE ON FILE?
TOGETHER WITH MAMAN WITHOUT IKETERU ONIISAN?!
HAVE A HEART, PEOPLE !!
?

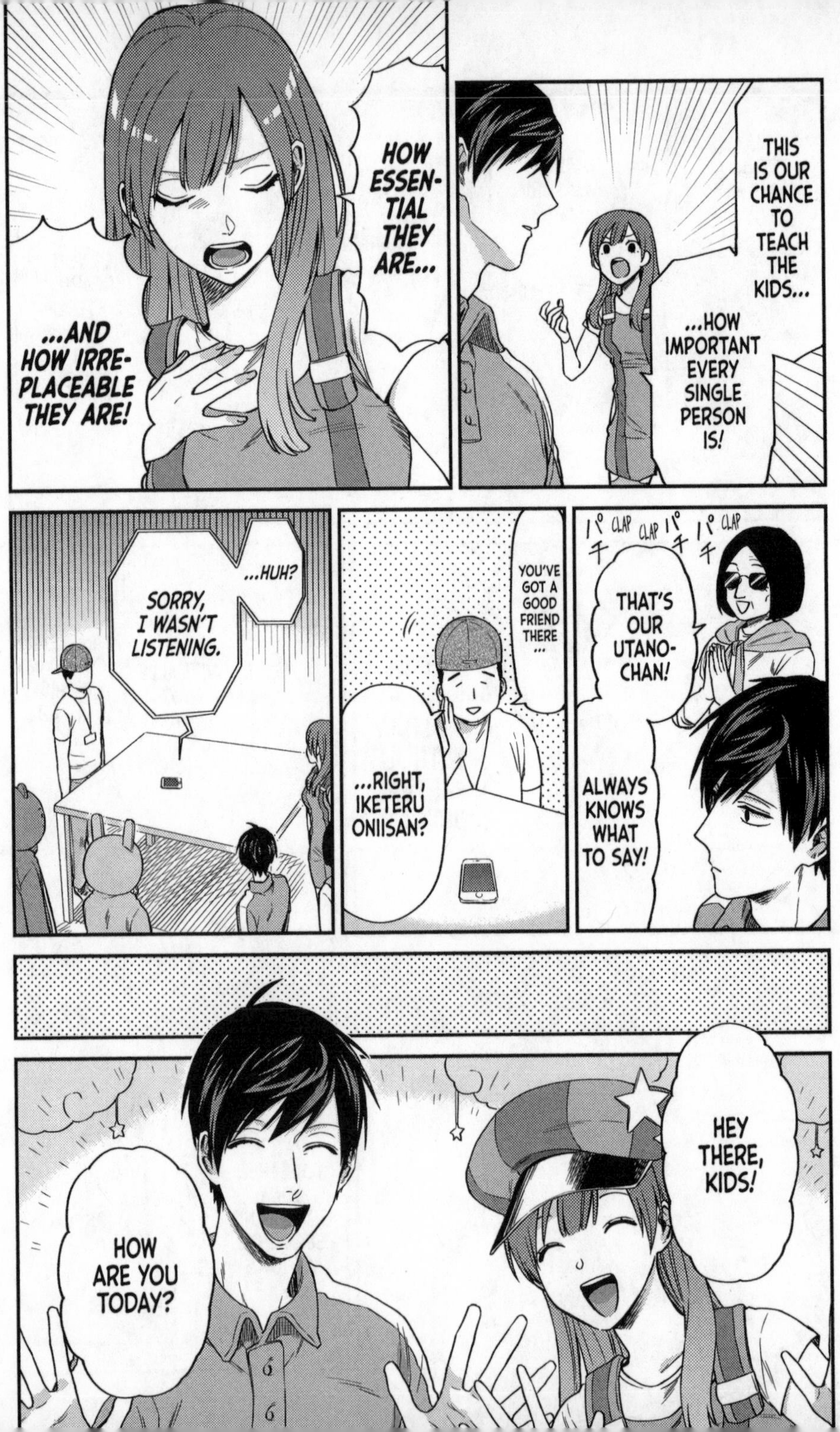
THIS IS OUR CHANCE TO TEACH THE KIDS...
...HOW IMPORTANT EVERY SINGLE PERSON IS!
HOW ESSENTIAL THEY ARE...
...AND HOW IRREPLACEABLE THEY ARE!
パチ CLAP パチ CLAP パチ CLAP
THAT'S OUR UTANO-CHAN!
ALWAYS KNOWS WHAT TO SAY!
YOU'VE GOT A GOOD FRIEND THERE...
...RIGHT, IKETERU ONIISAN?
...HUH?
SORRY, I WASN'T LISTENING.
HEY THERE, KIDS!
HOW ARE YOU TODAY?

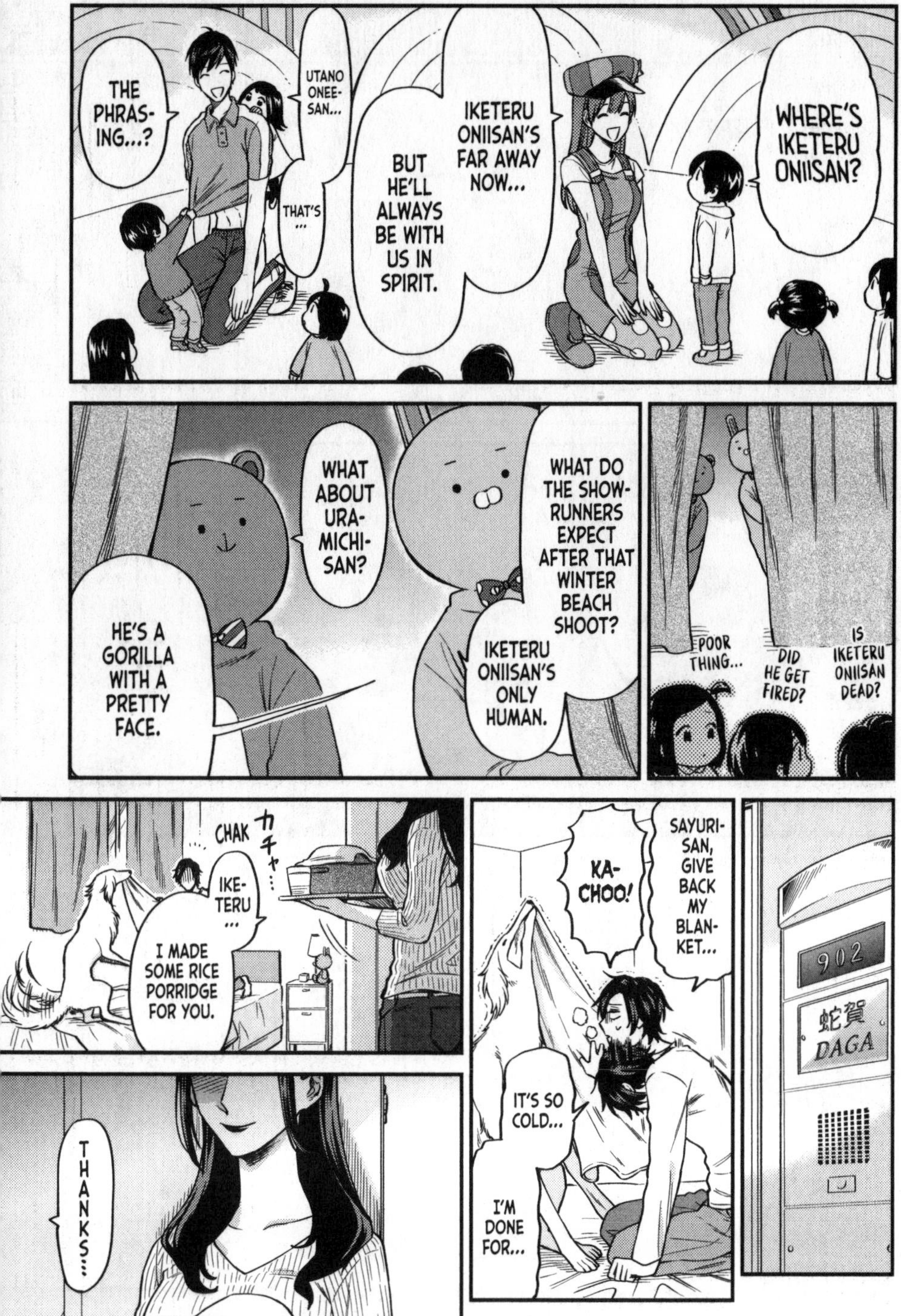
WHERE'S IKETERU ONIISAN?
IKETERU ONIISAN'S FAR AWAY NOW...
BUT HE'LL ALWAYS BE WITH US IN SPIRIT.
UTANO ONEE-SAN...
THAT'S ...
THE PHRASING...?
IS IKETERU ONIISAN DEAD?
DID HE GET FIRED?
POOR THING...
WHAT DO THE SHOWRUNNERS EXPECT AFTER THAT WINTER BEACH SHOOT?
IKETERU ONIISAN'S ONLY HUMAN.
WHAT ABOUT URAMICHI-SAN?
HE'S A GORILLA WITH A PRETTY FACE.
902
蛇賀
DAGA
SAYURI-SAN, GIVE BACK MY BLANKET...
KA-CHOO!
IT'S SO COLD...
I'M DONE FOR...
CHAK
カチャ
...
IKETERU...
I MADE SOME RICE PORRIDGE FOR YOU.
THANKS...

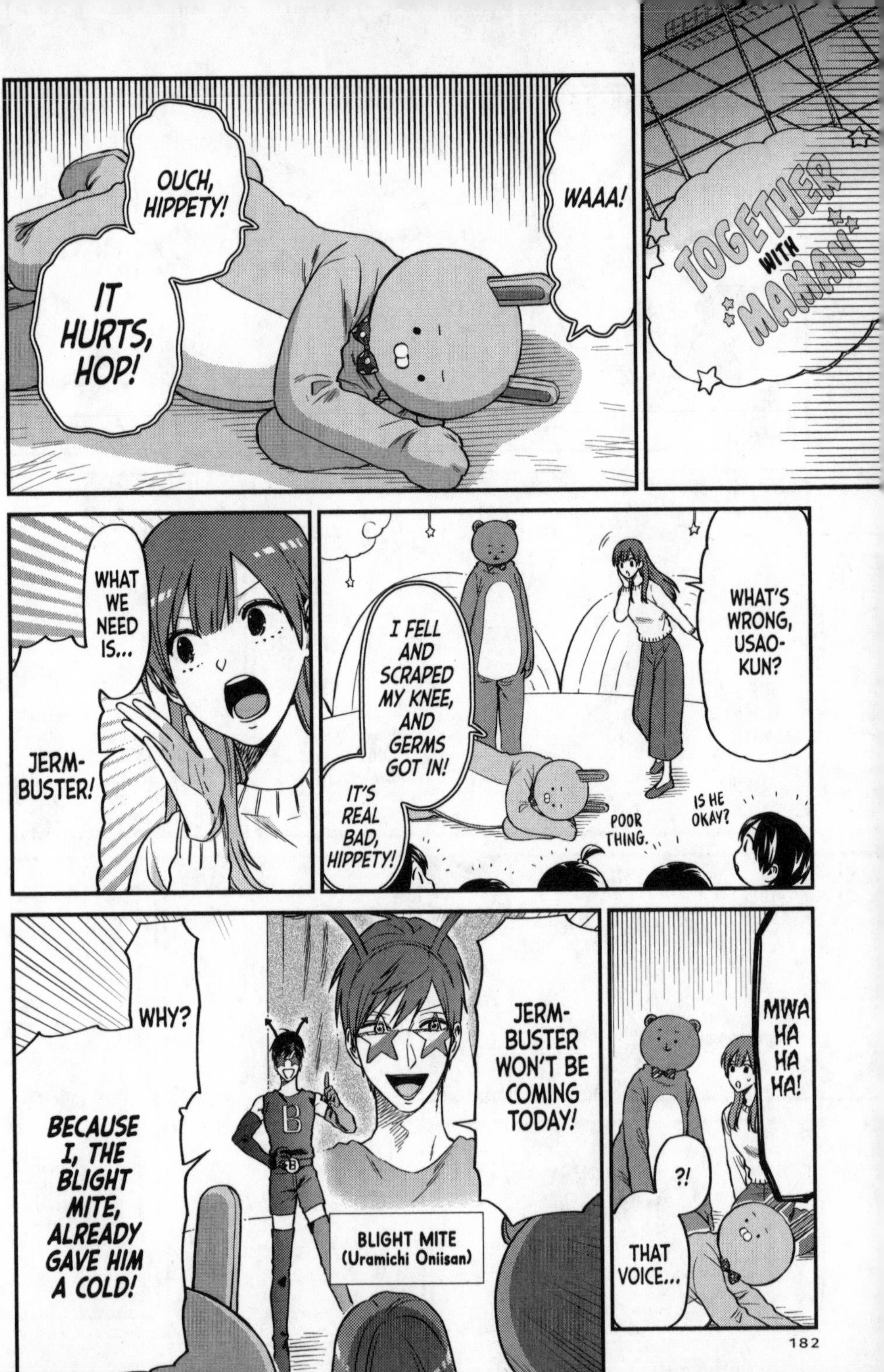

TOGETHER WITH MAMAN
WAAA!
OUCH, HIPPETY!
IT HURTS, HOP!
WHAT'S WRONG, USAO-KUN?
I FELL AND SCRAPED MY KNEE, AND GERMS GOT IN!
IT'S REAL BAD, HIPPETY!
IS HE OKAY?
POOR THING.
WHAT WE NEED IS...
JERM-BUSTER!
MWA HA HA HA!
?!
THAT VOICE...
JERM-BUSTER WON'T BE COMING TODAY!
WHY?
BECAUSE I, THE BLIGHT MITE, ALREADY GAVE HIM A COLD!
BLIGHT MITE (Uramichi Oniisan)

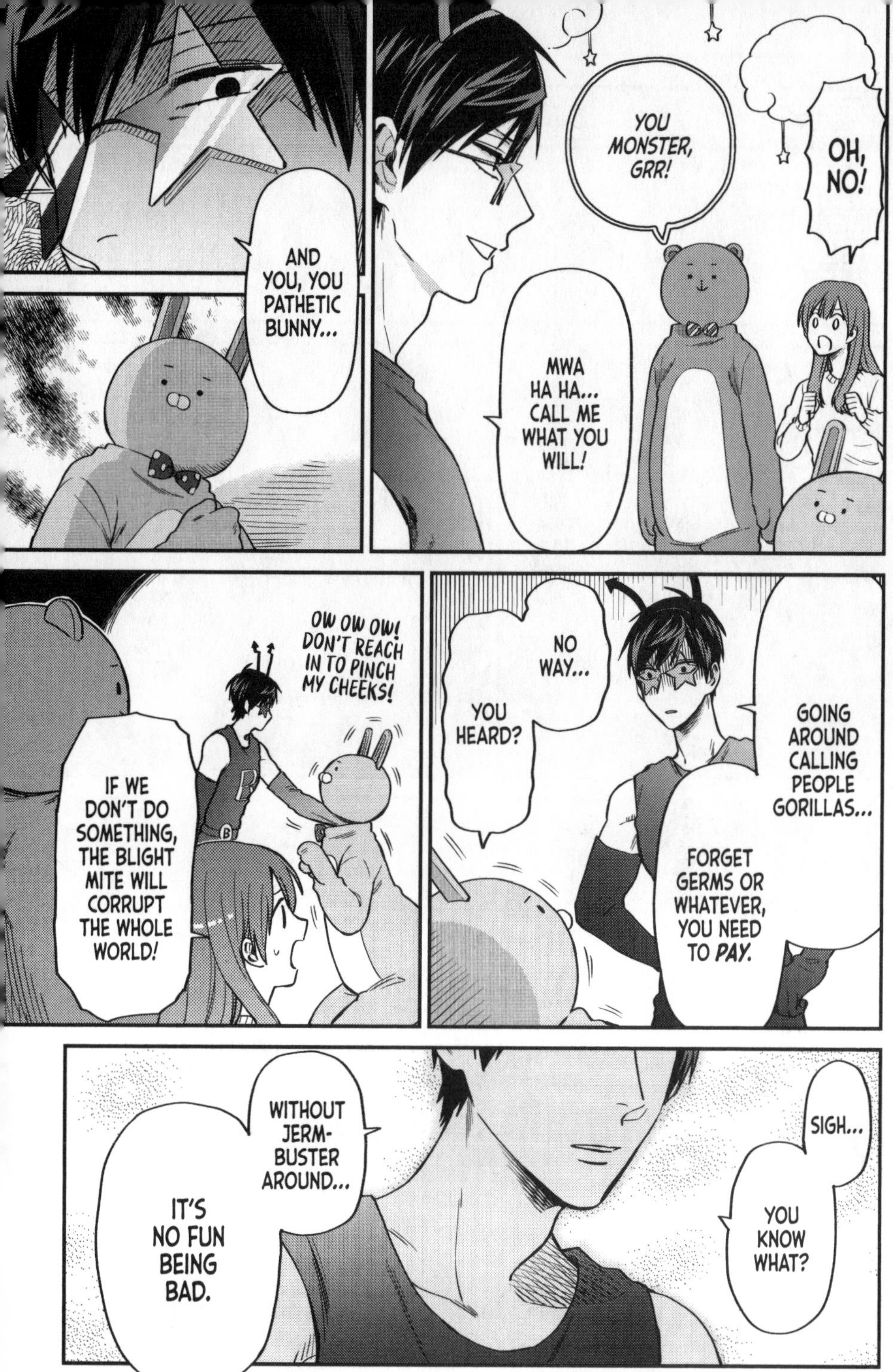
OH, NO!
YOU MONSTER, GRR!
MWA HA HA... CALL ME WHAT YOU WILL!
AND YOU, YOU PATHETIC BUNNY...
GOING AROUND CALLING PEOPLE GORILLAS...
FORGET GERMS OR WHATEVER, YOU NEED TO *PAY*.
NO WAY...
YOU HEARD?
OW OW OW! DON'T REACH IN TO PINCH MY CHEEKS!
IF WE DON'T DO SOMETHING, THE BLIGHT MITE WILL CORRUPT THE WHOLE WORLD!
SIGH...
YOU KNOW WHAT?
WITHOUT JERM-BUSTER AROUND...
IT'S NO FUN BEING BAD.

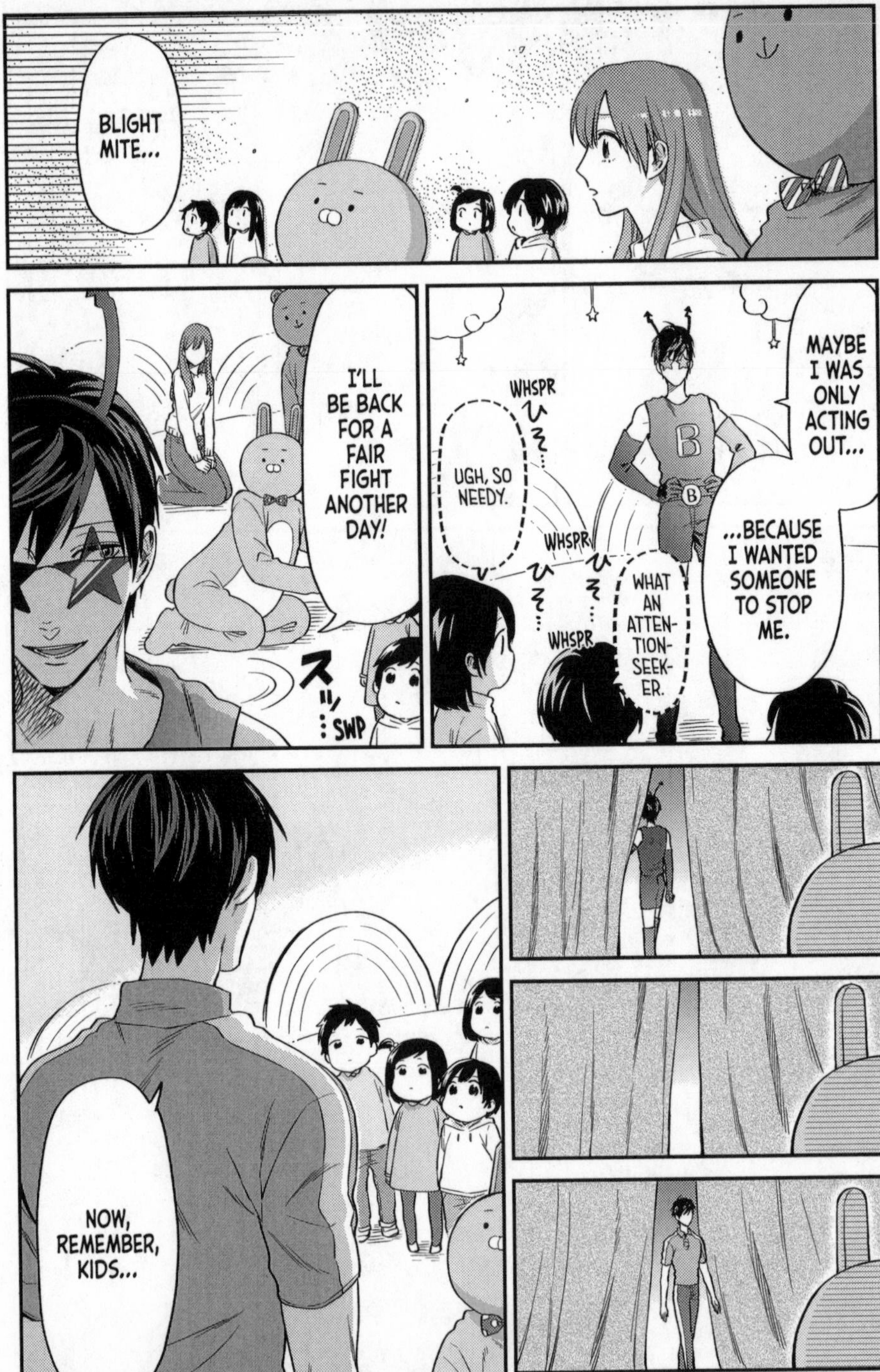
BLIGHT MITE...
MAYBE I WAS ONLY ACTING OUT...
...BECAUSE I WANTED SOMEONE TO STOP ME.
WHSPR
UGH, SO NEEDY.
WHSPR
WHSPR
WHAT AN ATTEN-TION-SEEK-ER.
I'LL BE BACK FOR A FAIR FIGHT ANOTHER DAY!
SWP
NOW, REMEMBER, KIDS...

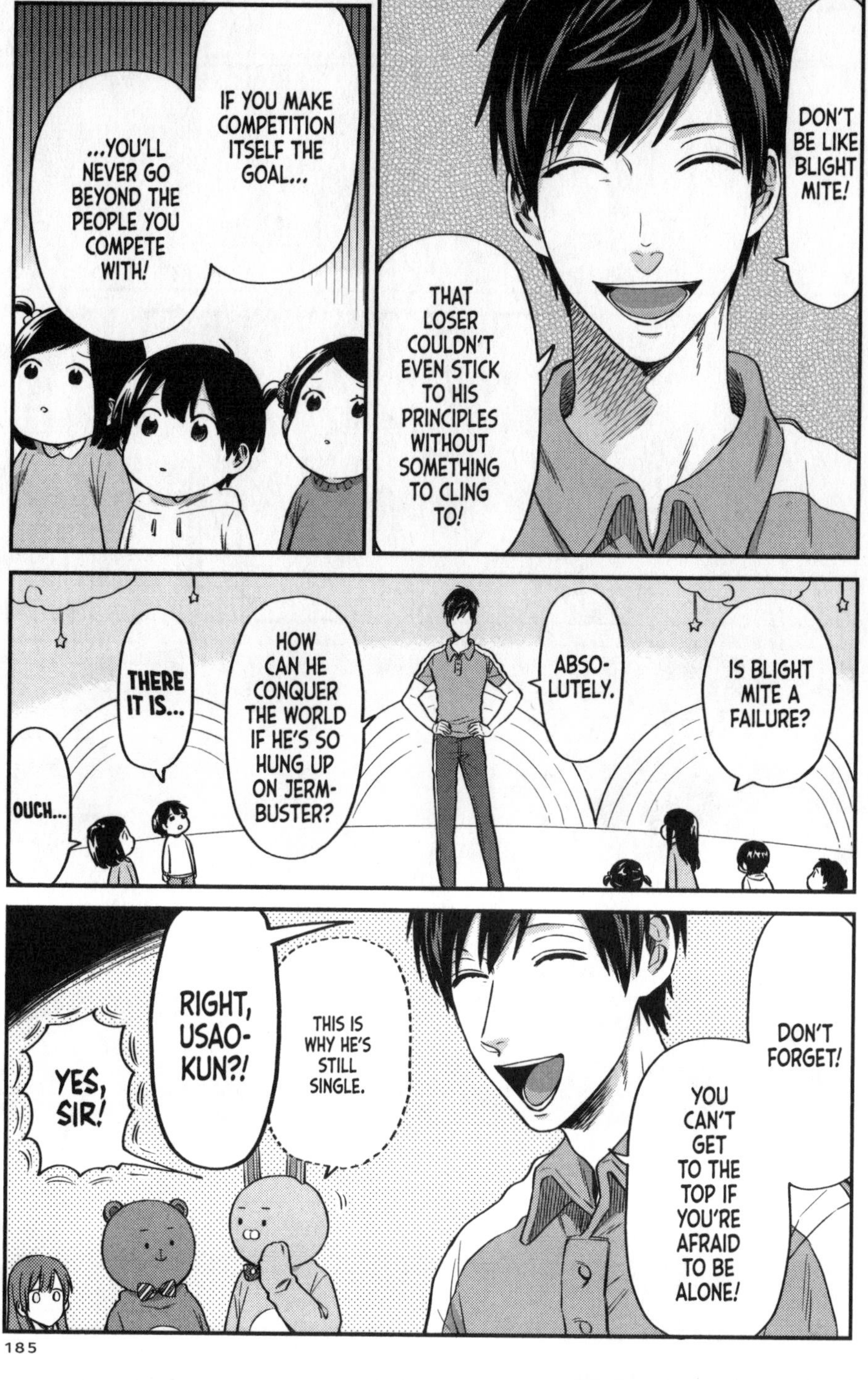
DON'T BE LIKE BLIGHT MITE!
THAT LOSER COULDN'T EVEN STICK TO HIS PRINCIPLES WITHOUT SOMETHING TO CLING TO!
IF YOU MAKE COMPETITION ITSELF THE GOAL...
...YOU'LL NEVER GO BEYOND THE PEOPLE YOU COMPETE WITH!
IS BLIGHT MITE A FAILURE?
ABSO-LUTELY.
HOW CAN HE CONQUER THE WORLD IF HE'S SO HUNG UP ON JERM-BUSTER?
THERE IT IS...
OUCH...
DON'T FORGET!
YOU CAN'T GET TO THE TOP IF YOU'RE AFRAID TO BE ALONE!
RIGHT, USAO-KUN?!
THIS IS WHY HE'S STILL SINGLE.
YES, SIR!

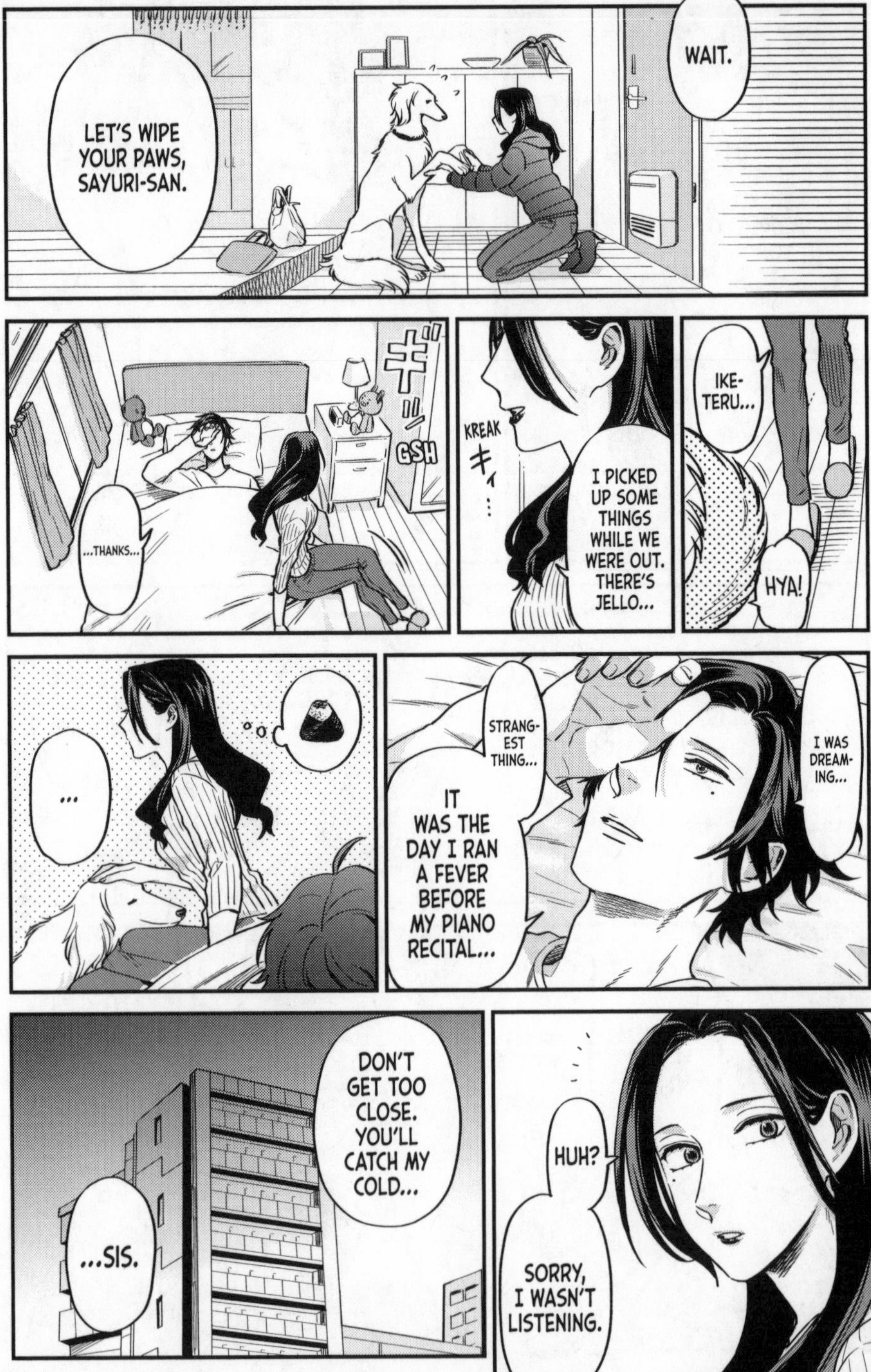
WAIT.
LET'S WIPE YOUR PAWS, SAYURI-SAN.
IKE-TERU...
HYA!
KREAK
キィ…
I PICKED UP SOME THINGS WHILE WE WERE OUT. THERE'S JELLO...
ギ
GSH
...THANKS...
I WAS DREAMING...
STRANGEST THING...
IT WAS THE DAY I RAN A FEVER BEFORE MY PIANO RECITAL...
...
HUH?
SORRY, I WASN'T LISTENING.
DON'T GET TOO CLOSE. YOU'LL CATCH MY COLD...
...SIS.

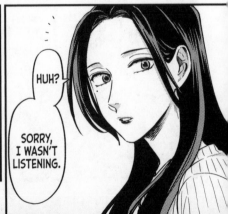

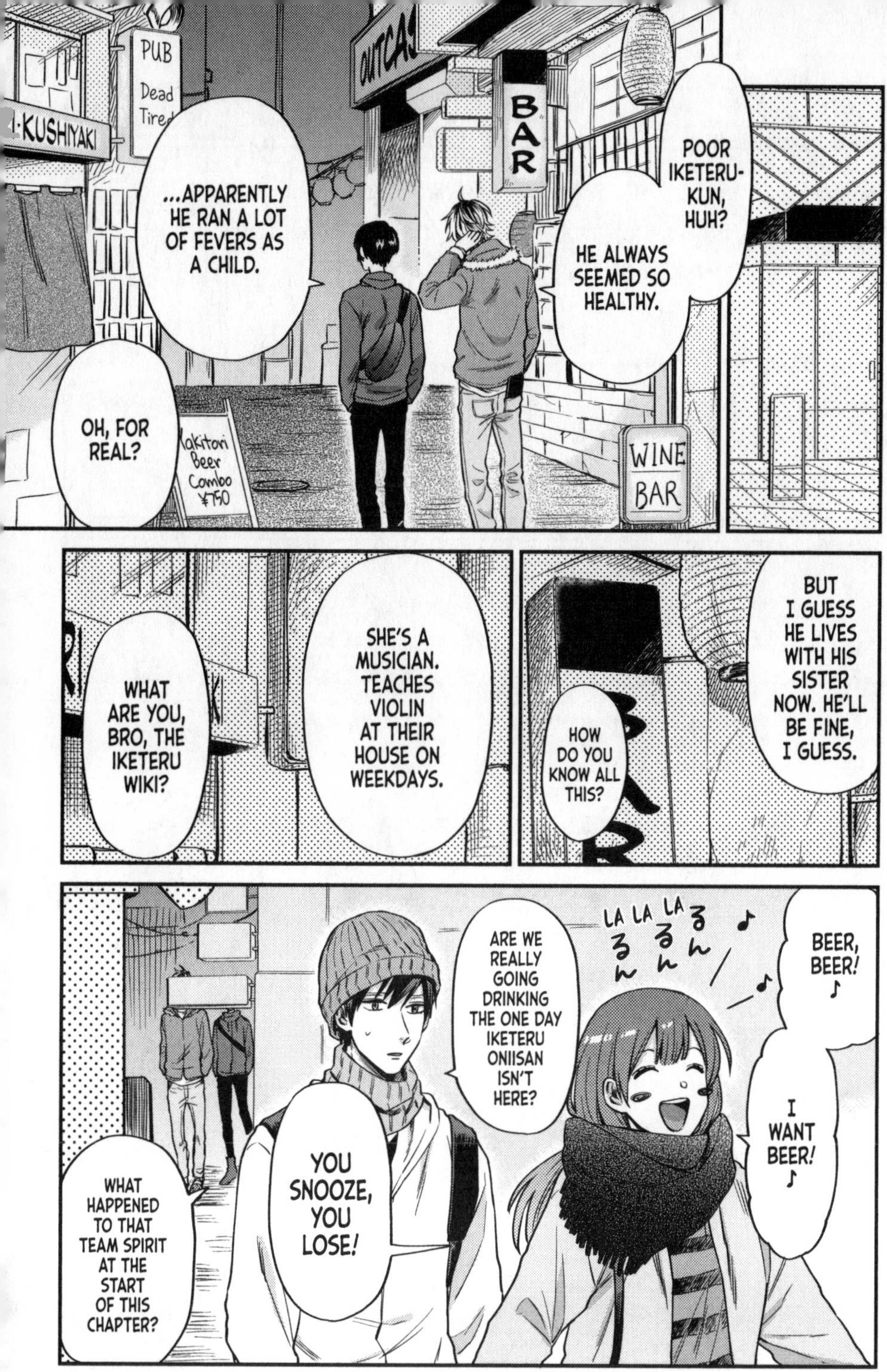
PUB
Dead Tired
KUSHIYAKI
BAR
POOR IKETERU-KUN, HUH?
HE ALWAYS SEEMED SO HEALTHY.
...APPARENTLY HE RAN A LOT OF FEVERS AS A CHILD.
OH, FOR REAL?
Yakitori Beer Combo ¥750
WINE BAR
BUT I GUESS HE LIVES WITH HIS SISTER NOW. HE'LL BE FINE, I GUESS.
HOW DO YOU KNOW ALL THIS?
SHE'S A MUSICIAN. TEACHES VIOLIN AT THEIR HOUSE ON WEEKDAYS.
WHAT ARE YOU, BRO, THE IKETERU WIKI?
BEER, BEER! ♪
LA LA LA るんるんるん ♪
I WANT BEER! ♪
ARE WE REALLY GOING DRINKING THE ONE DAY IKETERU ONIISAN ISN'T HERE?
YOU SNOOZE, YOU LOSE!
WHAT HAPPENED TO THAT TEAM SPIRIT AT THE START OF THIS CHAPTER?

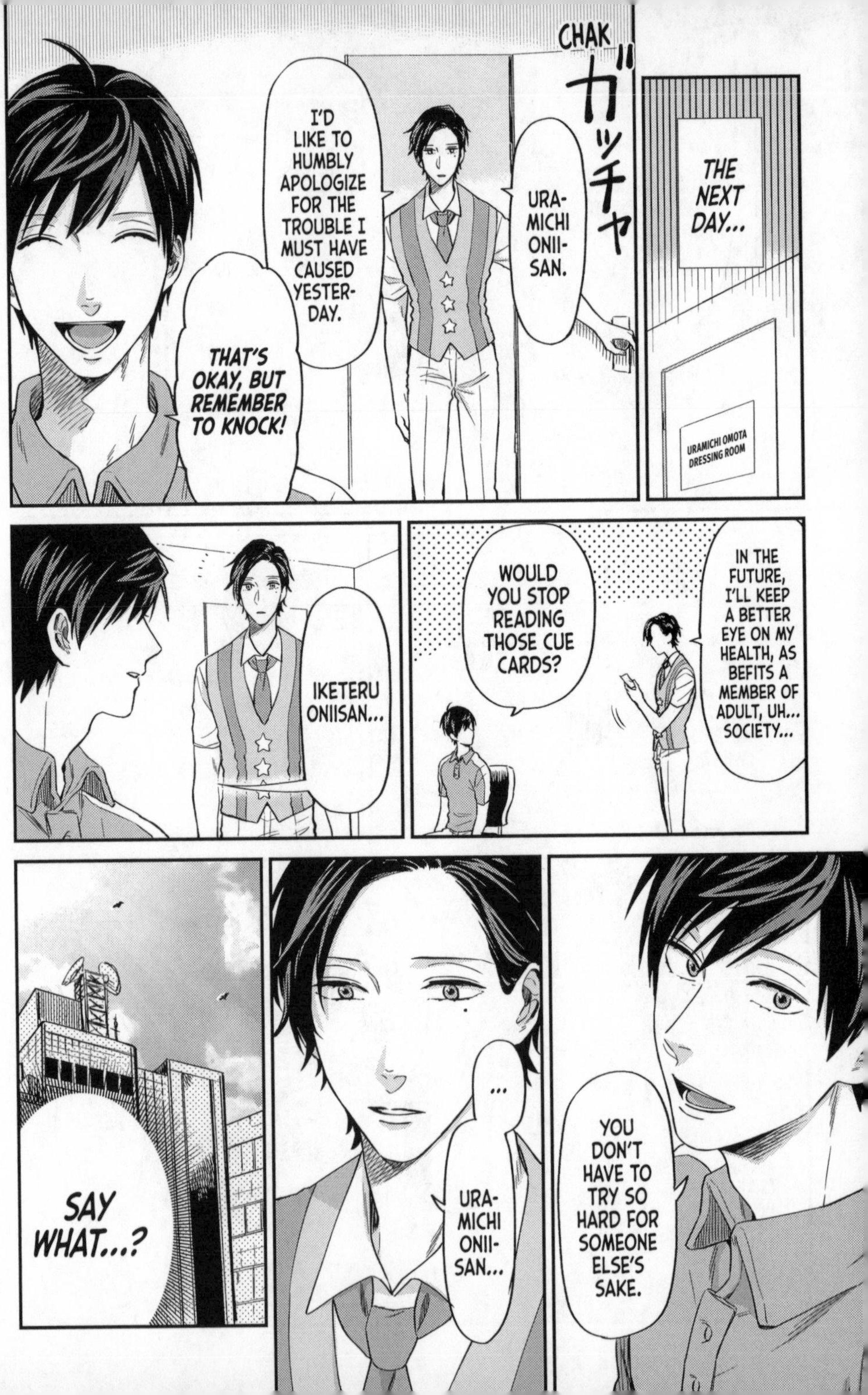
THE NEXT DAY...
URAMICHI OMOTA DRESSING ROOM
CHAK
ガッチャ
URA-MICHI ONII-SAN.
I'D LIKE TO HUMBLY APOLOGIZE FOR THE TROUBLE I MUST HAVE CAUSED YESTER-DAY.
THAT'S OKAY, BUT REMEMBER TO KNOCK!
IN THE FUTURE, I'LL KEEP A BETTER EYE ON MY HEALTH, AS BEFITS A MEMBER OF ADULT, UH... SOCIETY...
WOULD YOU STOP READING THOSE CUE CARDS?
IKETERU ONIISAN...
YOU DON'T HAVE TO TRY SO HARD FOR SOMEONE ELSE'S SAKE.
...
URA-MICHI ONII-SAN...
SAY WHAT...?

Life Lessons with
Uramichi Oniisan

The Cat's Staring at Nothing Again

Sung by Iketeru Oniisan and Utano Oneesan

What are you looking at?
What is it you see over there?

There's nothing there at all (nothing)
I don't have any furniture
Or money, or time
Or food in the fridge

Only my cat

He isn't any use at all, but at least he's here
That's enough for me

So tell me—what are you looking at?

What is it you see?
Nothing! There's nothing!

My life is all for nothing
I'm still alive, though I have nothing

Only my cat

Only my cat

He isn't any use at all

But at least he's here

I'm so glad he's here

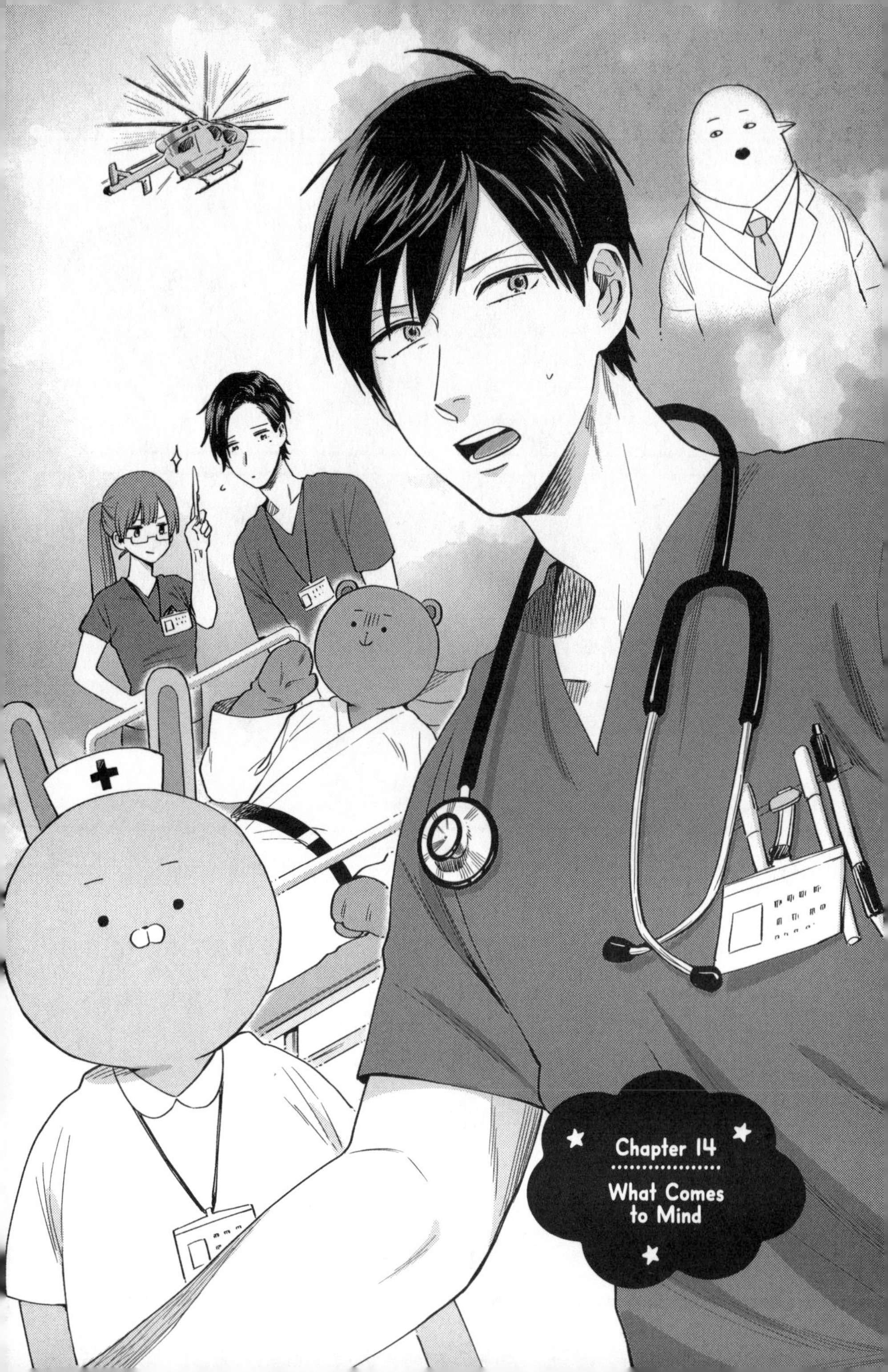
Chapter 14
What Comes to Mind

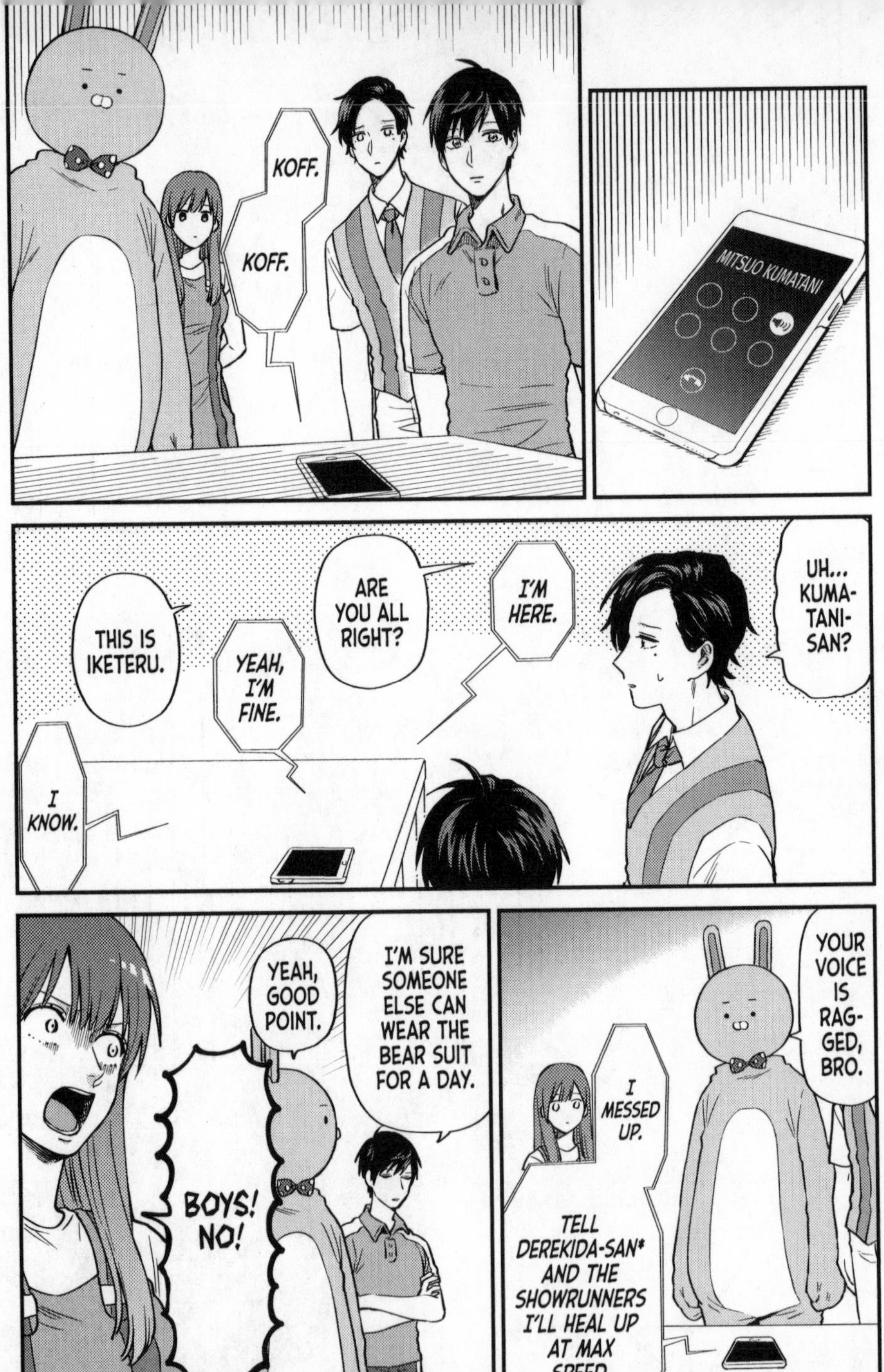
MITSUO KUMATANI
KOFF.
KOFF.
UH... KUMATANI-SAN?
I'M HERE.
ARE YOU ALL RIGHT?
YEAH, I'M FINE.
THIS IS IKETERU.
I KNOW.
YOUR VOICE IS RAGGED, BRO.
I MESSED UP.
TELL DEREKIDA-SAN* AND THE SHOWRUNNERS I'LL HEAL UP AT MAX SPEED.
I'M SURE SOMEONE ELSE CAN WEAR THE BEAR SUIT FOR A DAY.
YEAH, GOOD POINT.
BOYS! NO!

*Tekito Derekida, the show's director.

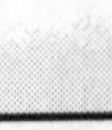

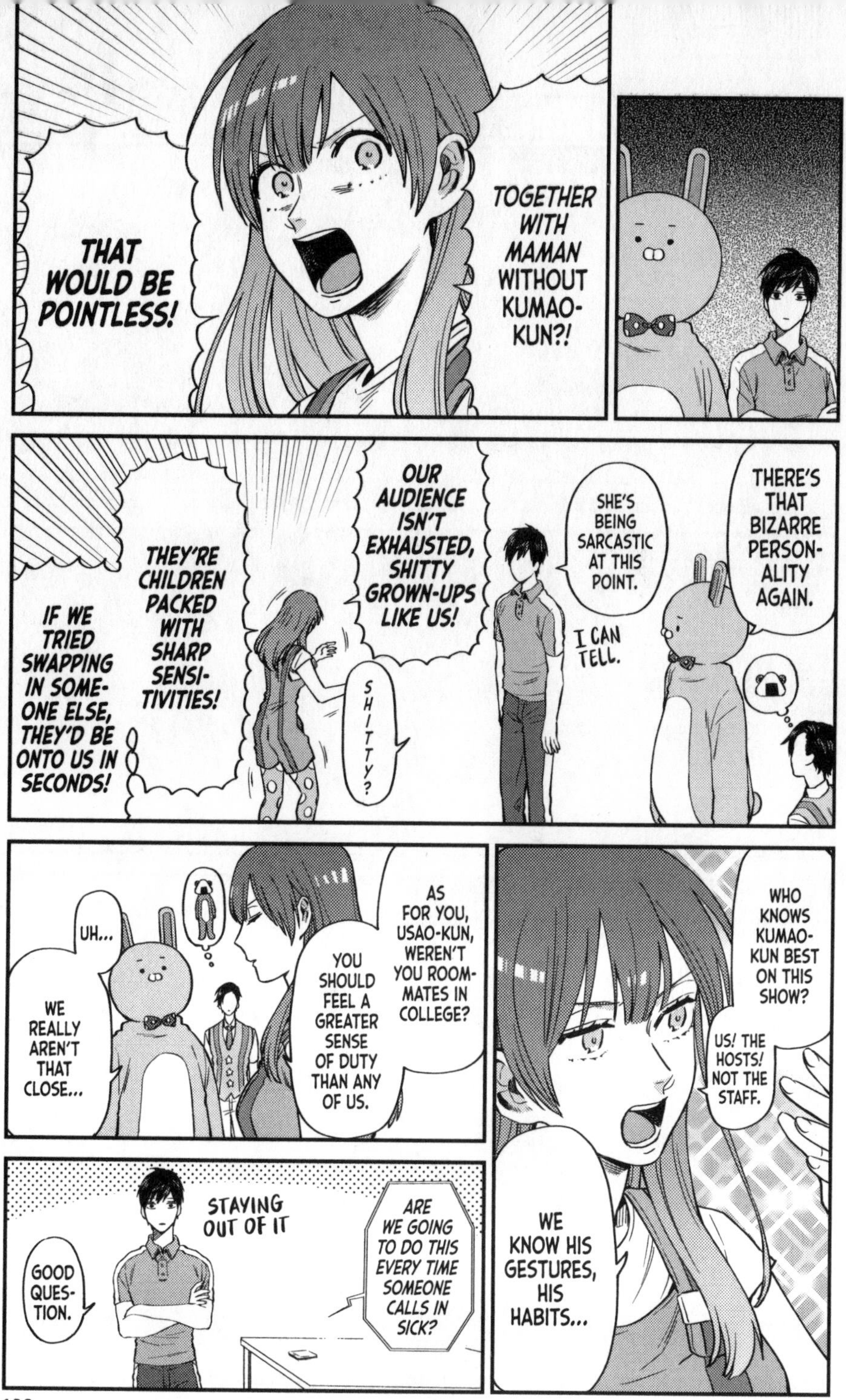
TOGETHER WITH MAMAN WITHOUT KUMAO-KUN?!
THAT WOULD BE POINTLESS!
THERE'S THAT BIZARRE PERSONALITY AGAIN.
SHE'S BEING SARCASTIC AT THIS POINT.
I CAN TELL.
OUR AUDIENCE ISN'T EXHAUSTED, SHITTY GROWN-UPS LIKE US!
SHITTY?
THEY'RE CHILDREN PACKED WITH SHARP SENSITIVITIES!
IF WE TRIED SWAPPING IN SOMEONE ELSE, THEY'D BE ONTO US IN SECONDS!
WHO KNOWS KUMAO-KUN BEST ON THIS SHOW?
US! THE HOSTS! NOT THE STAFF.
WE KNOW HIS GESTURES, HIS HABITS...
AS FOR YOU, USAO-KUN, WEREN'T YOU ROOMMATES IN COLLEGE?
YOU SHOULD FEEL A GREATER SENSE OF DUTY THAN ANY OF US.
UH...
WE REALLY AREN'T THAT CLOSE...
ARE WE GOING TO DO THIS EVERY TIME SOMEONE CALLS IN SICK?
STAYING OUT OF IT
GOOD QUESTION.

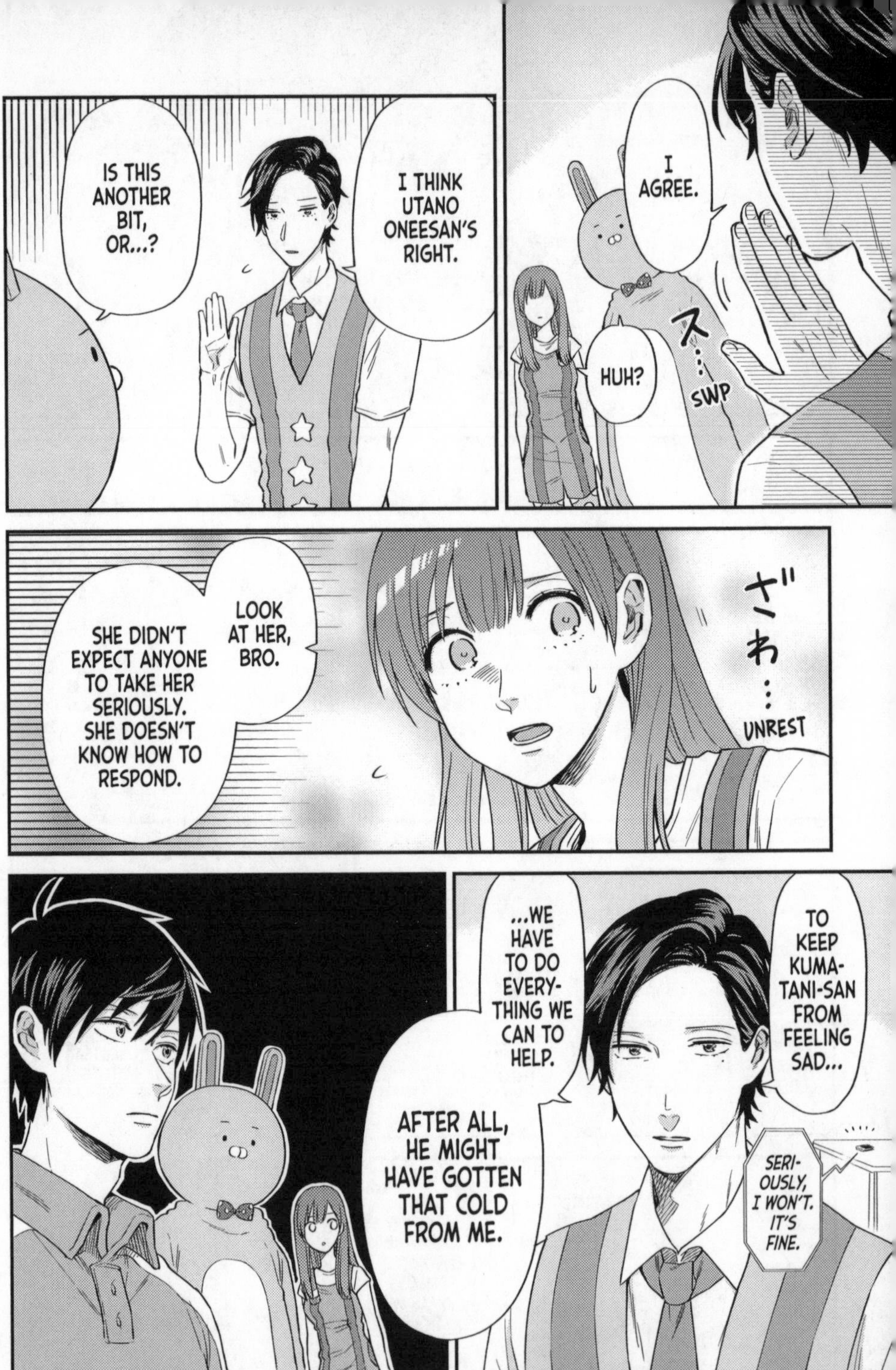
I AGREE.
ス…
SWP
HUH?
I THINK UTANO ONEESAN'S RIGHT.
IS THIS ANOTHER BIT, OR...?
ざわ…
UNREST
LOOK AT HER, BRO.
SHE DIDN'T EXPECT ANYONE TO TAKE HER SERIOUSLY. SHE DOESN'T KNOW HOW TO RESPOND.
TO KEEP KUMATANI-SAN FROM FEELING SAD...
...WE HAVE TO DO EVERYTHING WE CAN TO HELP.
SERIOUSLY, I WON'T. IT'S FINE.
AFTER ALL, HE MIGHT HAVE GOTTEN THAT COLD FROM ME.

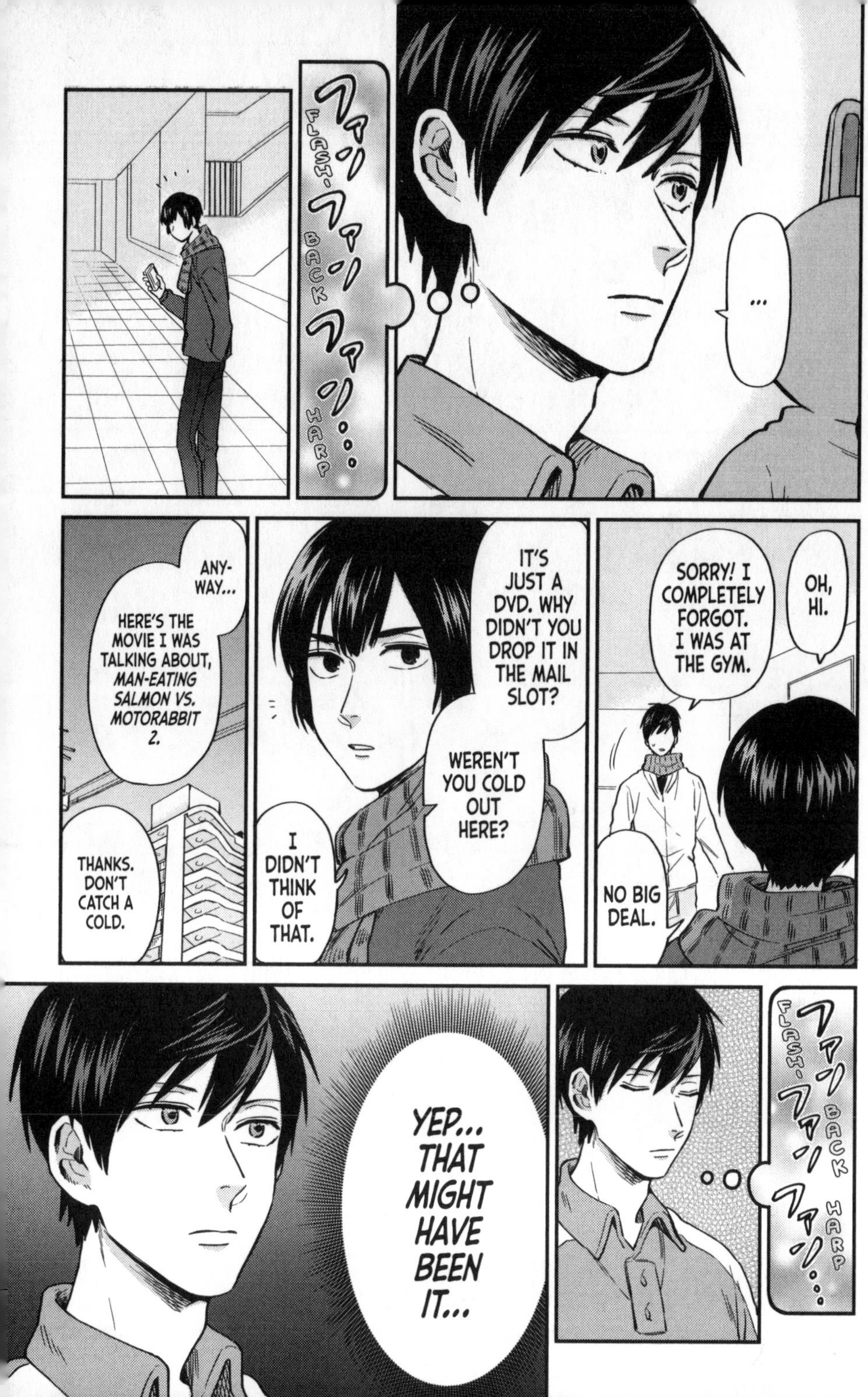
...
ファンファンファン...
FLASH-BACK HARP
OH, HI.
SORRY! I COMPLETELY FORGOT. I WAS AT THE GYM.
NO BIG DEAL.
IT'S JUST A DVD. WHY DIDN'T YOU DROP IT IN THE MAIL SLOT?
WEREN'T YOU COLD OUT HERE?
I DIDN'T THINK OF THAT.
ANY-WAY...
HERE'S THE MOVIE I WAS TALKING ABOUT, *MAN-EATING SALMON VS. MOTORABBIT 2.*
THANKS. DON'T CATCH A COLD.
ファンファンファン...
FLASH-BACK HARP
...
YEP... THAT MIGHT HAVE BEEN IT...

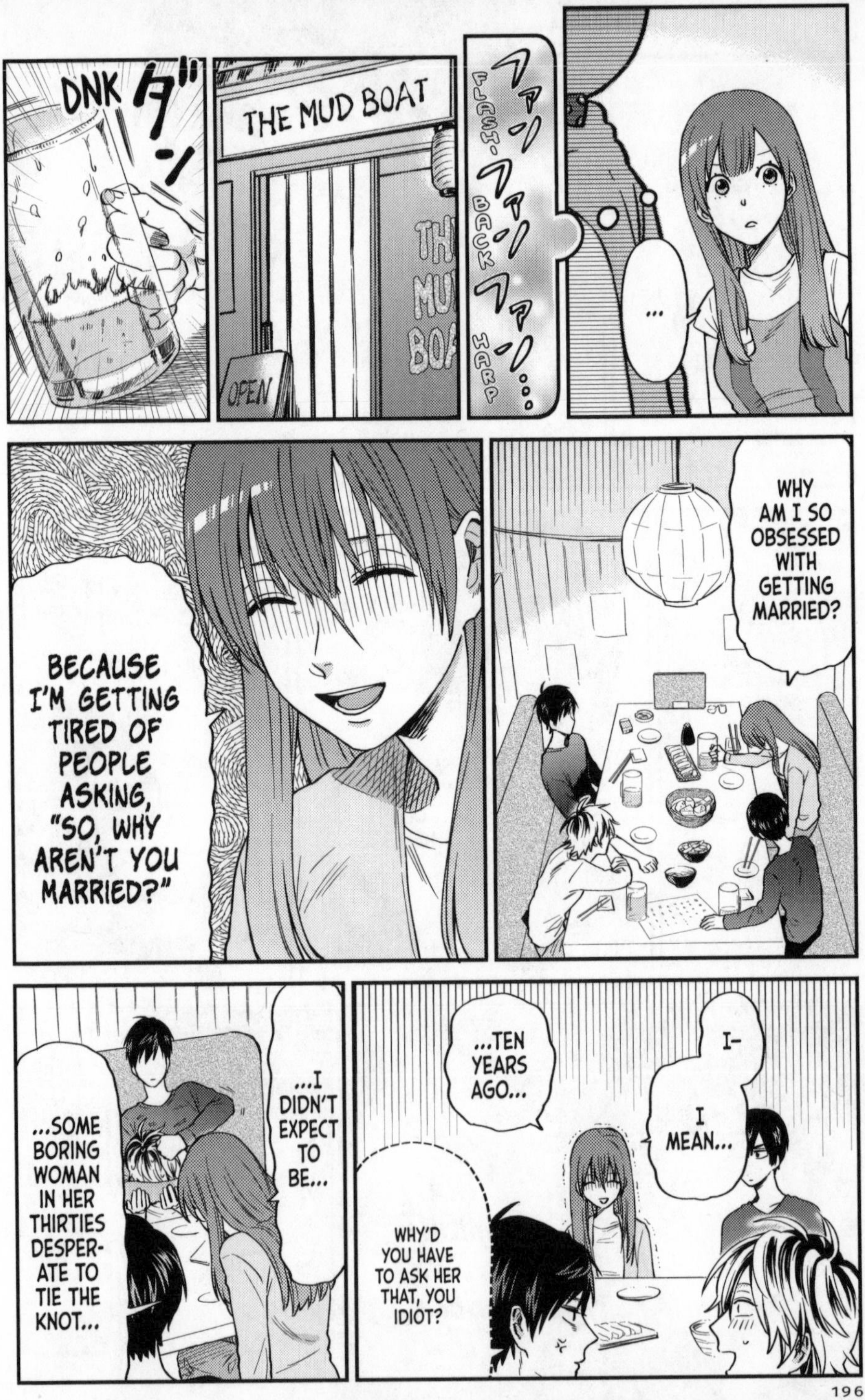
...
ファーンファーンファーン...
FLASH-BACK HARP
THE MUD BOAT
OPEN
DNK
ダン
WHY AM I SO OBSESSED WITH GETTING MARRIED?
BECAUSE I'M GETTING TIRED OF PEOPLE ASKING, "SO, WHY AREN'T YOU MARRIED?"
I-
I MEAN...
...TEN YEARS AGO...
WHY'D YOU HAVE TO ASK HER THAT, YOU IDIOT?
...I DIDN'T EXPECT TO BE...
...SOME BORING WOMAN IN HER THIRTIES DESPERATE TO TIE THE KNOT...

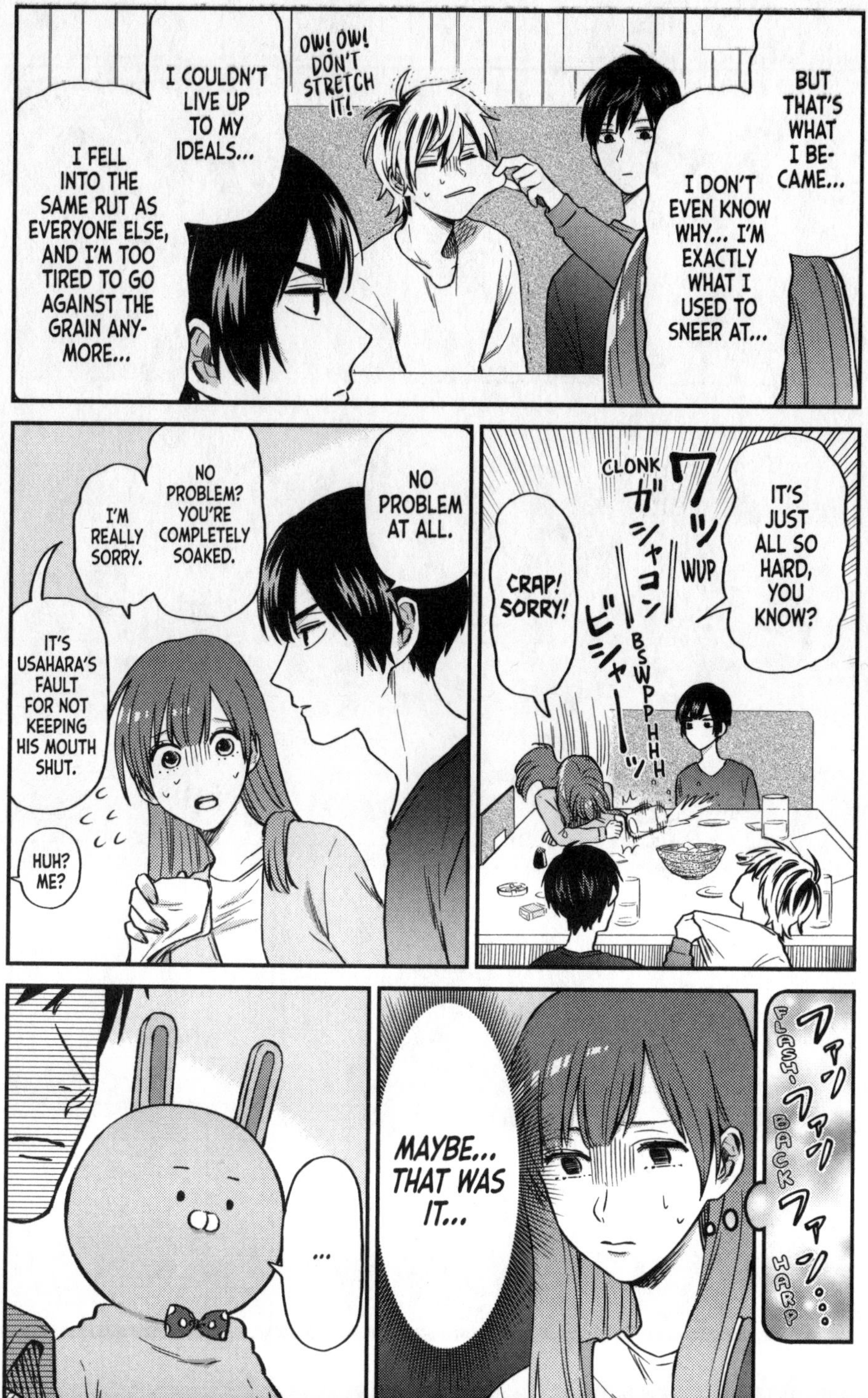
BUT THAT'S WHAT I BE-CAME...
I DON'T EVEN KNOW WHY... I'M EXACTLY WHAT I USED TO SNEER AT...
OW! OW! DON'T STRETCH IT!
I COULDN'T LIVE UP TO MY IDEALS...
I FELL INTO THE SAME RUT AS EVERYONE ELSE, AND I'M TOO TIRED TO GO AGAINST THE GRAIN ANY-MORE...
IT'S JUST ALL SO HARD, YOU KNOW?
ワッ WUP
ガシャコン CLONK
CRAP! SORRY!
ビシャーッ BSWPPHHH
NO PROBLEM AT ALL.
NO PROBLEM? YOU'RE COMPLETELY SOAKED.
I'M REALLY SORRY.
IT'S USAHARA'S FAULT FOR NOT KEEPING HIS MOUTH SHUT.
HUH? ME?
ファンファンファン... FLASH-BACK HARP
MAYBE... THAT WAS IT...
...

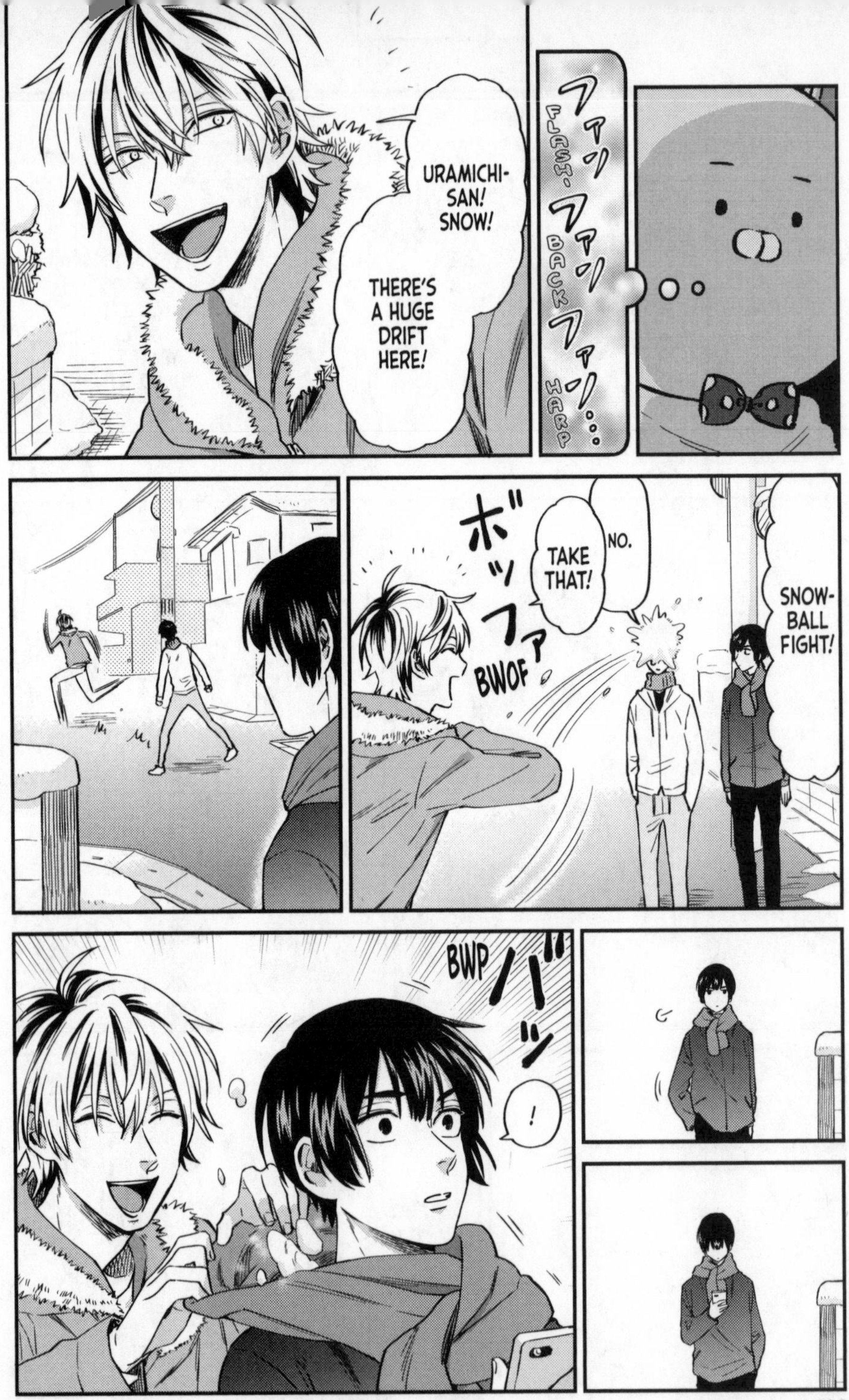
ファッファッファッ...
FLASH-BACK HARP
URAMICHI-SAN! SNOW!
THERE'S A HUGE DRIFT HERE!
SNOW-BALL FIGHT!
NO.
TAKE THAT!
ボッファ
BWOF
バッ
BWP
!

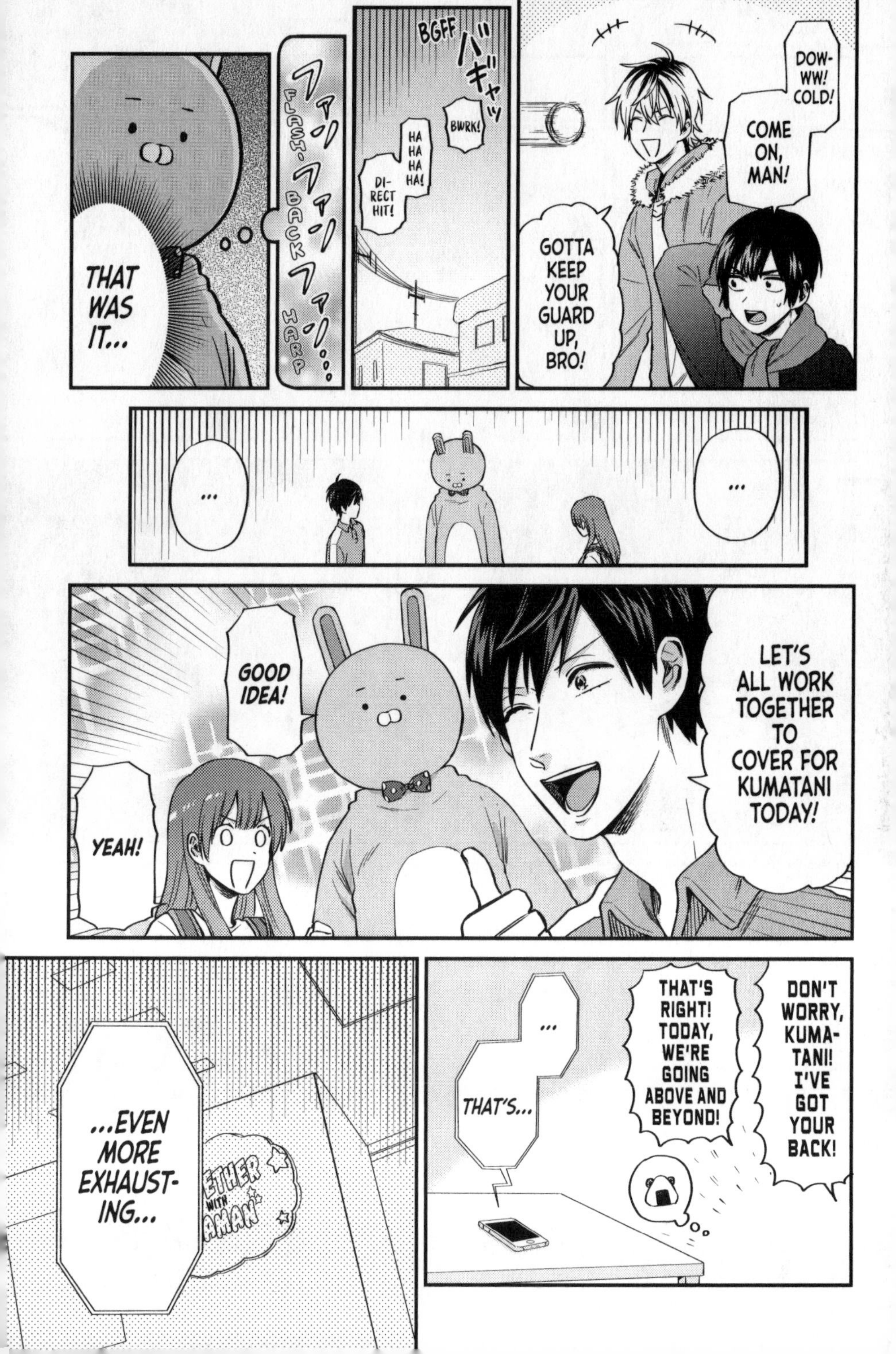
DOW-WW! COLD!
COME ON, MAN!
GOTTA KEEP YOUR GUARD UP, BRO!
BGFF
バギャッ
BWRK!
HA HA HA HA!
DI-RECT HIT!
FLASH-BACK HARP
THAT WAS IT...
...
...
LET'S ALL WORK TOGETHER TO COVER FOR KUMATANI TODAY!
GOOD IDEA!
YEAH!
DON'T WORRY, KUMA-TANI! I'VE GOT YOUR BACK!
THAT'S RIGHT! TODAY, WE'RE GOING ABOVE AND BEYOND!
...
THAT'S...
...EVEN MORE EXHAUST-ING...

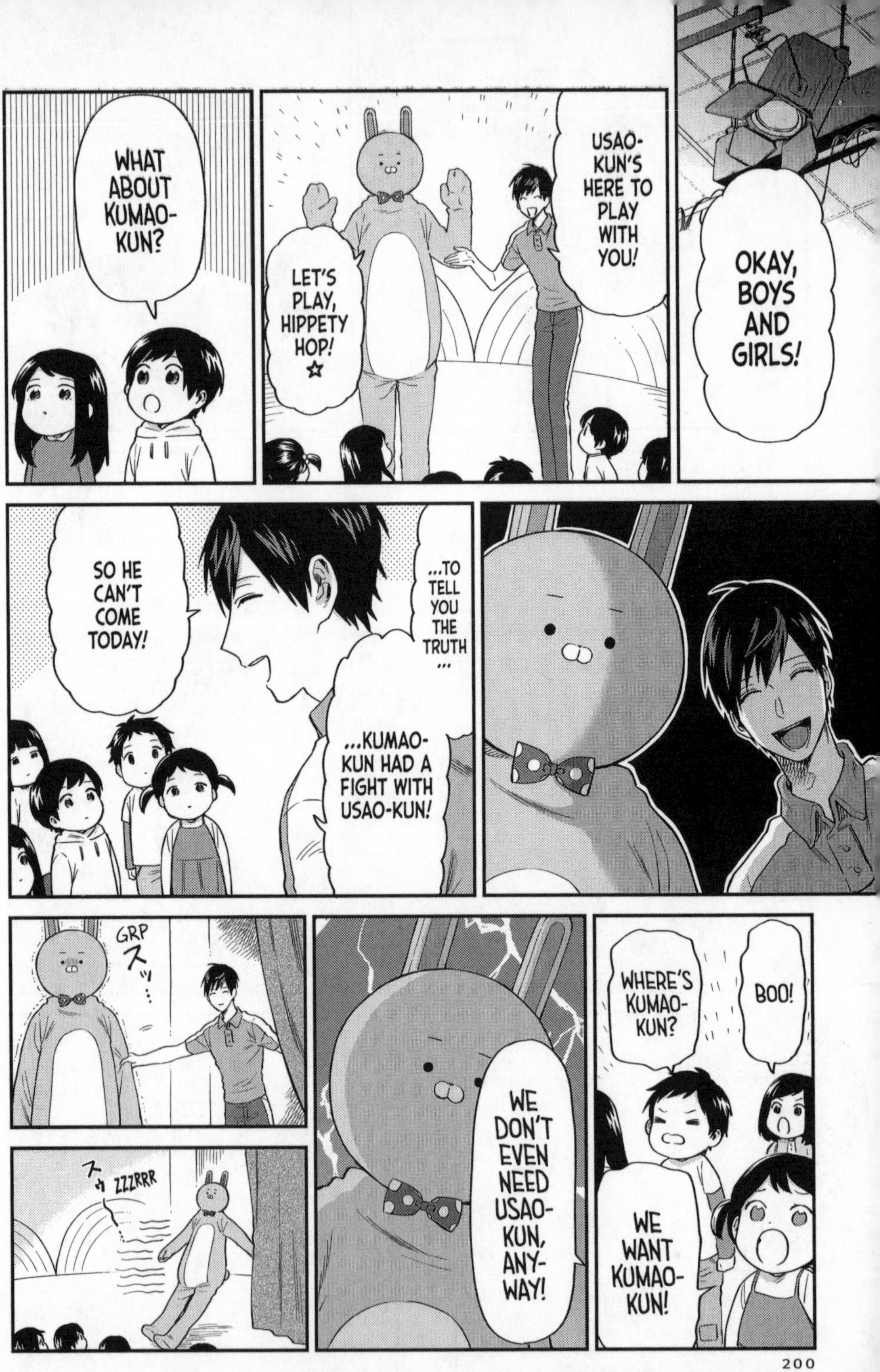
OKAY, BOYS AND GIRLS!
USAO-KUN'S HERE TO PLAY WITH YOU!
LET'S PLAY, HIPPETY HOP! ☆
WHAT ABOUT KUMAO-KUN?
...TO TELL YOU THE TRUTH...
...KUMAO-KUN HAD A FIGHT WITH USAO-KUN!
SO HE CAN'T COME TODAY!
BOO!
WHERE'S KUMAO-KUN?
WE WANT KUMAO-KUN!
WE DON'T EVEN NEED USAO-KUN, ANYWAY!
GRP スッ…
スゥ ZZZRRR

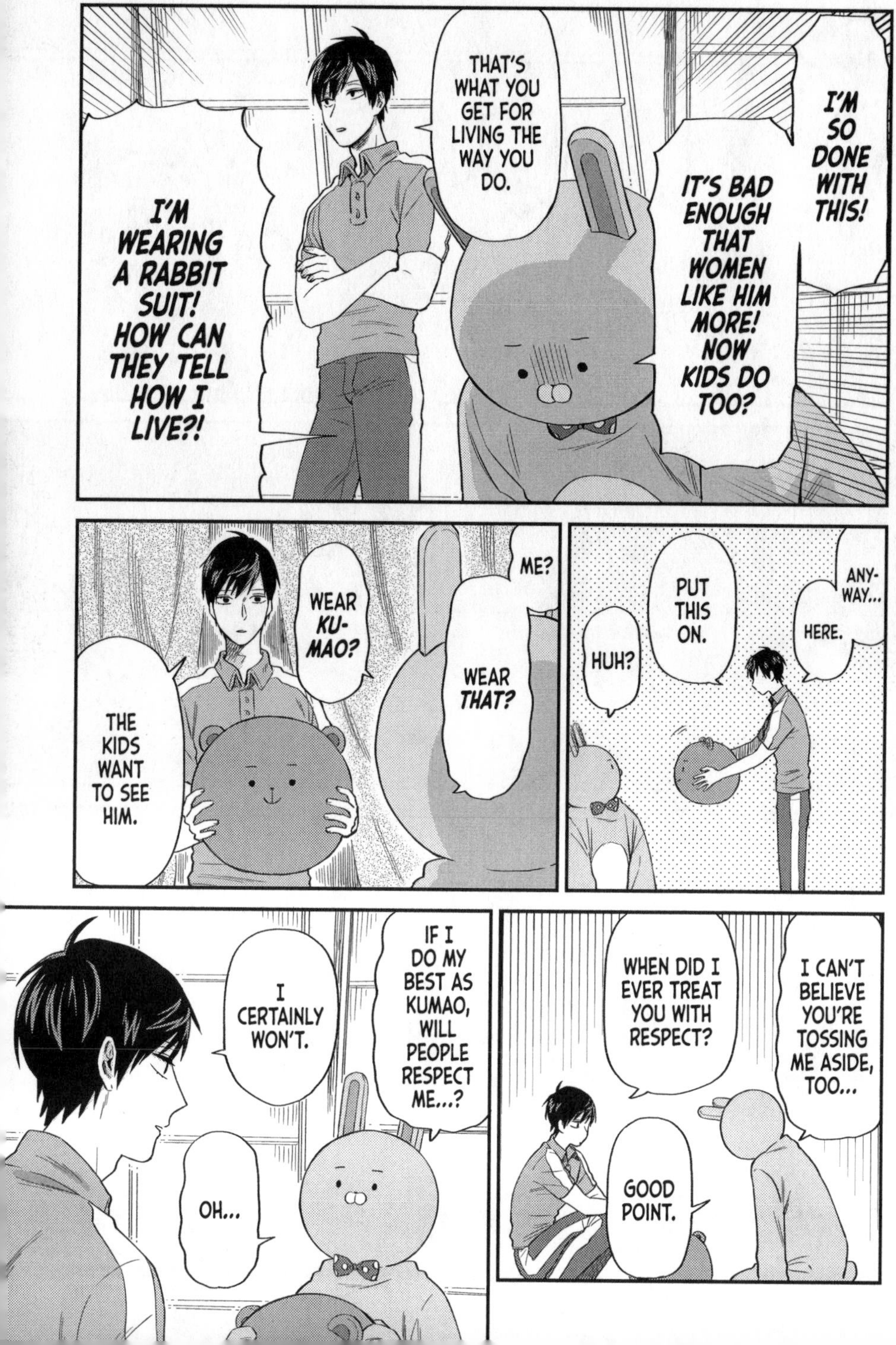

I'M SO DONE WITH THIS!
IT'S BAD ENOUGH THAT WOMEN LIKE HIM MORE! NOW KIDS DO TOO?
THAT'S WHAT YOU GET FOR LIVING THE WAY YOU DO.
I'M WEARING A RABBIT SUIT! HOW CAN THEY TELL HOW I LIVE?!
ANYWAY... HERE.
PUT THIS ON.
HUH?
ME?
WEAR THAT?
WEAR KUMAO?
THE KIDS WANT TO SEE HIM.
I CAN'T BELIEVE YOU'RE TOSSING ME ASIDE, TOO...
WHEN DID I EVER TREAT YOU WITH RESPECT?
GOOD POINT.
IF I DO MY BEST AS KUMAO, WILL PEOPLE RESPECT ME...?
I CERTAINLY WON'T.
OH...

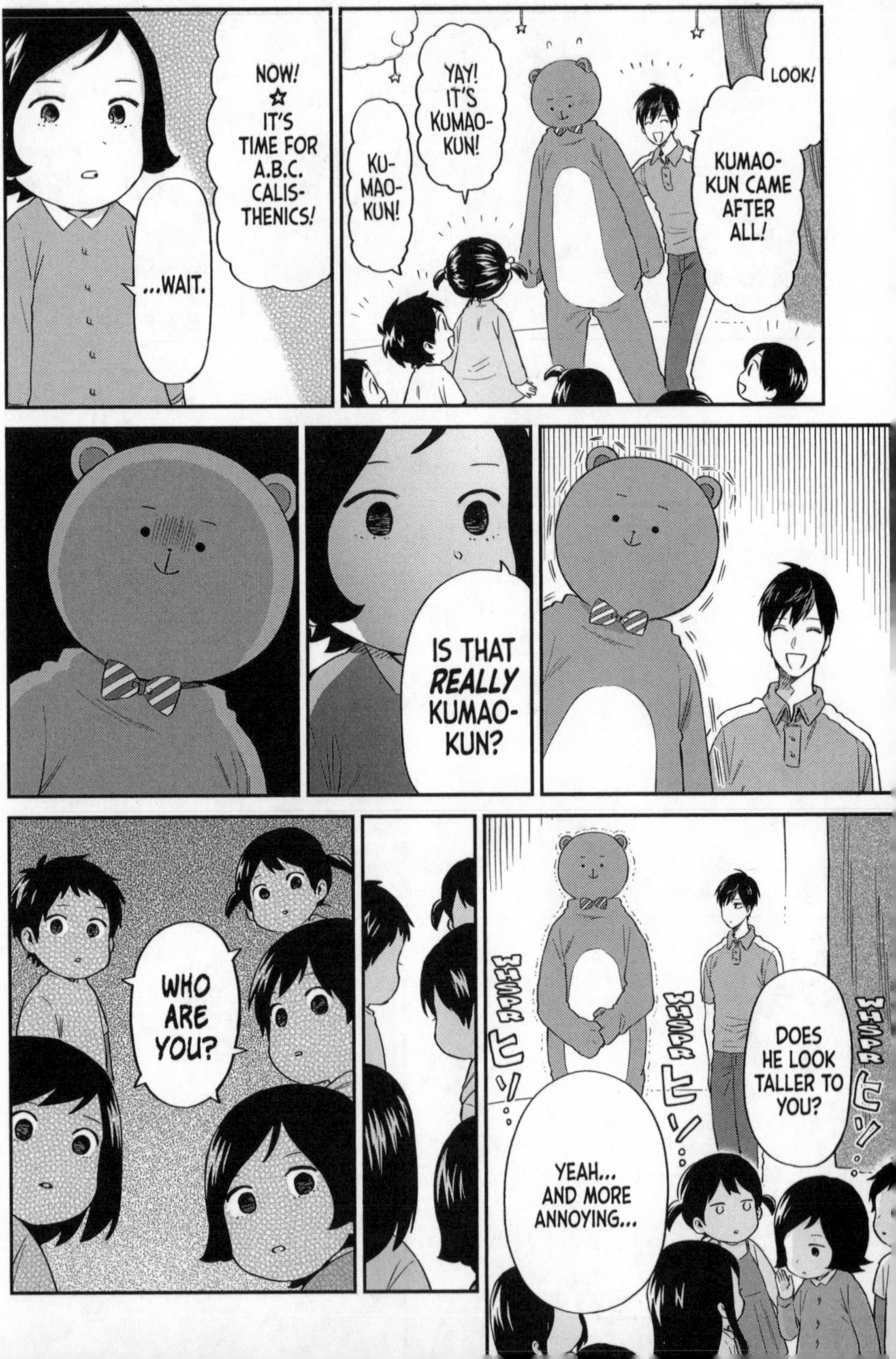
LOOK!
KUMAO-KUN CAME AFTER ALL!
YAY! IT'S KUMAO-KUN!
KU-MAO-KUN!
NOW! ☆ IT'S TIME FOR A.B.C. CALIS-THENICS!
...WAIT.
IS THAT *REALLY* KUMAO-KUN?
WHSPR ヒソ…
DOES HE LOOK TALLER TO YOU?
WHSPR ヒソ…
WHSPR ヒソ…
YEAH... AND MORE ANNOYING...
WHO ARE YOU?

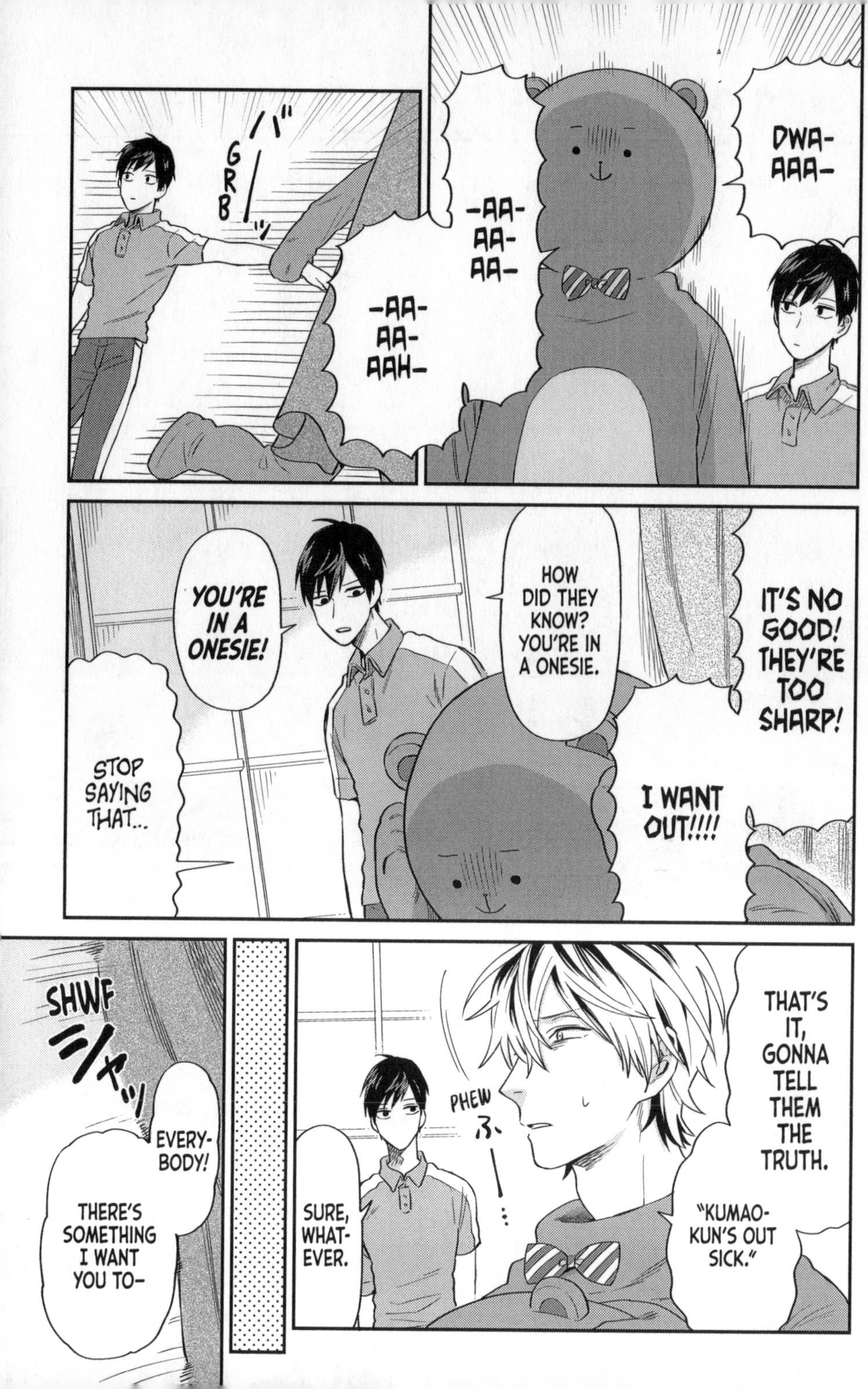
DWAA-AAA-
-AA-AA-AA-
-AA-AA-AAH-
GRB
バッ
IT'S NO GOOD! THEY'RE TOO SHARP!
I WANT OUT!!!!
HOW DID THEY KNOW? YOU'RE IN A ONESIE.
YOU'RE IN A ONESIE!
STOP SAYING THAT...
THAT'S IT, GONNA TELL THEM THE TRUTH.
"KUMAO-KUN'S OUT SICK."
PHEW
ふー…
SURE, WHATEVER.
SHWF
シャッ
EVERY-BODY!
THERE'S SOMETHING I WANT YOU TO-

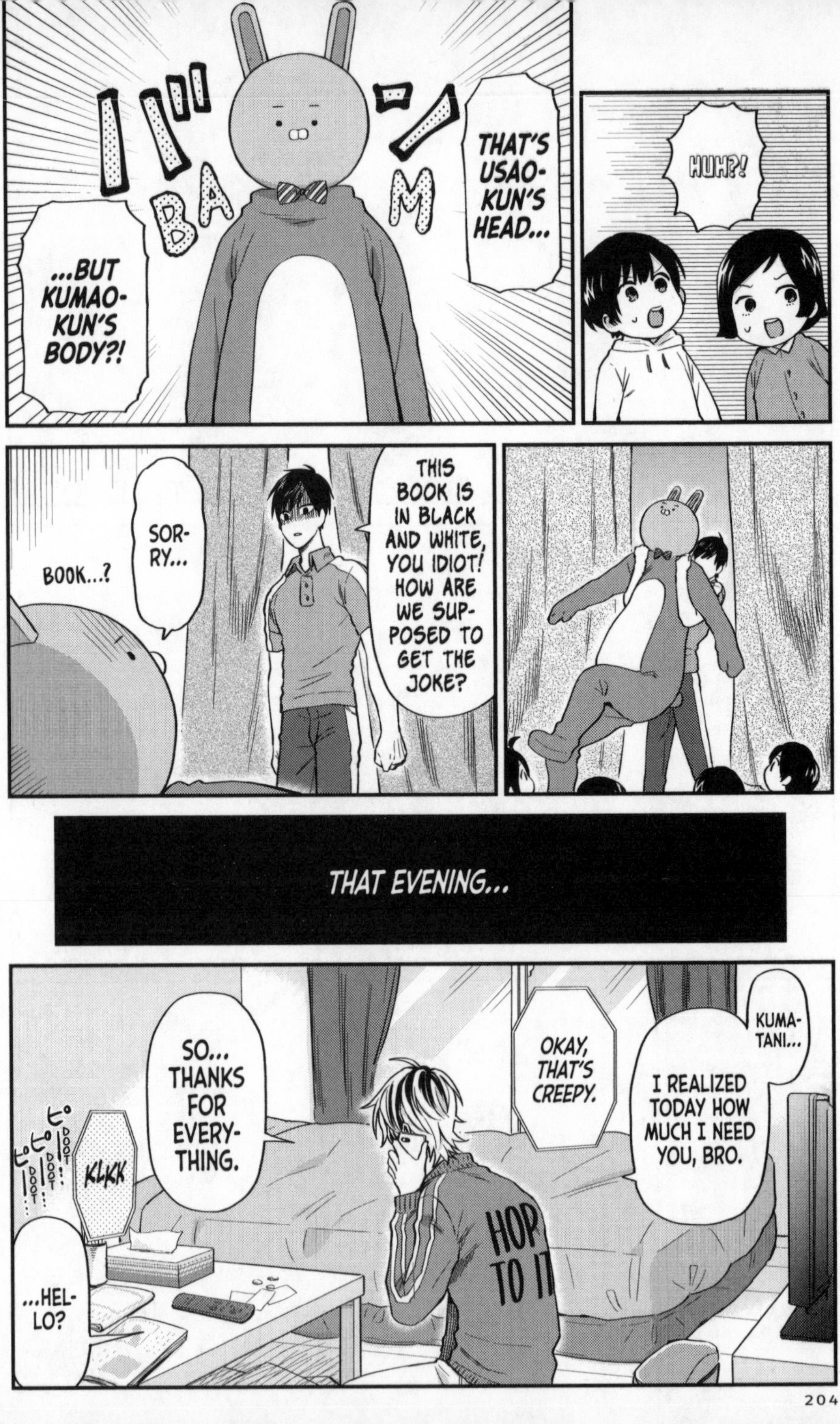
HUH?!
BAM
THAT'S USAO-KUN'S HEAD...
...BUT KUMAO-KUN'S BODY?!
THIS BOOK IS IN BLACK AND WHITE, YOU IDIOT! HOW ARE WE SUPPOSED TO GET THE JOKE?
SORRY...
BOOK...?
THAT EVENING...
KUMATANI...
I REALIZED TODAY HOW MUCH I NEED YOU, BRO.
OKAY, THAT'S CREEPY.
SO... THANKS FOR EVERYTHING.
KLKK
ピ DOOT ピ DOOT ピ DOOT...
...HELLO?
HOP TO IT

Life Lessons with
Uramichi Oniisan

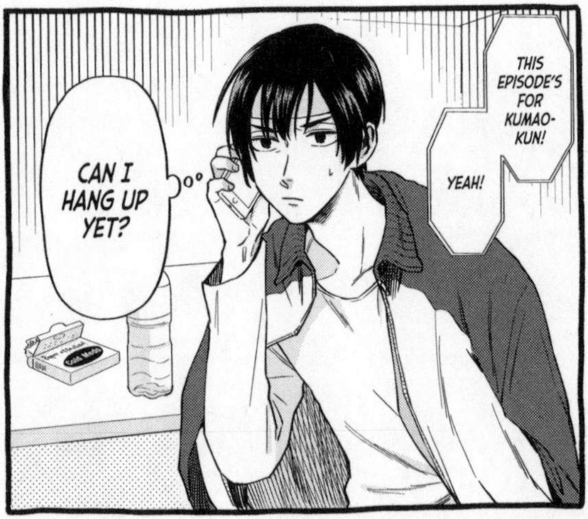
THIS EPISODE'S FOR KUMAO-KUN!
YEAH!
CAN I HANG UP YET?

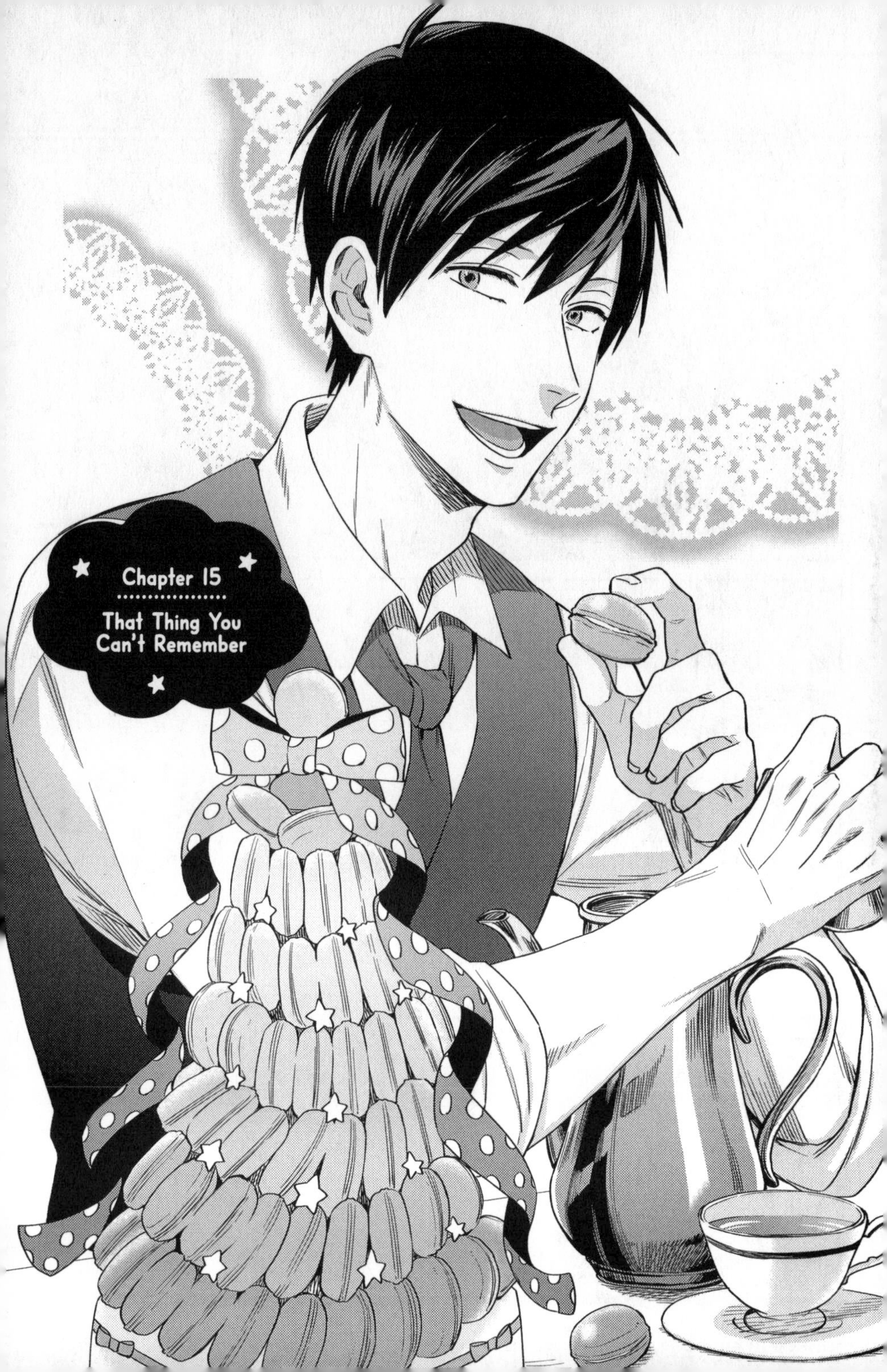
Chapter 15
That Thing You Can't Remember

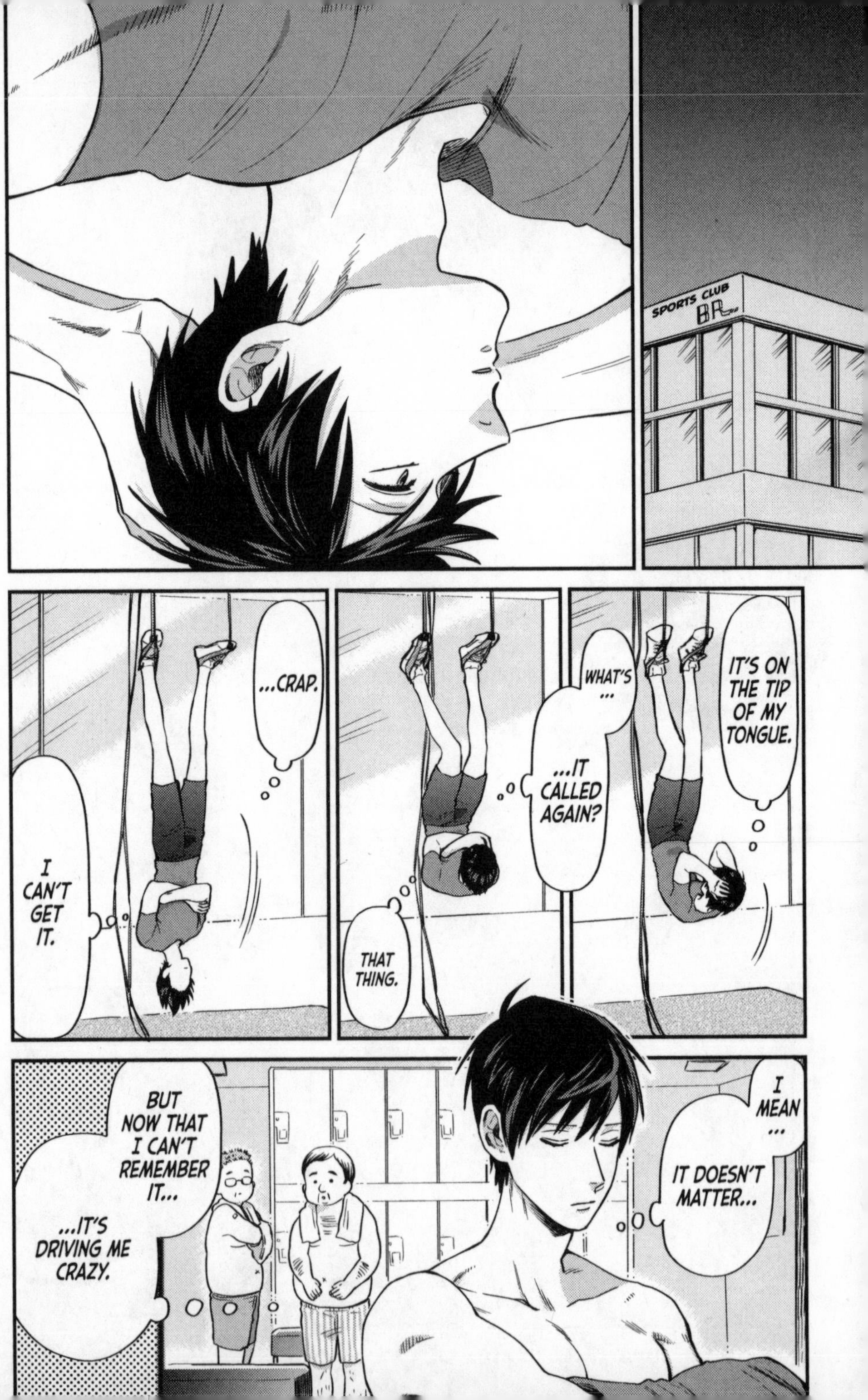
SPORTS CLUB
BR
IT'S ON THE TIP OF MY TONGUE.
WHAT'S ...
...IT CALLED AGAIN?
THAT THING.
...CRAP.
I CAN'T GET IT.
I MEAN ...
IT DOESN'T MATTER...
BUT NOW THAT I CAN'T REMEMBER IT...
...IT'S DRIVING ME CRAZY.

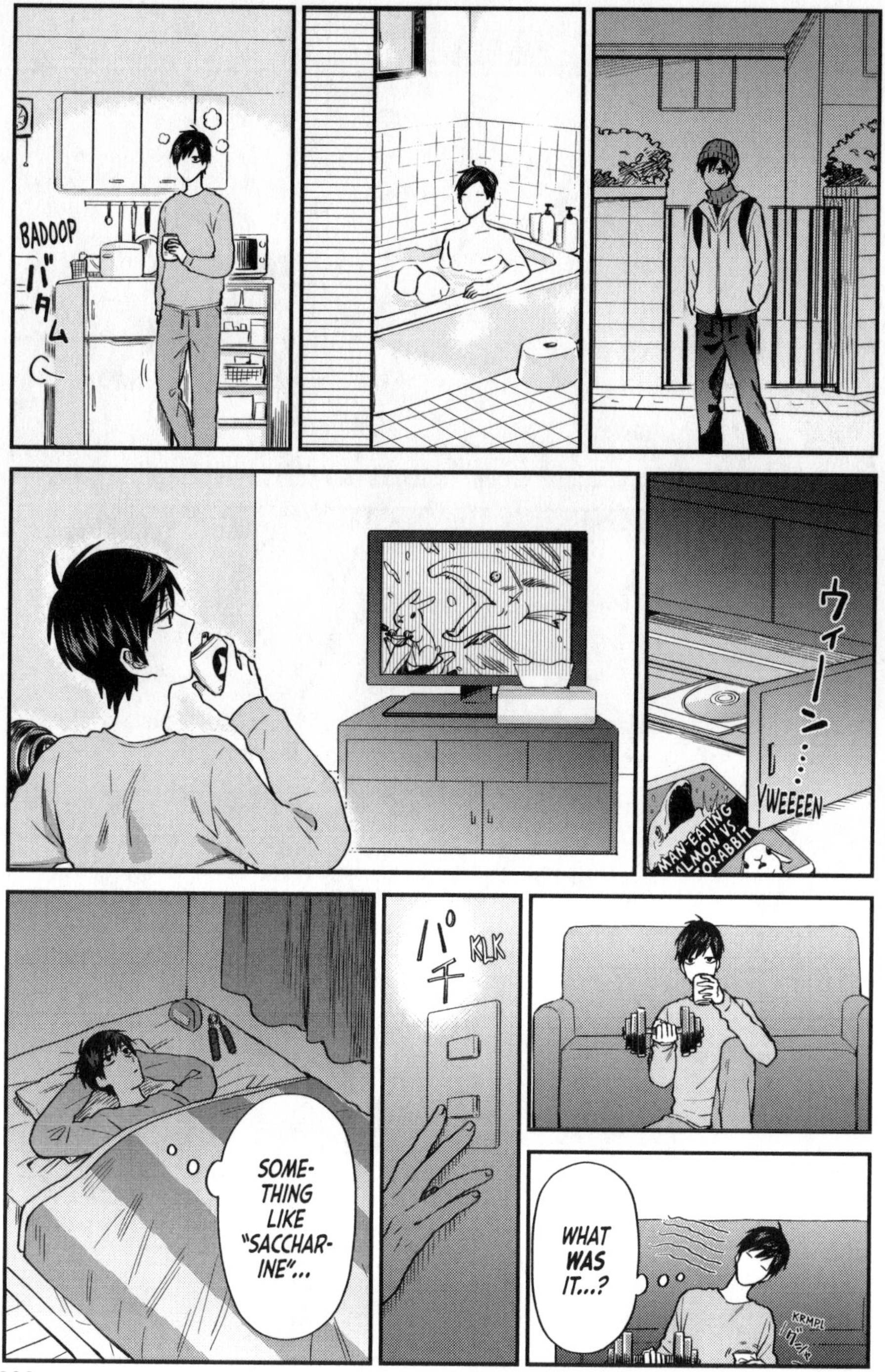
BADOOP
バタム
ウィーン…
VWEEEEN
MAN-EATING
ALMON VS
ORABBIT
WHAT WAS IT...?
KRMPL
グシャ
パチ
KLK
SOME-THING LIKE "SACCHAR-INE"...

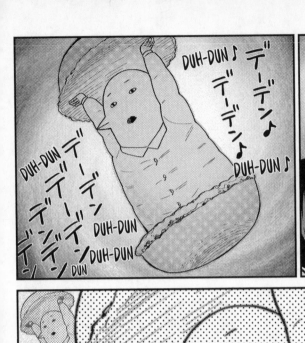

DUH-DUN♪ デーデン♪
デーデン♪
DUH-DUN♪
DUH-DUN デーデン♪
デーデン♪
デーデン♪
デーデン♪
DUH-DUN
DUH-DUN
DUN

デーデン♪
デーデン♪
デーデン♪
デーデン♪
DUH-DUN♪
DUH-DUN♪
DUH-DUN♪
DUH-DUN♪

Think the "Jaws" theme.

TWEET チュン
TWEET チュン...

OH...

...IT'S MORN- ING...

ハッ
GASP

210

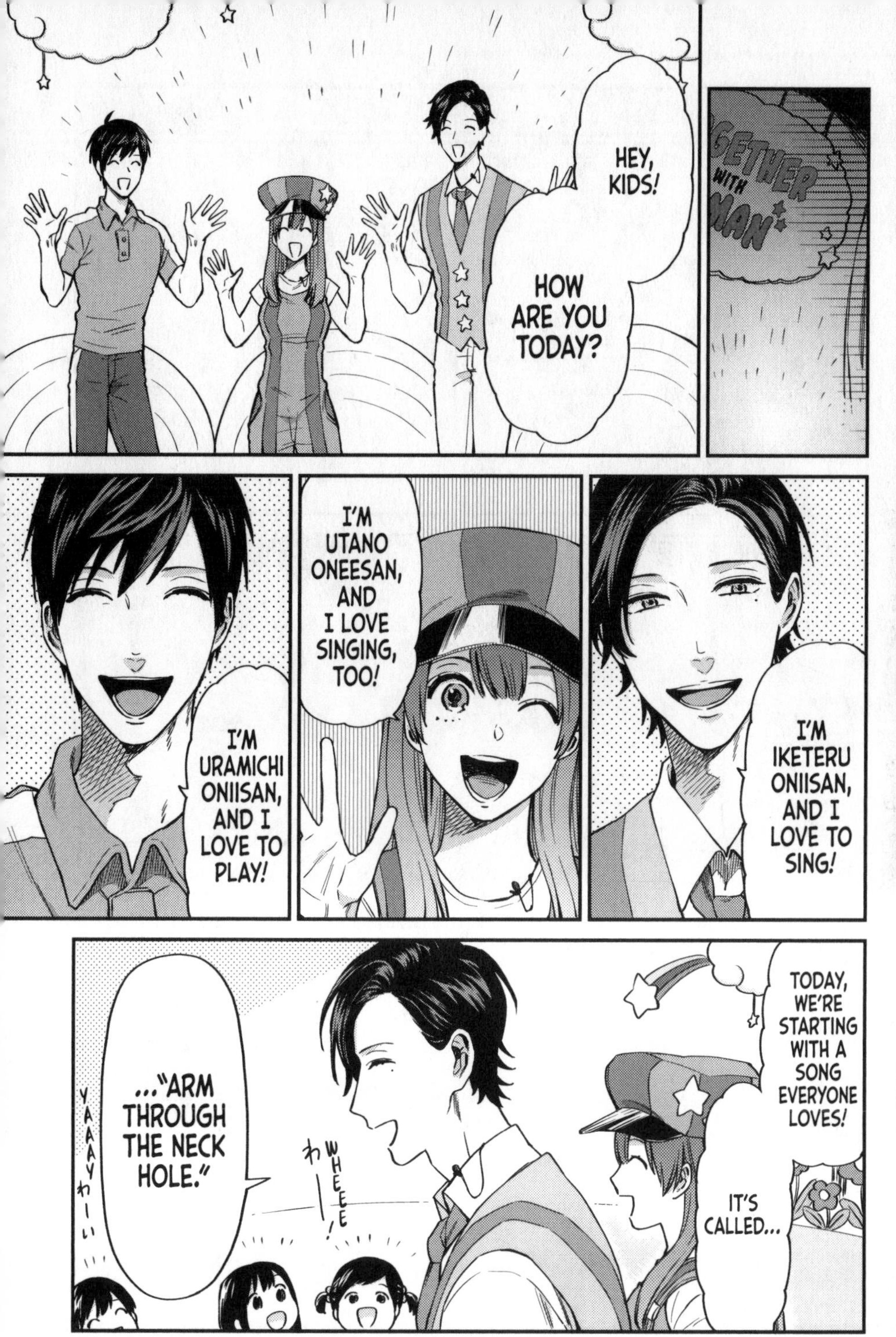
GETHER WITH MAN
HEY, KIDS!
HOW ARE YOU TODAY?
I'M IKETERU ONIISAN, AND I LOVE TO SING!
I'M UTANO ONEESAN, AND I LOVE SINGING, TOO!
I'M URAMICHI ONIISAN, AND I LOVE TO PLAY!
TODAY, WE'RE STARTING WITH A SONG EVERYONE LOVES!
IT'S CALLED...
...“ARM THROUGH THE NECK HOLE.”
WHEEE わーー!
YAAAY わーい

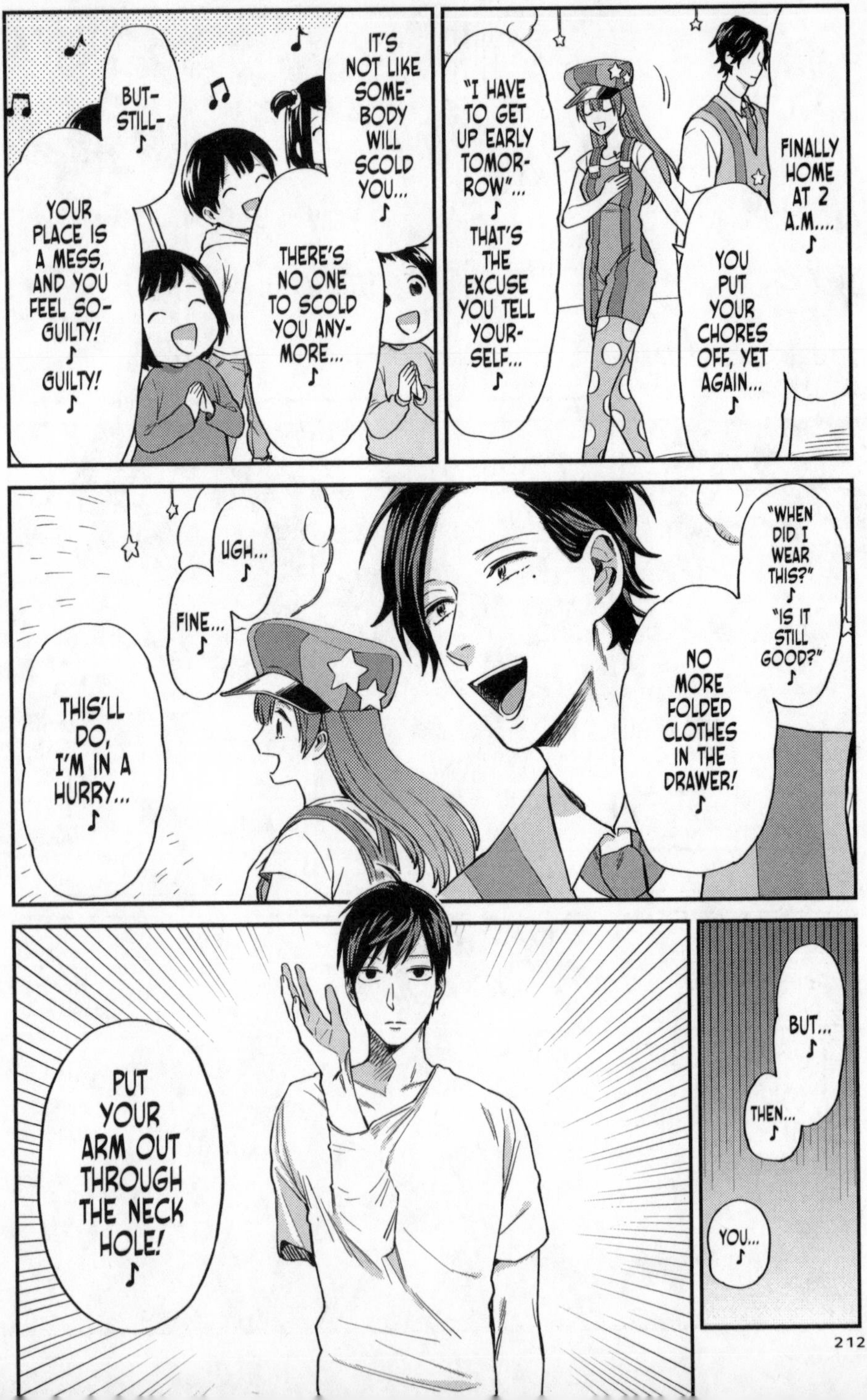
FINALLY HOME AT 2 A.M.... ♪
YOU PUT YOUR CHORES OFF, YET AGAIN... ♪
"I HAVE TO GET UP EARLY TOMORROW"... ♪ THAT'S THE EXCUSE YOU TELL YOURSELF... ♪
IT'S NOT LIKE SOMEBODY WILL SCOLD YOU... ♪
THERE'S NO ONE TO SCOLD YOU ANYMORE... ♪
BUT-STILL- ♪
YOUR PLACE IS A MESS, AND YOU FEEL SO-GUILTY! ♪ GUILTY! ♪
"WHEN DID I WEAR THIS?" ♪ "IS IT STILL GOOD?" ♪
NO MORE FOLDED CLOTHES IN THE DRAWER! ♪
UGH... ♪
FINE... ♪
THIS'LL DO, I'M IN A HURRY... ♪
BUT... ♪
THEN... ♪
YOU... ♪
PUT YOUR ARM OUT THROUGH THE NECK HOLE! ♪

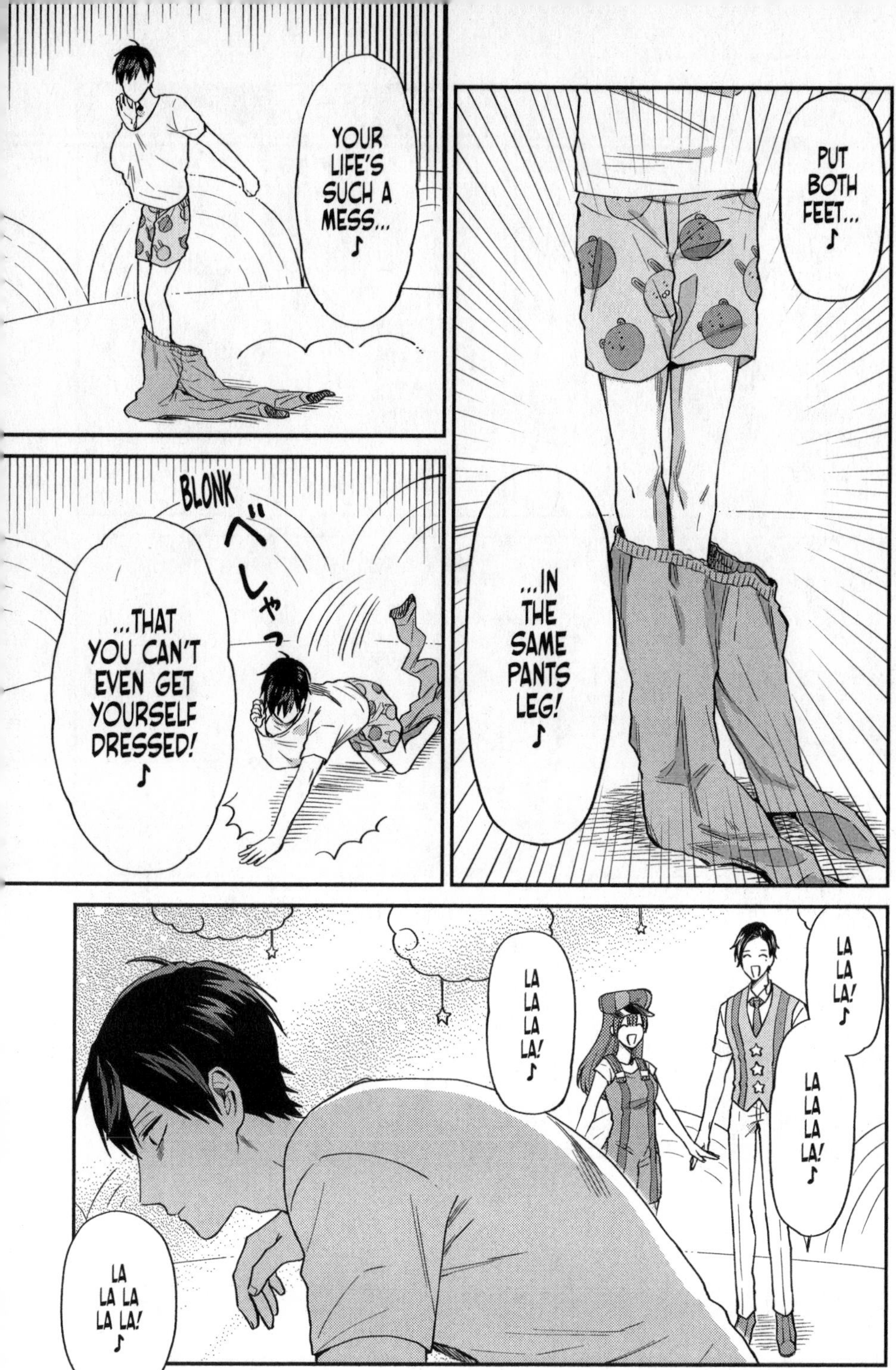
PUT BOTH FEET... ♪
...IN THE SAME PANTS LEG! ♪
YOUR LIFE'S SUCH A MESS... ♪
BLONK
べしゃっ
...THAT YOU CAN'T EVEN GET YOURSELF DRESSED! ♪
LA LA LA! ♪
LA LA LA LA! ♪
LA LA LA LA! ♪
LA LA LA LA LA! ♪

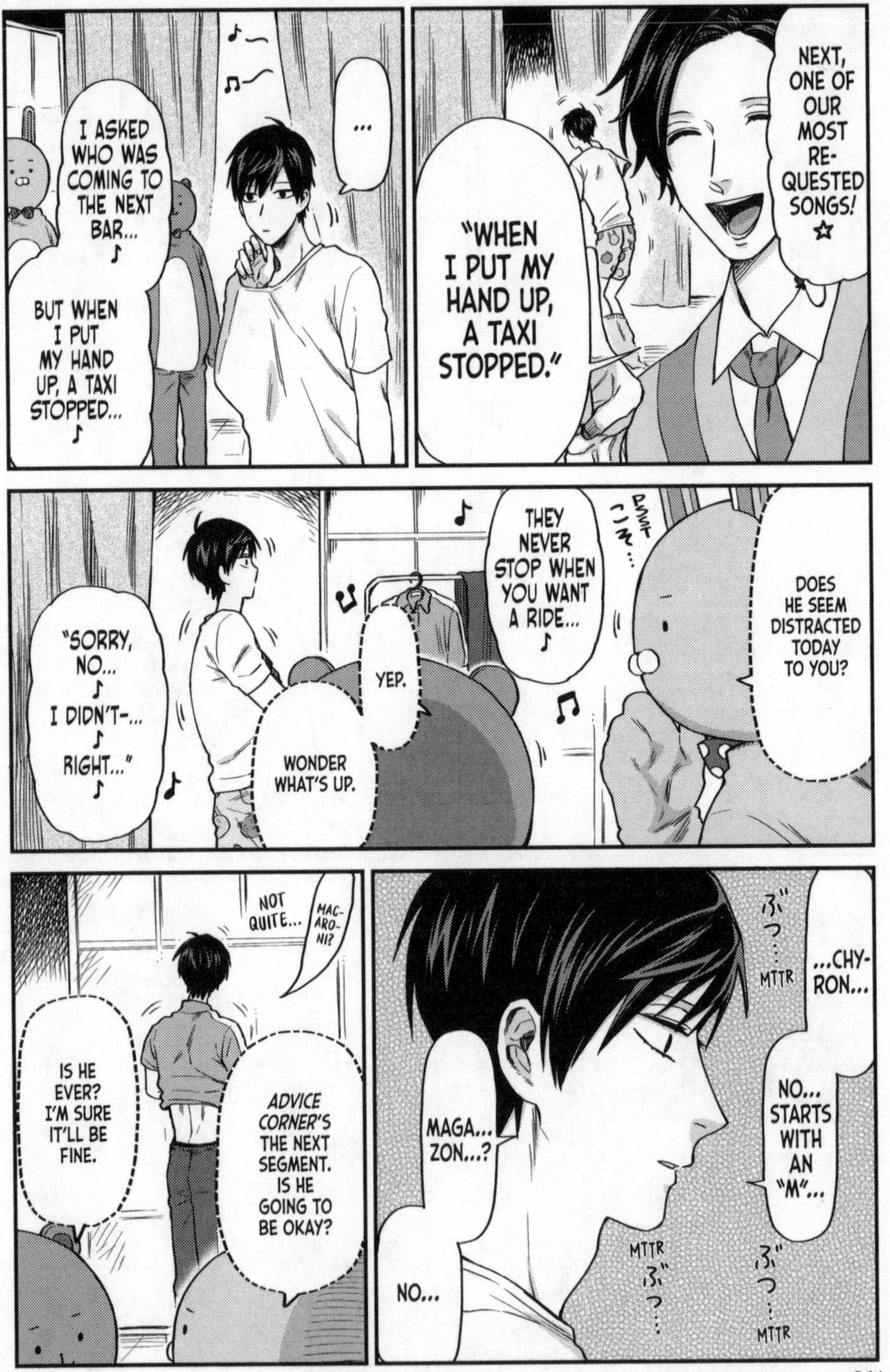
NEXT, ONE OF OUR MOST RE-QUESTED SONGS! ☆
"WHEN I PUT MY HAND UP, A TAXI STOPPED."
♪~ ♪~
...
I ASKED WHO WAS COMING TO THE NEXT BAR... ♪
BUT WHEN I PUT MY HAND UP, A TAXI STOPPED... ♪
PSST こそ...
DOES HE SEEM DISTRACTED TODAY TO YOU?
THEY NEVER STOP WHEN YOU WANT A RIDE... ♪
YEP.
WONDER WHAT'S UP.
"SORRY, NO... ♪ I DIDN'T-... ♪ RIGHT..." ♪
ぶつ... MTTR
...CHY-RON...
NO... STARTS WITH AN "M"...
MAGA... ZON...?
NO...
MTTR ぶつ...
ぶつ... MTTR
NOT QUITE...
MAC-ARO-NI?
ADVICE CORNER'S THE NEXT SEGMENT. IS HE GOING TO BE OKAY?
IS HE EVER? I'M SURE IT'LL BE FINE.

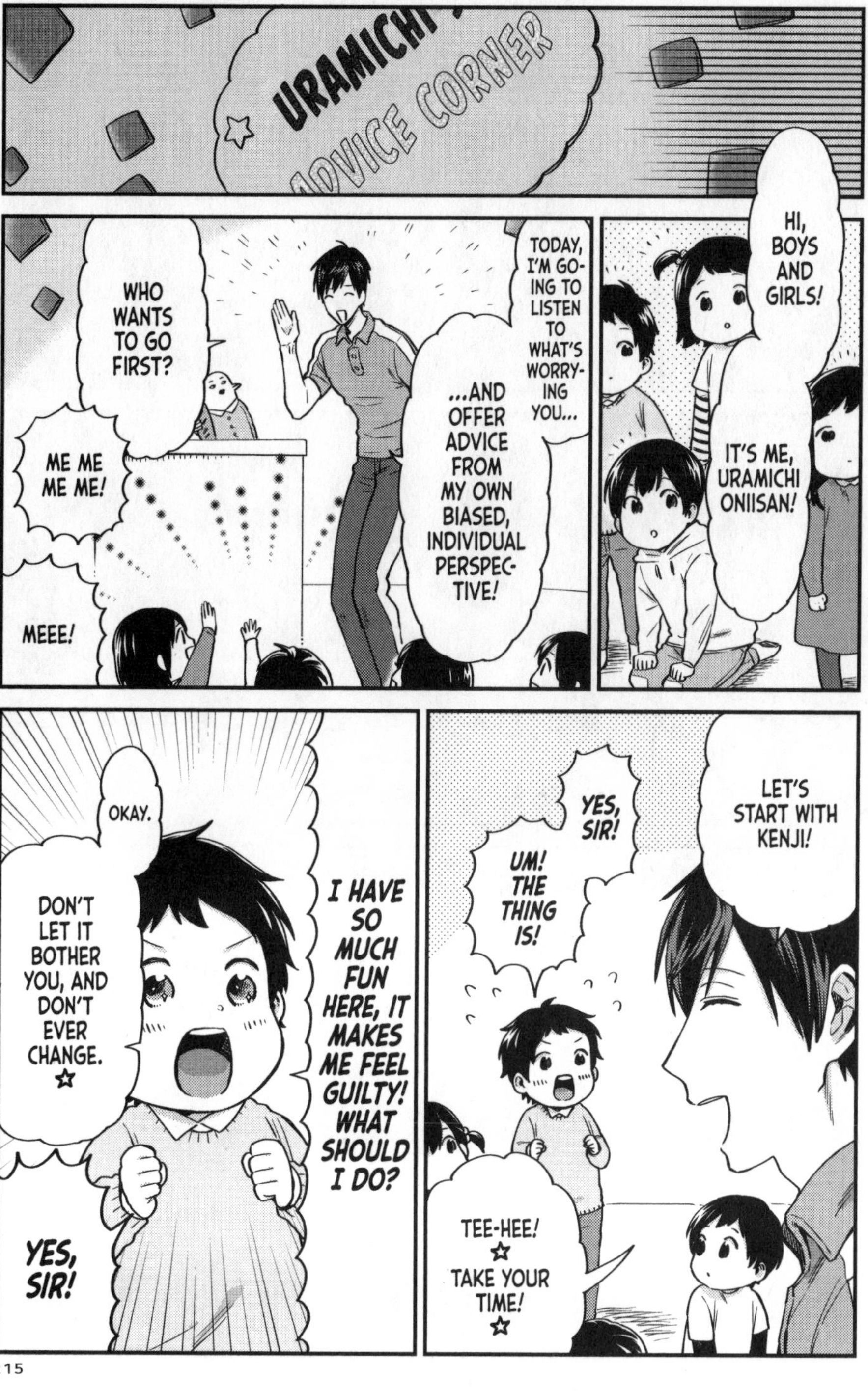
URAMICHI
ADVICE CORNER
HI, BOYS AND GIRLS!
IT'S ME, URAMICHI ONIISAN!
TODAY, I'M GOING TO LISTEN TO WHAT'S WORRYING YOU...
...AND OFFER ADVICE FROM MY OWN BIASED, INDIVIDUAL PERSPECTIVE!
WHO WANTS TO GO FIRST?
ME ME ME ME!
MEEE!
LET'S START WITH KENJI!
YES, SIR!
UM! THE THING IS!
TEE-HEE! ☆ TAKE YOUR TIME! ☆
I HAVE SO MUCH FUN HERE, IT MAKES ME FEEL GUILTY! WHAT SHOULD I DO?
OKAY.
DON'T LET IT BOTHER YOU, AND DON'T EVER CHANGE. ☆
YES, SIR!

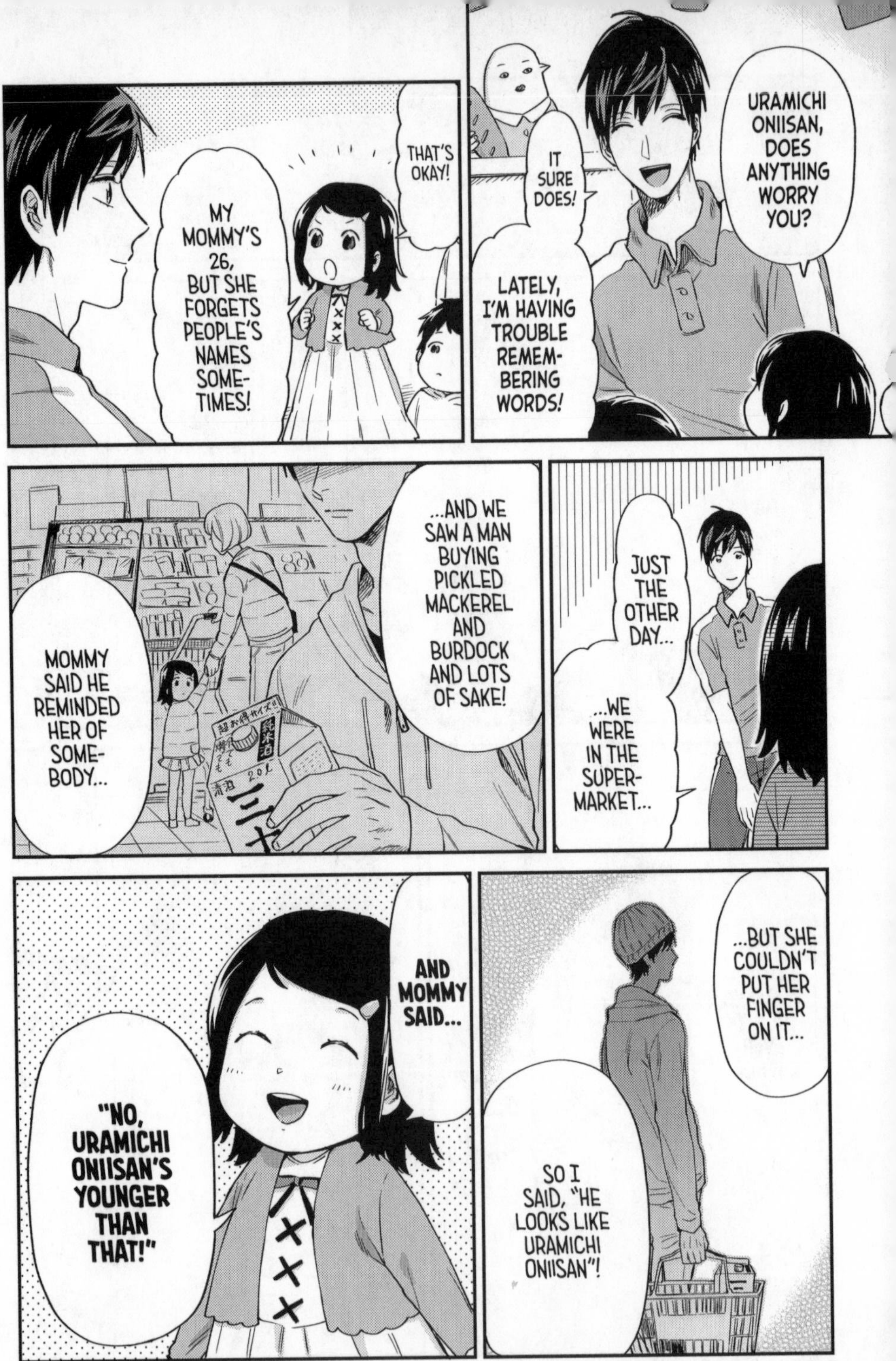
URAMICHI ONIISAN, DOES ANYTHING WORRY YOU?
IT SURE DOES!
LATELY, I'M HAVING TROUBLE REMEMBERING WORDS!
THAT'S OKAY!
MY MOMMY'S 26, BUT SHE FORGETS PEOPLE'S NAMES SOMETIMES!
JUST THE OTHER DAY...
...WE WERE IN THE SUPERMARKET...
...AND WE SAW A MAN BUYING PICKLED MACKEREL AND BURDOCK AND LOTS OF SAKE!
MOMMY SAID HE REMINDED HER OF SOMEBODY...
...BUT SHE COULDN'T PUT HER FINGER ON IT...
SO I SAID, "HE LOOKS LIKE URAMICHI ONIISAN"!
AND MOMMY SAID...
"NO, URAMICHI ONIISAN'S YOUNGER THAN THAT!"

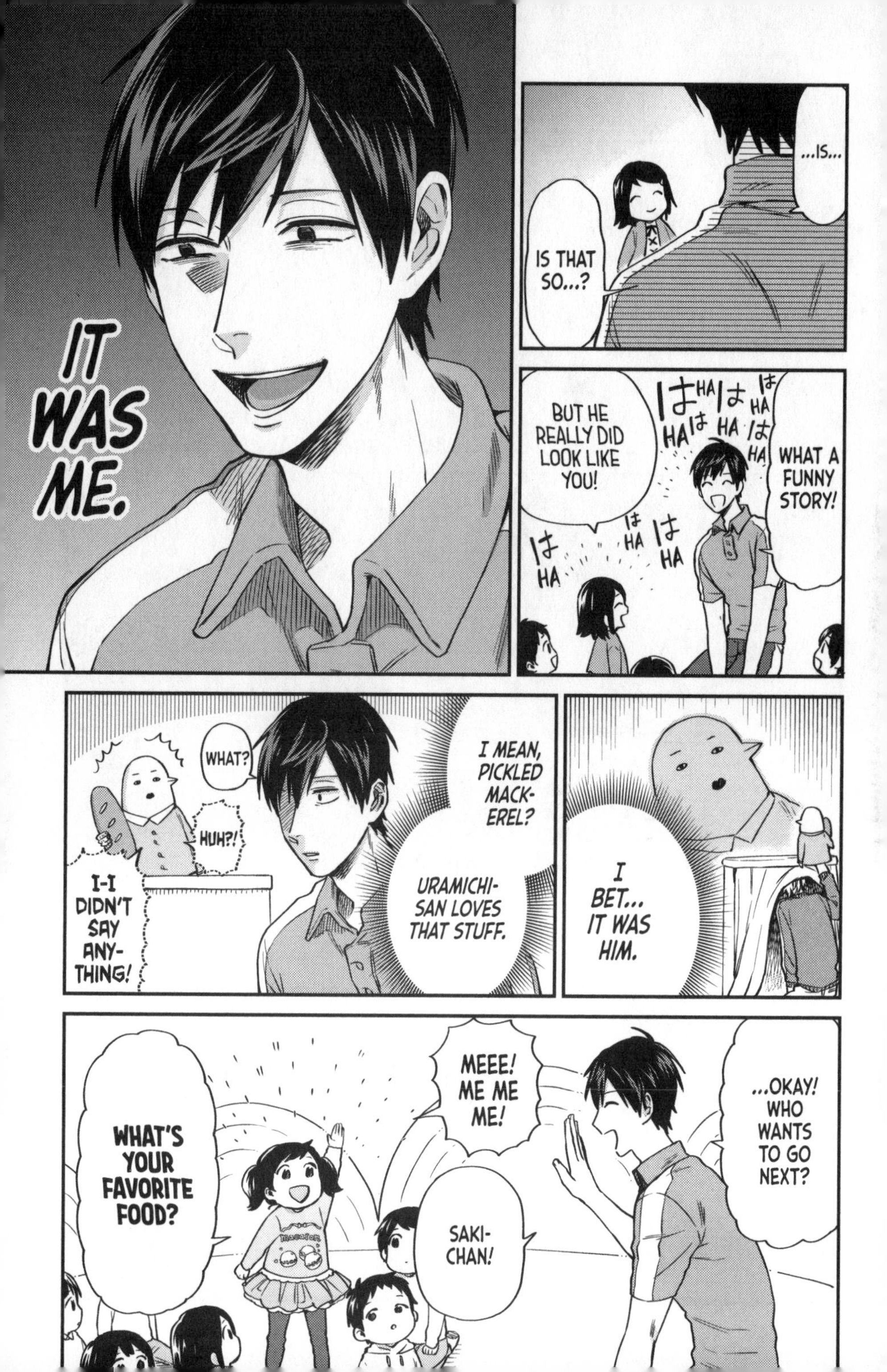
...IS...
IS THAT SO...?
WHAT A FUNNY STORY!
は HA は HA は HA は HA
BUT HE REALLY DID LOOK LIKE YOU!
は HA は HA は HA
IT WAS ME.
I BET... IT WAS HIM.
I MEAN, PICKLED MACK-EREL?
URAMICHI-SAN LOVES THAT STUFF.
WHAT?
HUH?!
I-I DIDN'T SAY ANY-THING!
...OKAY! WHO WANTS TO GO NEXT?
MEEE! ME ME ME!
SAKI-CHAN!
WHAT'S YOUR FAVORITE FOOD?

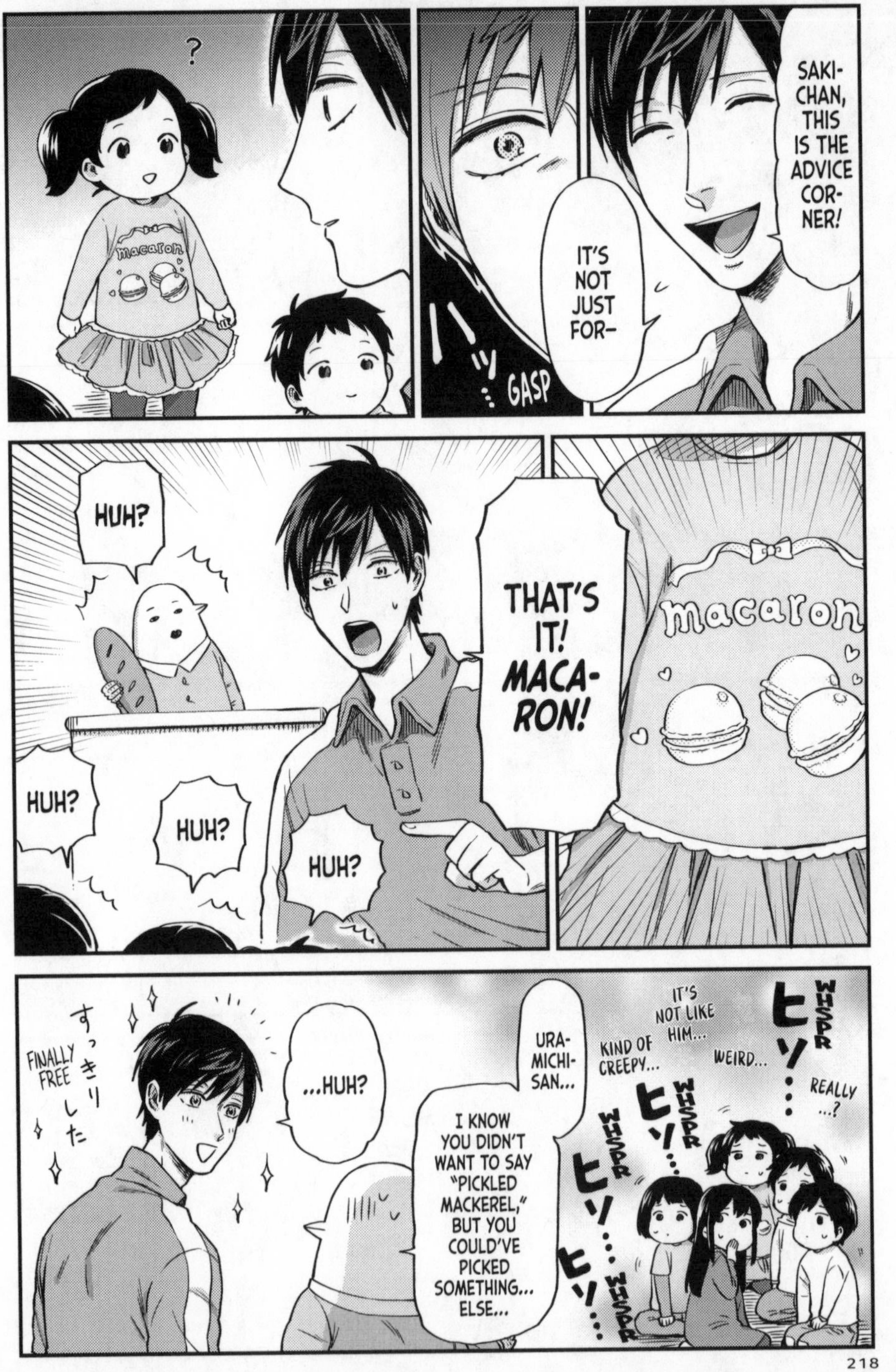
SAKI-CHAN, THIS IS THE ADVICE CORNER!
IT'S NOT JUST FOR–
ハッ… GASP
?
THAT'S IT! MACARON!
HUH?
HUH?
HUH?
HUH?
macaron
ヒソ… WHSPR
IT'S NOT LIKE HIM...
WEIRD...
REALLY ...?
KIND OF CREEPY...
ヒソ… WHSPR
ヒソ… WHSPR
ヒソ… WHSPR
URA-MICHI-SAN...
I KNOW YOU DIDN'T WANT TO SAY "PICKLED MACKEREL," BUT YOU COULD'VE PICKED SOMETHING... ELSE...
...HUH?
すっきりした FINALLY FREE

Life Lessons with
Uramichi Oniisan

Arm Through the Neck Hole

Sung by Iketeru Oniisan and Utano Oneesan

Finally home at 2 a.m.
Time to put your chores off again

"I have to get up early tomorrow"
That's the excuse you tell yourself

It's not like somebody will scold you
There's no one to scold you anymore

But still

Your place is a mess, and you feel so guilty (guilty)

"When did I wear this?" "Is it still good?"
No more folded clothes in the drawer!

Ugh, fine
This'll do, I'm in a hurry

But then you

Put your arm out through the neck hole
Put both feet in the same pants leg

Your life's such a mess
That you can't even get yourself dressed

La la la, la la la la...

Stretched-out neck holes,
black and blue knees
Songs and gloves, both different colors

La la la, la la la la...

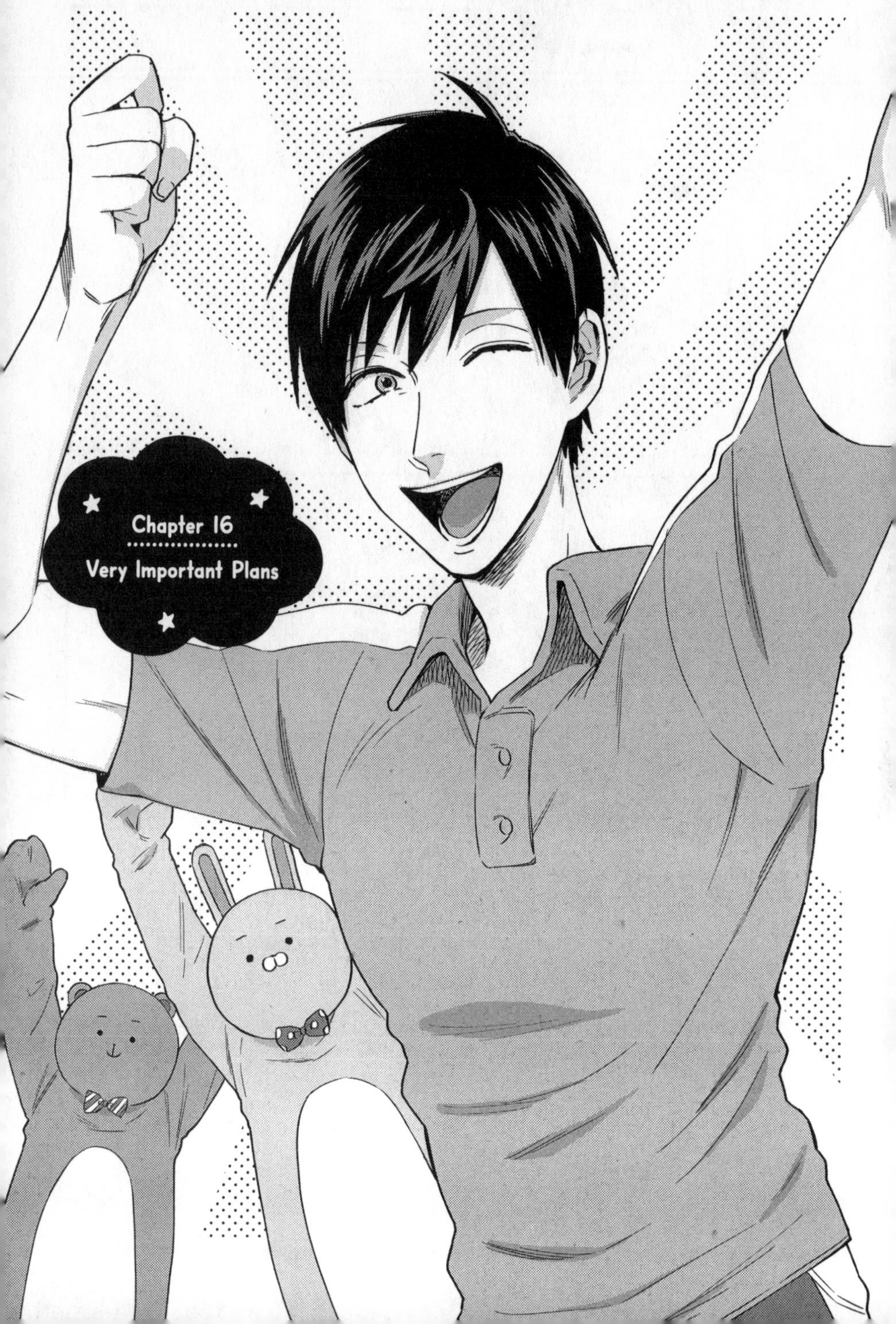
Chapter 16
Very Important Plans

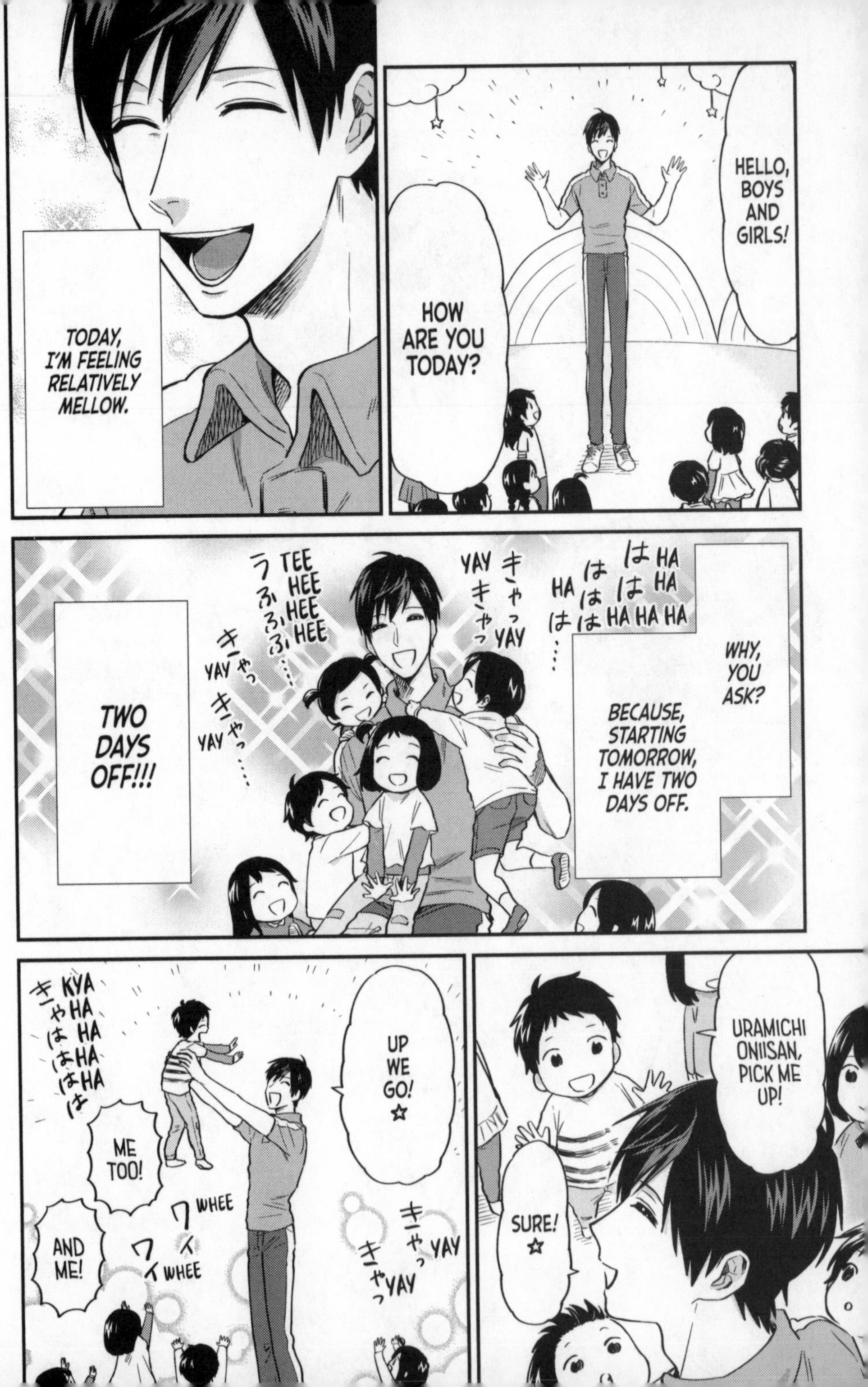
HELLO, BOYS AND GIRLS!
HOW ARE YOU TODAY?
TODAY, I'M FEELING RELATIVELY MELLOW.
HA HA HA HA HA はははは…
WHY, YOU ASK?
BECAUSE, STARTING TOMORROW, I HAVE TWO DAYS OFF.
YAY YAY きゃっきゃっ
TEE HEE HEE HEE うふふふ…
YAY YAY きゃっきゃっ…
TWO DAYS OFF!!!
URAMICHI ONIISAN, PICK ME UP!
SURE! ☆
UP WE GO! ☆
YAY YAY きゃっきゃっ
KYA HA HA HA HA きゃははは
ME TOO!
WHEE WHEE ワイワイ
AND ME!

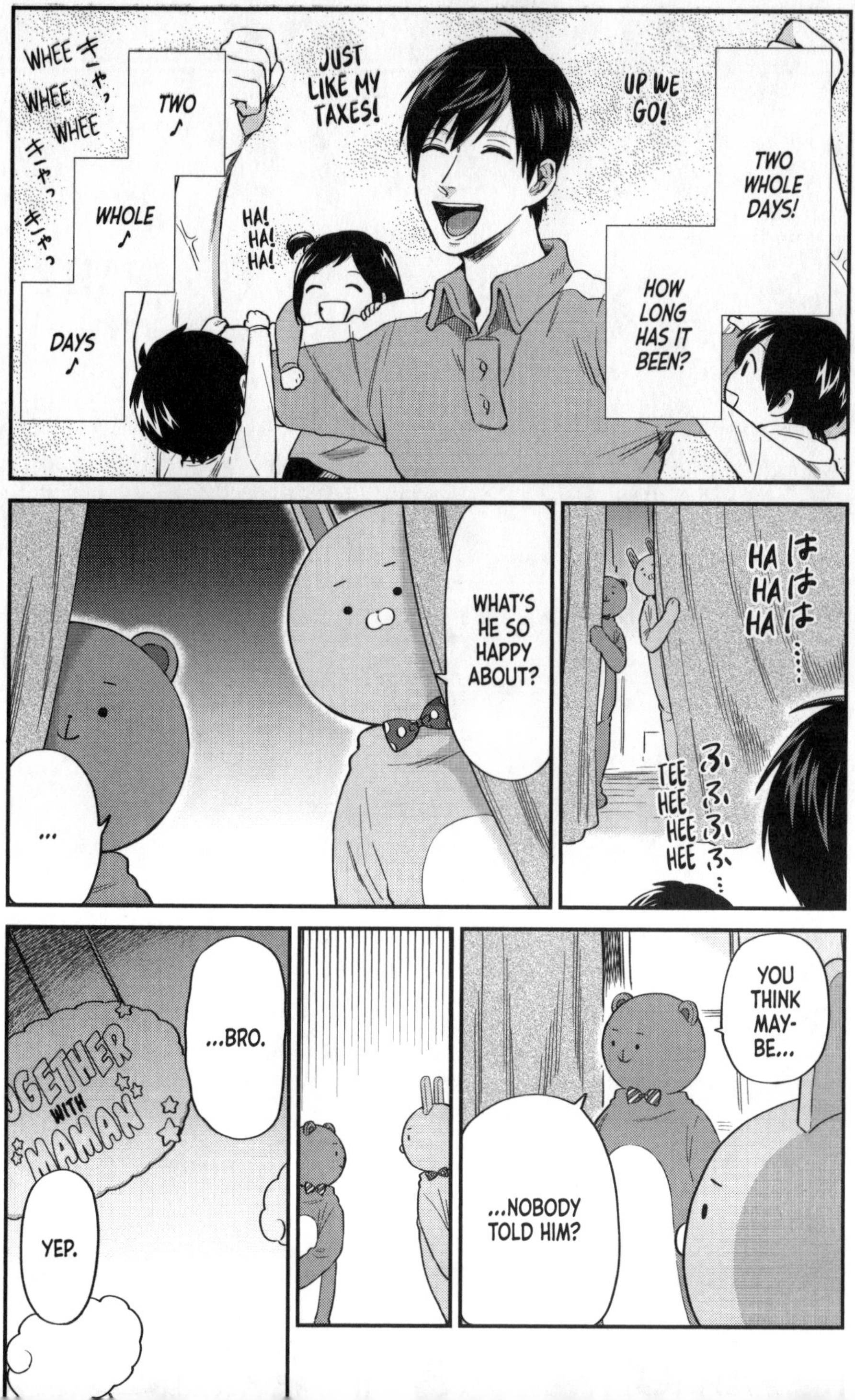
TWO WHOLE DAYS!
UP WE GO!
HOW LONG HAS IT BEEN?
JUST LIKE MY TAXES!
HA! HA! HA!
TWO ♪
WHOLE ♪
DAYS ♪
WHEE WHEE WHEE キャッ キャッ キャッ
HA HA HA ははは……
TEE HEE HEE HEE ふふふふ…
WHAT'S HE SO HAPPY ABOUT?
...
YOU THINK MAY-BE...
...NOBODY TOLD HIM?
...BRO.
OGETHER WITH MAMAN
YEP.

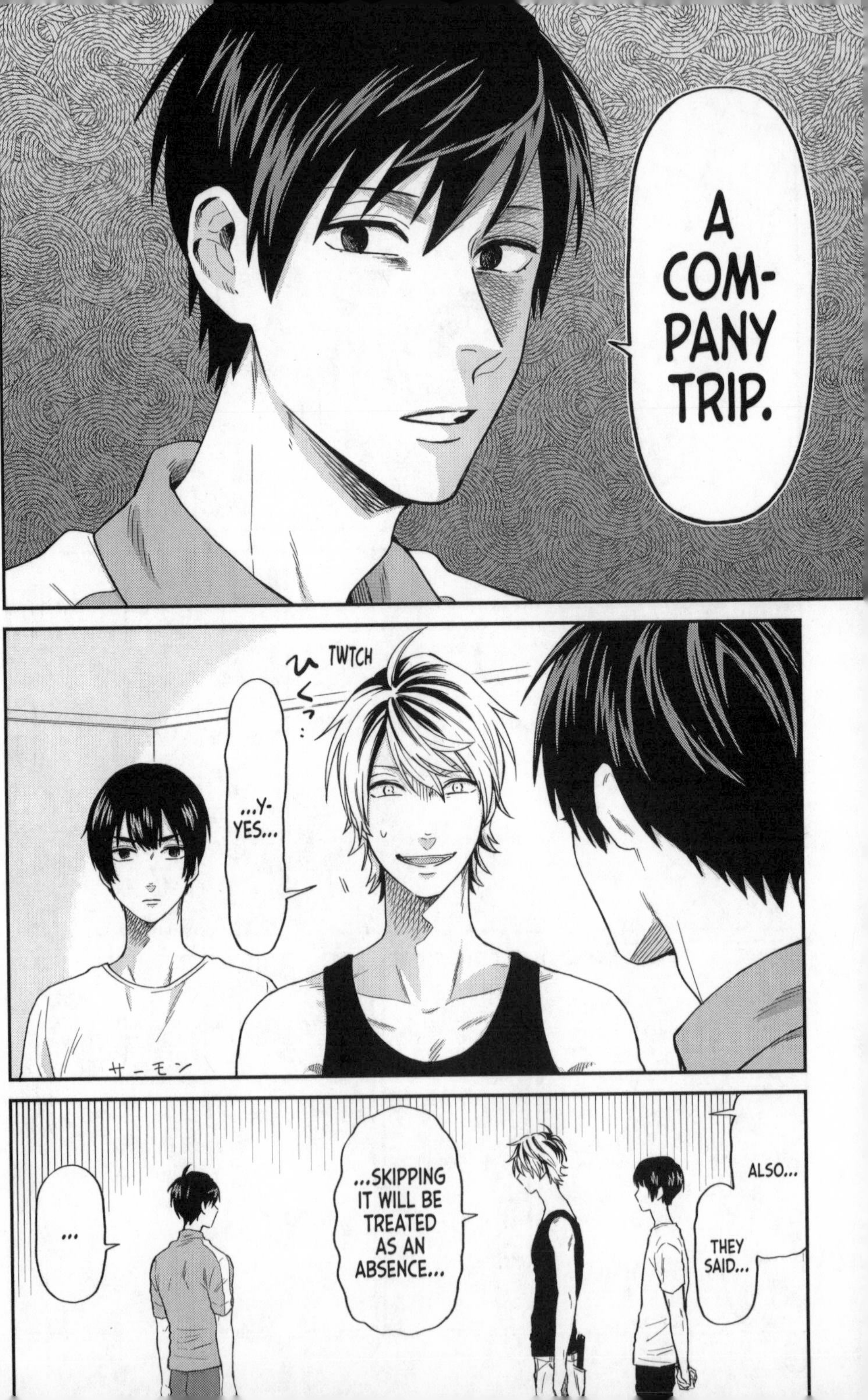
A COMPANY TRIP.
ひくっ
TWTCH
...Y-YES...
サーモン
ALSO... THEY SAID...
...SKIPPING IT WILL BE TREATED AS AN ABSENCE...
...

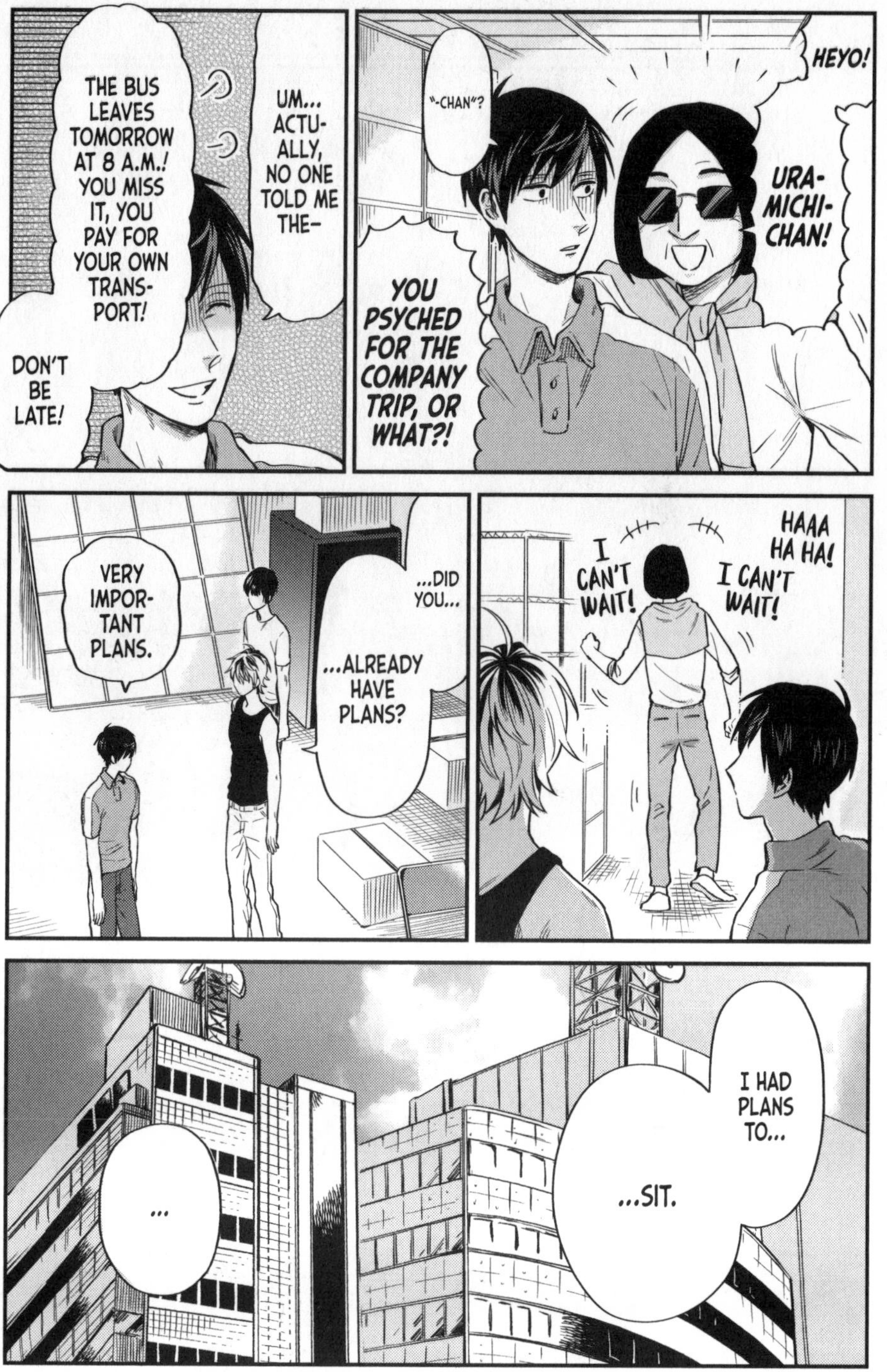
HEYO!
URA-MICHI-CHAN!
YOU PSYCHED FOR THE COMPANY TRIP, OR WHAT?!
"-CHAN"?
UM... ACTUALLY, NO ONE TOLD ME THE-
THE BUS LEAVES TOMORROW AT 8 A.M.! YOU MISS IT, YOU PAY FOR YOUR OWN TRANSPORT!
DON'T BE LATE!
HAAA HA HA! I CAN'T WAIT!
I CAN'T WAIT!
...DID YOU...
...ALREADY HAVE PLANS?
VERY IMPORTANT PLANS.
I HAD PLANS TO...
...SIT.
...

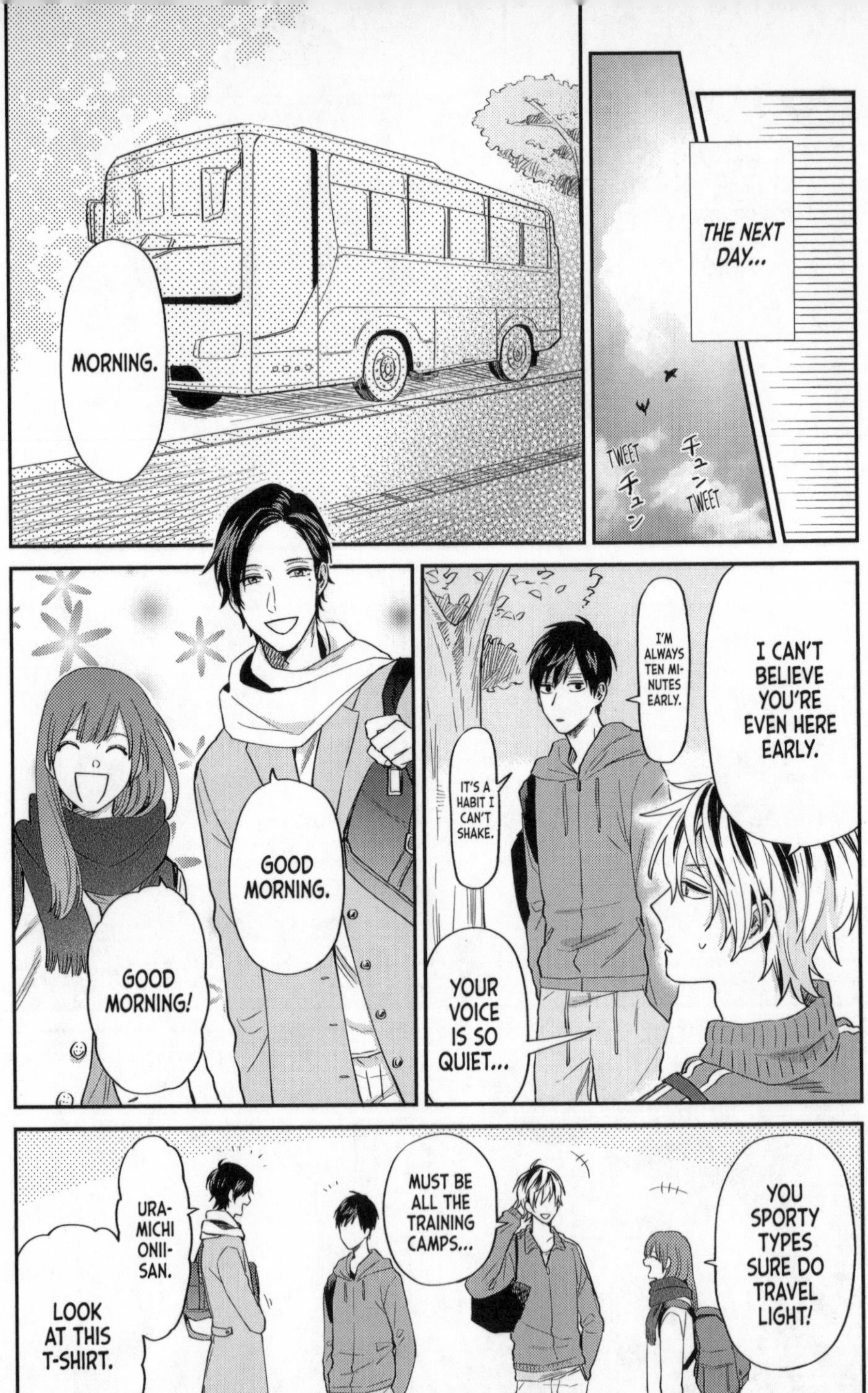
THE NEXT DAY...
チュン
TWEET
TWEET
チュン
MORNING.
I CAN'T BELIEVE YOU'RE EVEN HERE EARLY.
I'M ALWAYS TEN MINUTES EARLY.
IT'S A HABIT I CAN'T SHAKE.
YOUR VOICE IS SO QUIET...
GOOD MORNING.
GOOD MORNING!
YOU SPORTY TYPES SURE DO TRAVEL LIGHT!
MUST BE ALL THE TRAINING CAMPS...
URA-MICHI ONII-SAN.
LOOK AT THIS T-SHIRT.

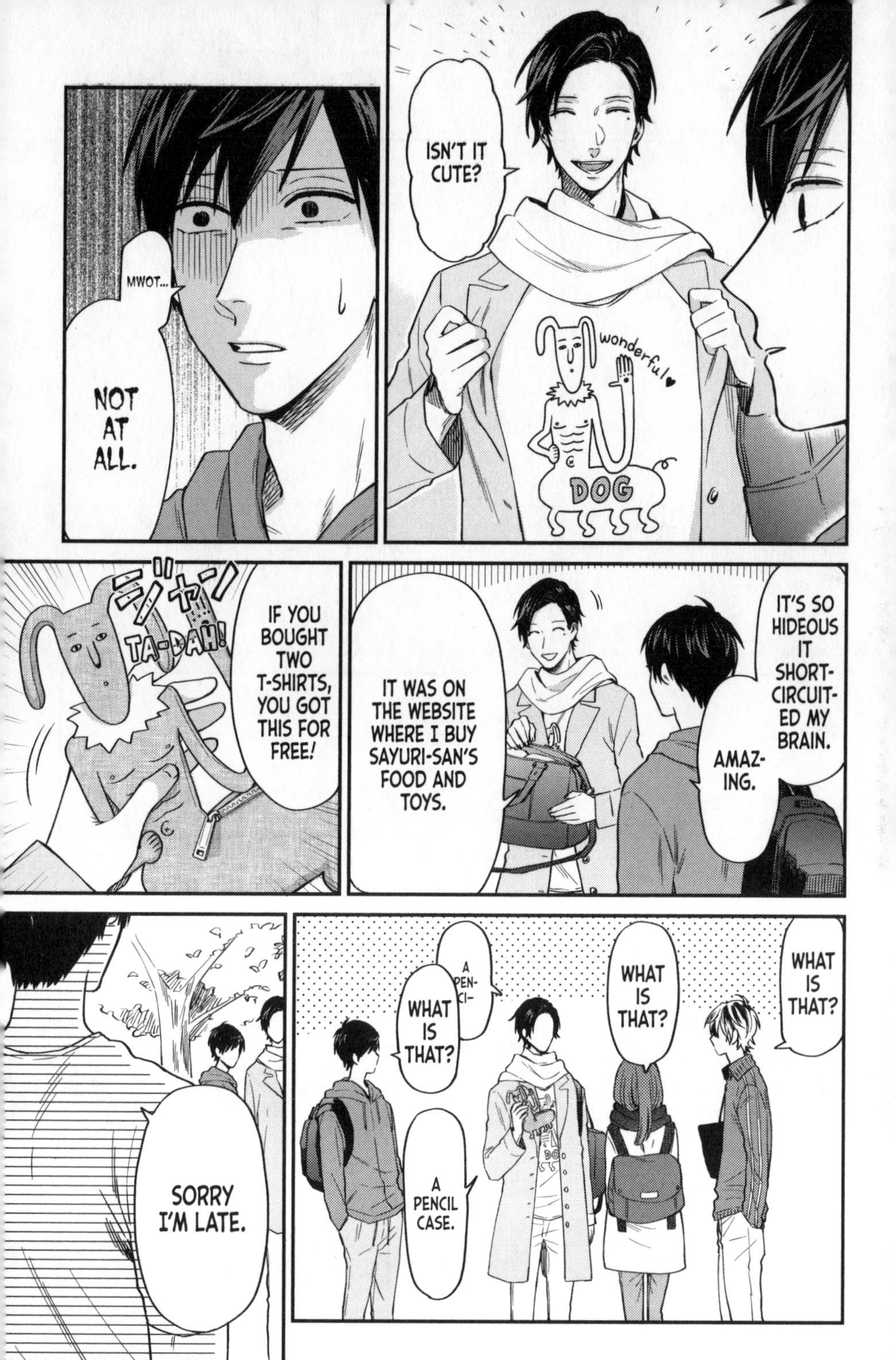
ISN'T IT CUTE?
wonderful♥
DOG
MWOT...
NOT AT ALL.
IT'S SO HIDEOUS IT SHORT-CIRCUITED MY BRAIN.
AMAZ-ING.
IT WAS ON THE WEBSITE WHERE I BUY SAYURI-SAN'S FOOD AND TOYS.
IF YOU BOUGHT TWO T-SHIRTS, YOU GOT THIS FOR FREE!
ジャーン
TA-DAH!
WHAT IS THAT?
WHAT IS THAT?
A PENCI-
WHAT IS THAT?
A PENCIL CASE.
SORRY I'M LATE.

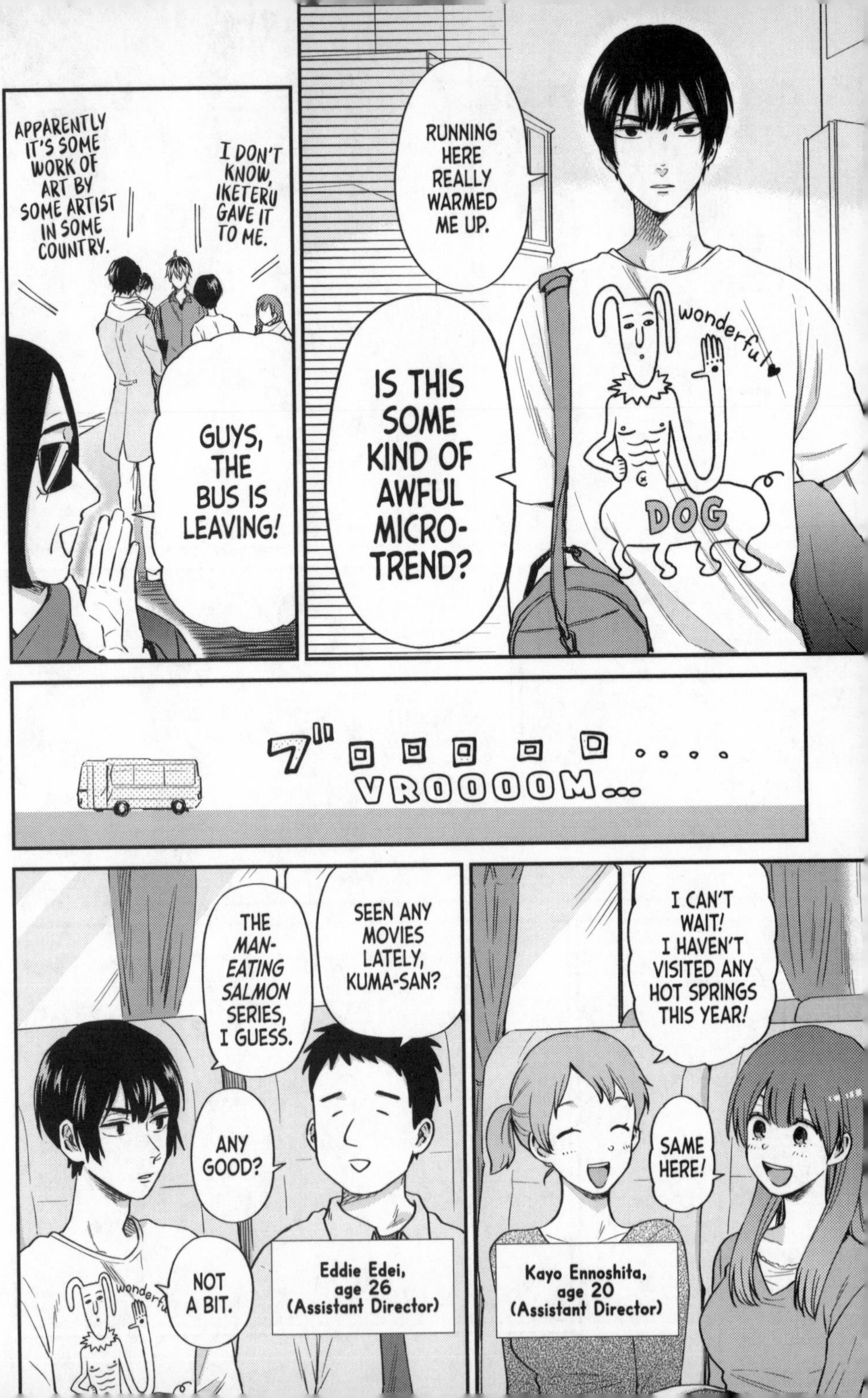
RUNNING HERE REALLY WARMED ME UP.
IS THIS SOME KIND OF AWFUL MICRO-TREND?
wonderful
DOG
I DON'T KNOW, IKETERU GAVE IT TO ME.
APPARENTLY IT'S SOME WORK OF ART BY SOME ARTIST IN SOME COUNTRY.
GUYS, THE BUS IS LEAVING!
VROOOOOM...
I CAN'T WAIT! I HAVEN'T VISITED ANY HOT SPRINGS THIS YEAR!
SAME HERE!
Kayo Ennoshita, age 20 (Assistant Director)
SEEN ANY MOVIES LATELY, KUMA-SAN?
THE MAN-EATING SALMON SERIES, I GUESS.
ANY GOOD?
NOT A BIT.
Eddie Edei, age 26 (Assistant Director)

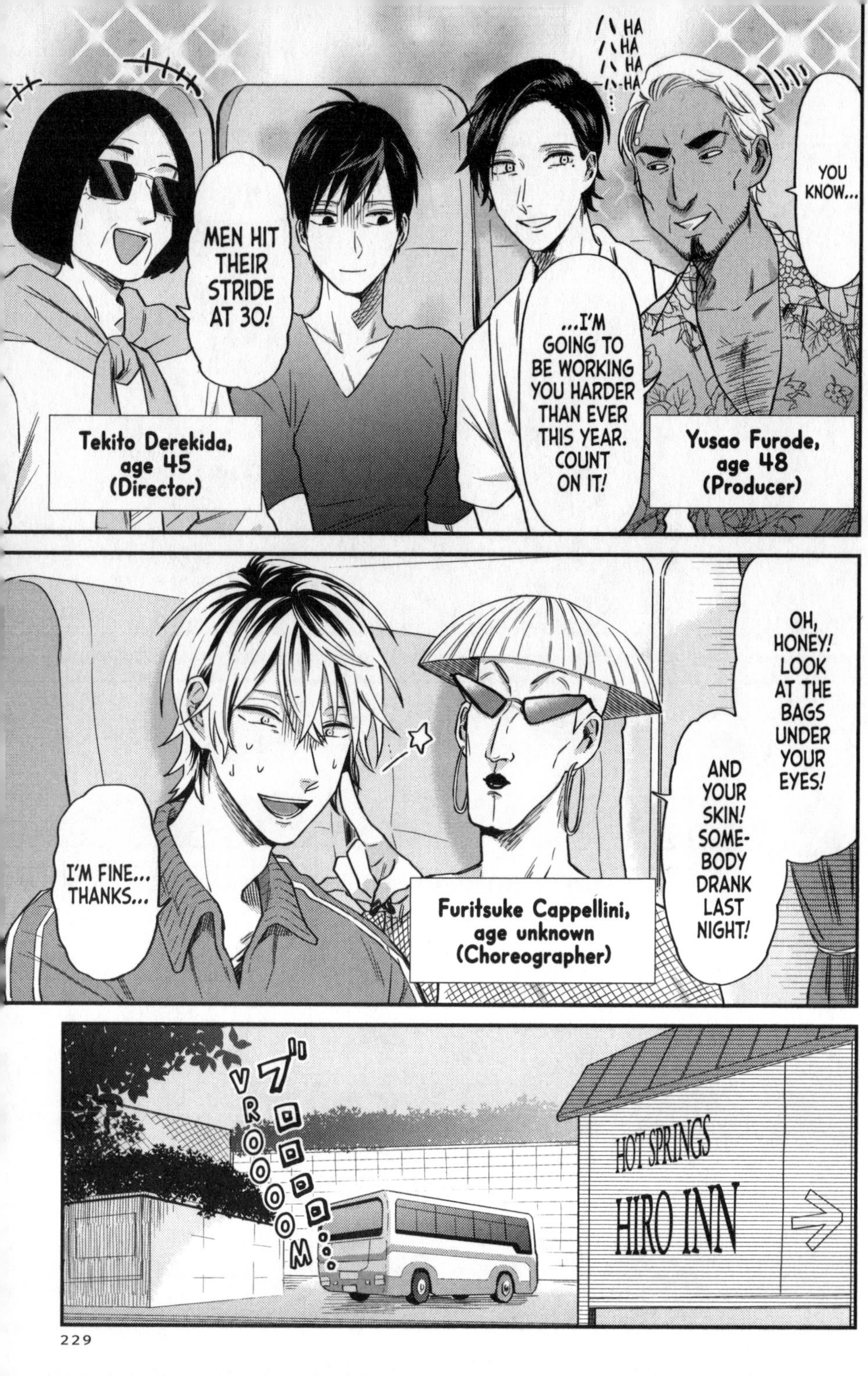
HA HA HA HA...
YOU KNOW...
...I'M GOING TO BE WORKING YOU HARDER THAN EVER THIS YEAR. COUNT ON IT!
Yusao Furode, age 48 (Producer)
MEN HIT THEIR STRIDE AT 30!
Tekito Derekida, age 45 (Director)
OH, HONEY! LOOK AT THE BAGS UNDER YOUR EYES!
AND YOUR SKIN! SOMEBODY DRANK LAST NIGHT!
Furitsuke Cappellini, age unknown (Choreographer)
I'M FINE... THANKS...
HOT SPRINGS
HIRO INN
VROOOOOM

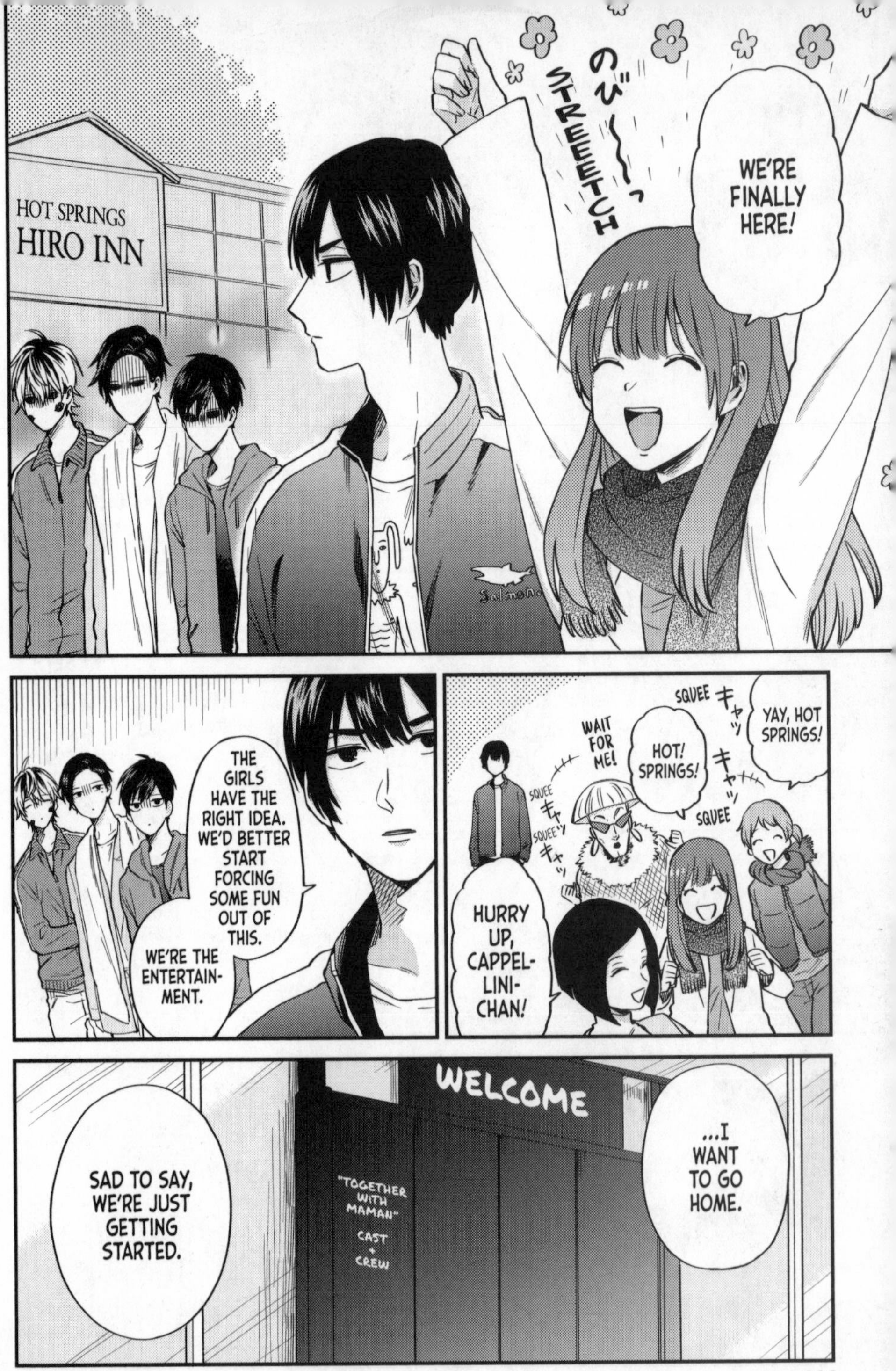
WE'RE FINALLY HERE!
のび～～っ
STREEEETCH
HOT SPRINGS HIRO INN
YAY, HOT SPRINGS!
SQUEE キャッ
キャッ SQUEE
HOT! SPRINGS!
WAIT FOR ME!
SQUEE キャッ
SQUEE キャッ
HURRY UP, CAPPEL-LINI-CHAN!
THE GIRLS HAVE THE RIGHT IDEA. WE'D BETTER START FORCING SOME FUN OUT OF THIS.
WE'RE THE ENTERTAIN-MENT.
...I WANT TO GO HOME.
WELCOME
"TOGETHER WITH MAMAN" CAST + CREW
SAD TO SAY, WE'RE JUST GETTING STARTED.

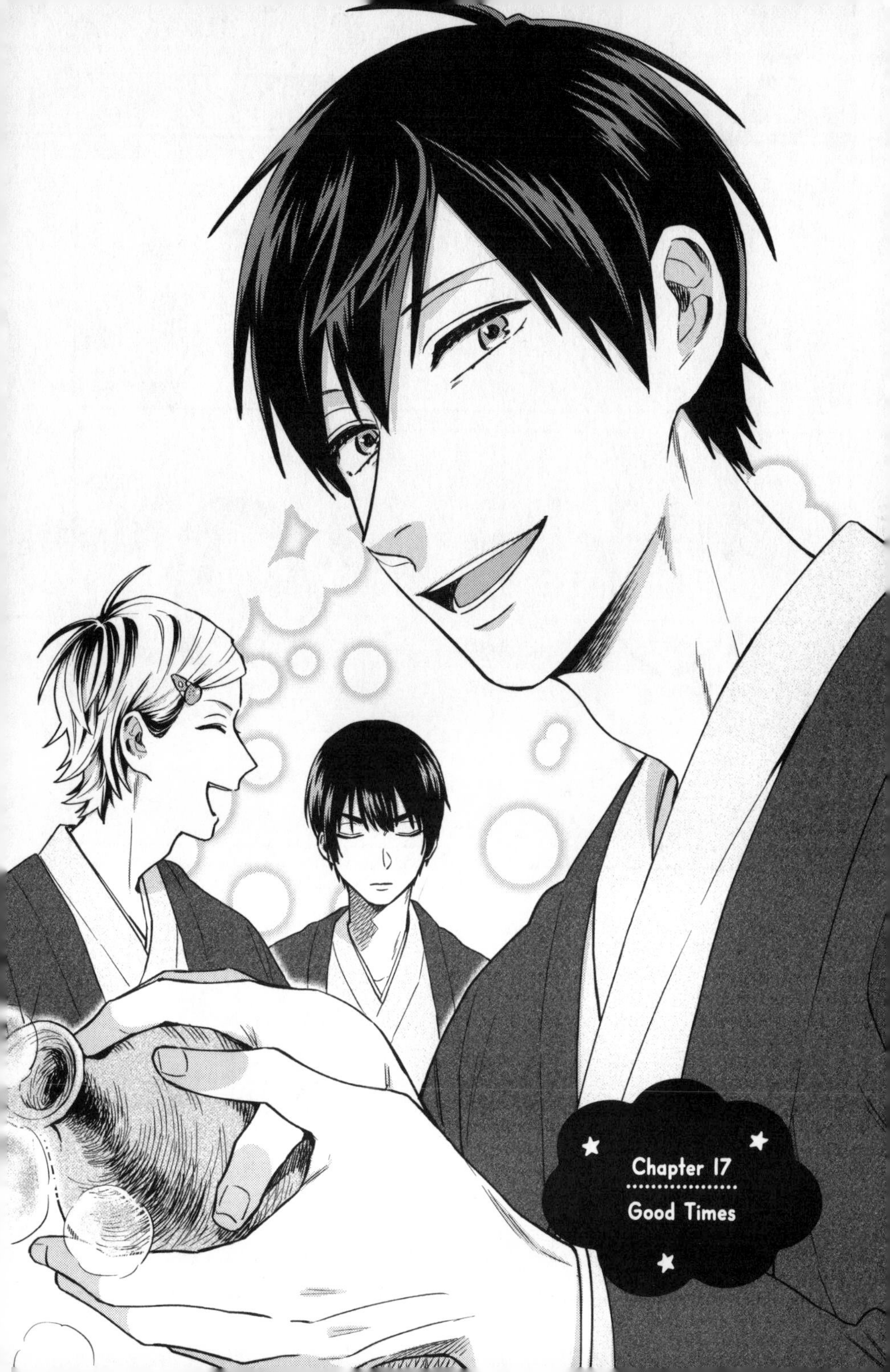
Chapter 17
Good Times

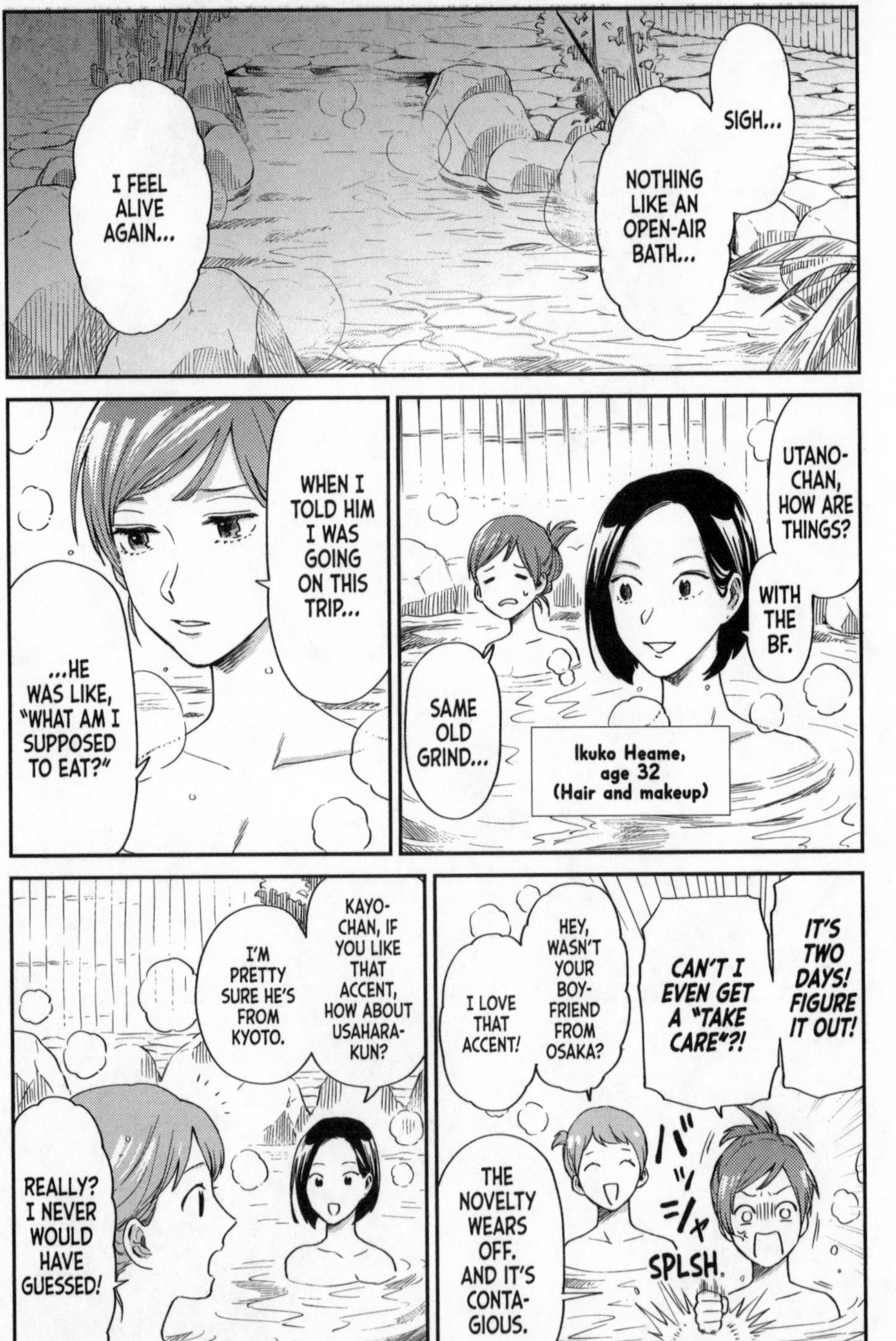
SIGH...
NOTHING LIKE AN OPEN-AIR BATH...
I FEEL ALIVE AGAIN...
UTANO-CHAN, HOW ARE THINGS?
WITH THE BF.
SAME OLD GRIND...
Ikuko Heame, age 32 (Hair and makeup)
WHEN I TOLD HIM I WAS GOING ON THIS TRIP...
...HE WAS LIKE, "WHAT AM I SUPPOSED TO EAT?"
IT'S TWO DAYS! FIGURE IT OUT!
CAN'T I EVEN GET A "TAKE CARE"?!
HEY, WASN'T YOUR BOY-FRIEND FROM OSAKA?
I LOVE THAT ACCENT!
バッシャ
SPLSH
THE NOVELTY WEARS OFF. AND IT'S CONTA-GIOUS.
KAYO-CHAN, IF YOU LIKE THAT ACCENT, HOW ABOUT USAHARA-KUN?
I'M PRETTY SURE HE'S FROM KYOTO.
REALLY? I NEVER WOULD HAVE GUESSED!

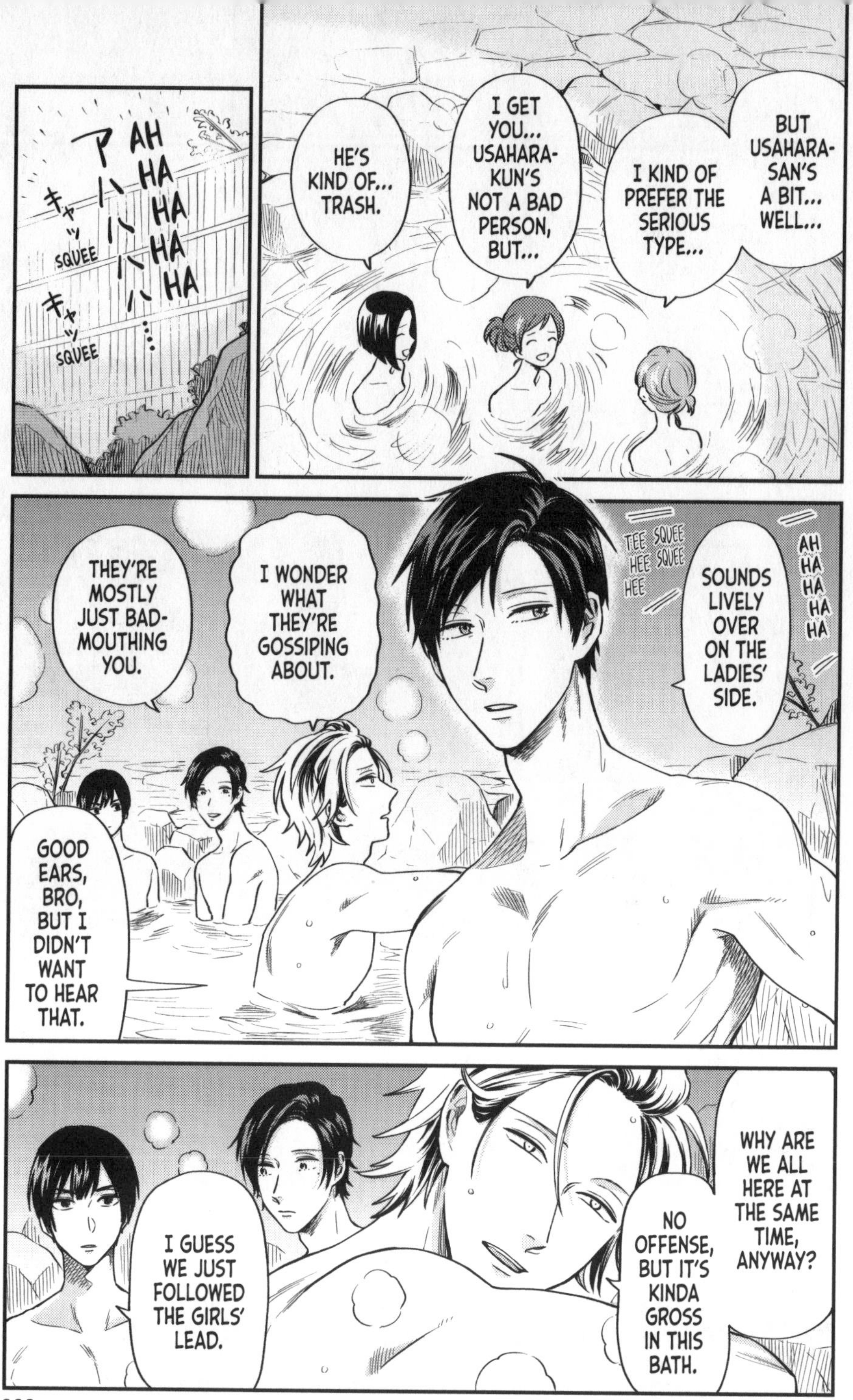
BUT USAHARA-SAN'S A BIT... WELL...
I KIND OF PREFER THE SERIOUS TYPE...
I GET YOU... USAHARA-KUN'S NOT A BAD PERSON, BUT...
HE'S KIND OF... TRASH.
アハハハ… AH HA HA HA HA
キャッ SQUEE
キャッ SQUEE
AH HA HA HA HA
TEE HEE HEE
SQUEE SQUEE
SOUNDS LIVELY OVER ON THE LADIES' SIDE.
I WONDER WHAT THEY'RE GOSSIPING ABOUT.
THEY'RE MOSTLY JUST BAD-MOUTHING YOU.
GOOD EARS, BRO, BUT I DIDN'T WANT TO HEAR THAT.
WHY ARE WE ALL HERE AT THE SAME TIME, ANYWAY?
NO OFFENSE, BUT IT'S KINDA GROSS IN THIS BATH.
I GUESS WE JUST FOLLOWED THE GIRLS' LEAD.

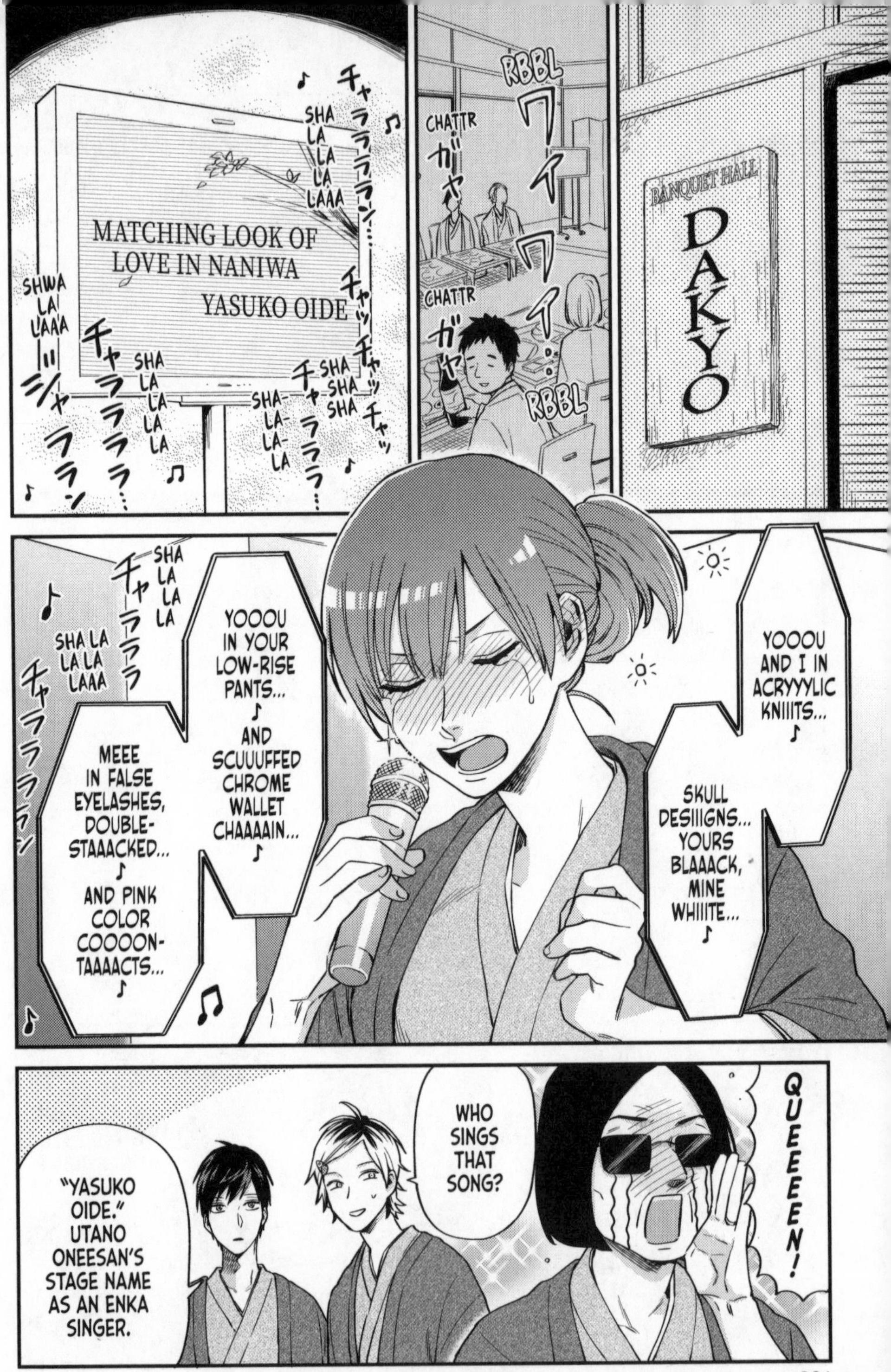
BANQUET HALL
DAKYO
RBBL
CHATTR
CHATTR
RBBL
♪
SHA LA LA LA LAAA
♪
MATCHING LOOK OF LOVE IN NANIWA
YASUKO OIDE
SHWA LA LAAA
SHA LA LA LA LA
SHA SHA SHA
SHA-LA-LA-LA
♪
♪
YOOOU AND I IN ACRYYYLIC KNIIITS... ♪
SKULL DESIIIGNS... YOURS BLAAACK, MINE WHIIITE... ♪
YOOOU IN YOUR LOW-RISE PANTS... ♪ AND SCUUUFFED CHROME WALLET CHAAAAIN... ♪
MEEE IN FALSE EYELASHES, DOUBLE-STAAACKED... ♪ AND PINK COLOR COOOON-TAAAACTS... ♪
SHA LA LA LA
SHA LA LA LA LAAA
♪
♪
QUEEEEN!
WHO SINGS THAT SONG?
"YASUKO OIDE." UTANO ONEESAN'S STAGE NAME AS AN ENKA SINGER.

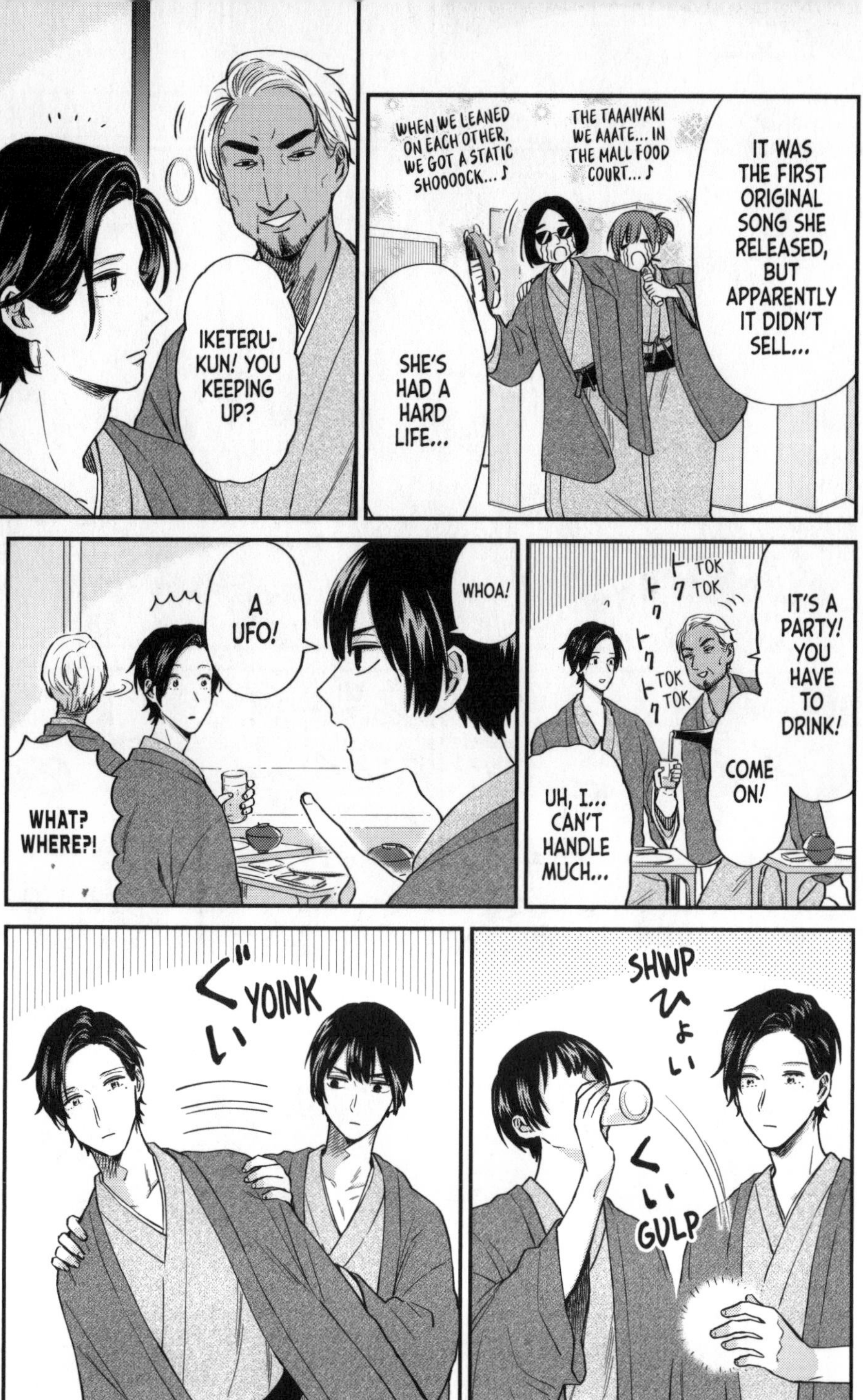
IT WAS THE FIRST ORIGINAL SONG SHE RELEASED, BUT APPARENTLY IT DIDN'T SELL...
THE TAAAIYAKI WE AAATE... IN THE MALL FOOD COURT... ♪
WHEN WE LEANED ON EACH OTHER, WE GOT A STATIC SHOOOCK... ♪
SHE'S HAD A HARD LIFE...
IKETERU-KUN! YOU KEEPING UP?
トクトク TOK TOK
トクトク TOK TOK
IT'S A PARTY! YOU HAVE TO DRINK!
COME ON!
UH, I... CAN'T HANDLE MUCH...
WHOA!
A UFO!
WHAT? WHERE?!
ひょい SHWP
くい GULP
ぐい YOINK

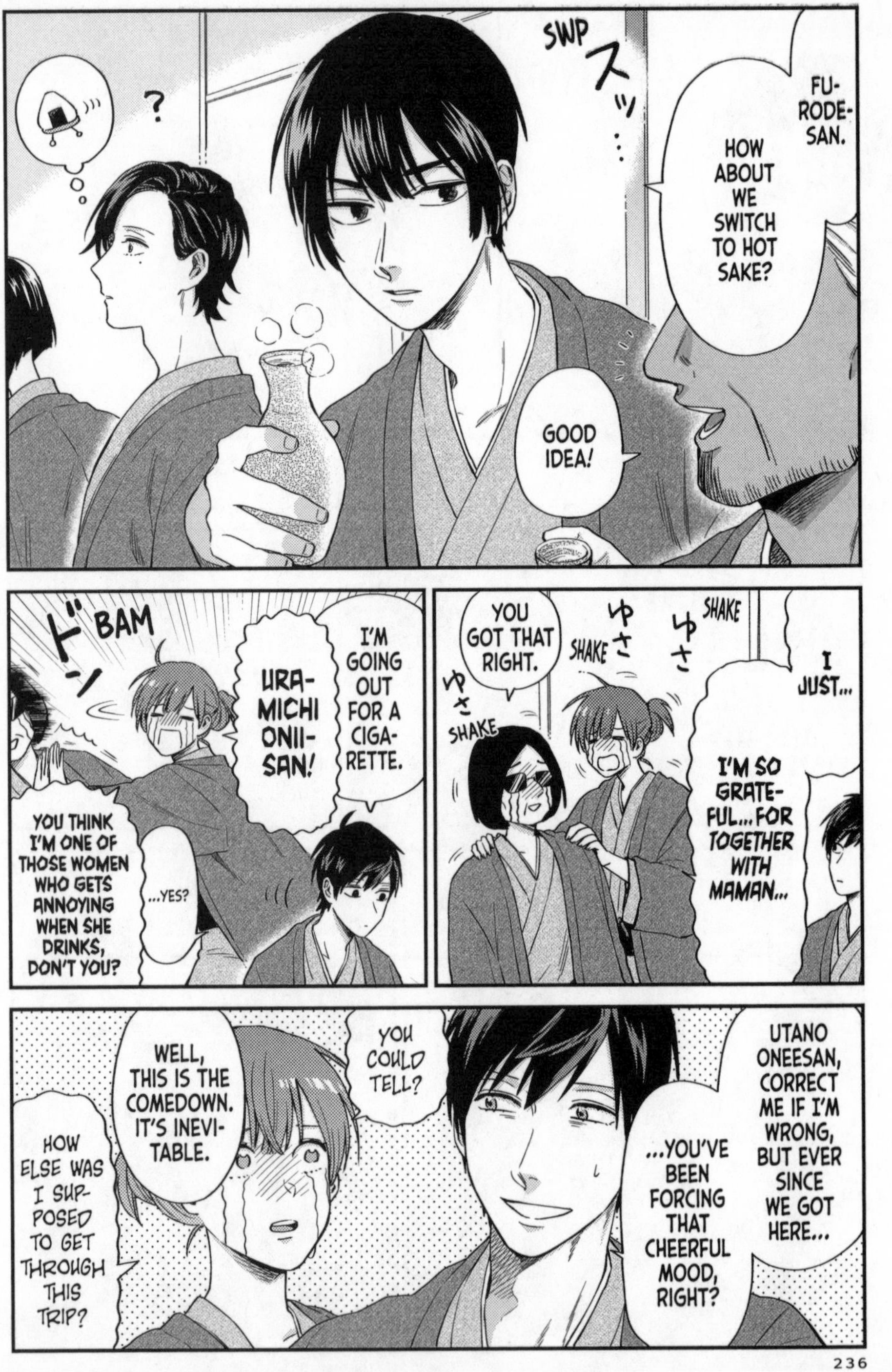
FU-RODE-SAN.
HOW ABOUT WE SWITCH TO HOT SAKE?
SWP スッ
GOOD IDEA!
?
I JUST...
I'M SO GRATEFUL... FOR TOGETHER WITH MAMAN...
SHAKE ゆさ
SHAKE ゆさ
SHAKE ゆさ
YOU GOT THAT RIGHT.
I'M GOING OUT FOR A CIGARETTE.
URA-MICHI ONII-SAN!
BAM ドン
YOU THINK I'M ONE OF THOSE WOMEN WHO GETS ANNOYING WHEN SHE DRINKS, DON'T YOU?
...YES?
UTANO ONEESAN, CORRECT ME IF I'M WRONG, BUT EVER SINCE WE GOT HERE...
...YOU'VE BEEN FORCING THAT CHEERFUL MOOD, RIGHT?
YOU COULD TELL?
WELL, THIS IS THE COMEDOWN. IT'S INEVITABLE.
HOW ELSE WAS I SUPPOSED TO GET THROUGH THIS TRIP?

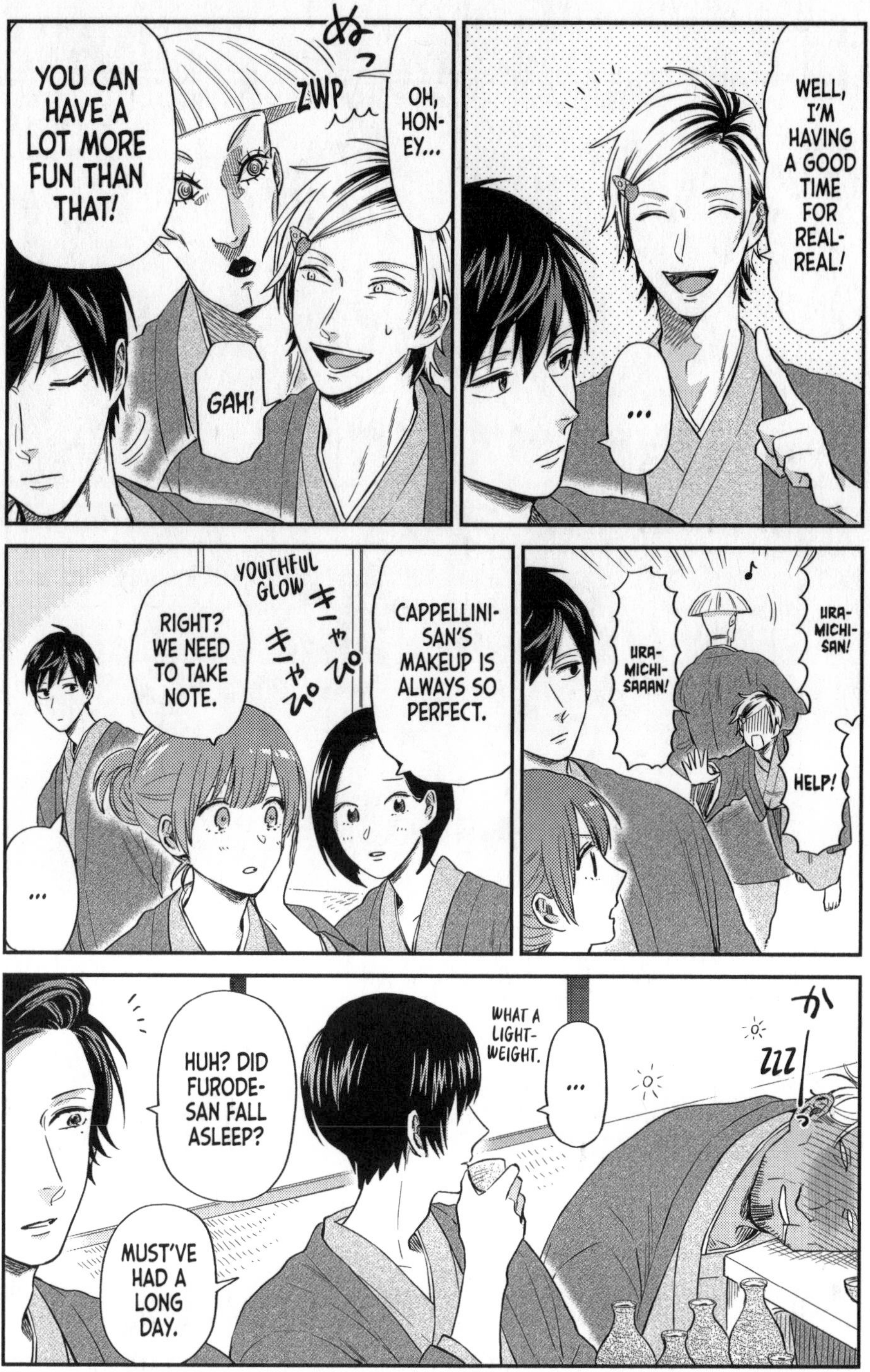
WELL, I'M HAVING A GOOD TIME FOR REAL-REAL!
...
ぬっ
ZWP
OH, HONEY...
YOU CAN HAVE A LOT MORE FUN THAN THAT!
GAH!
URA-MICHI-SAN!
URA-MICHI-SAAAN!
HELP!
CAPPELLINI-SAN'S MAKEUP IS ALWAYS SO PERFECT.
キャピキャピ
YOUTHFUL GLOW
RIGHT? WE NEED TO TAKE NOTE.
...
かー
ZZZ
WHAT A LIGHT-WEIGHT.
...
HUH? DID FURODE-SAN FALL ASLEEP?
MUST'VE HAD A LONG DAY.

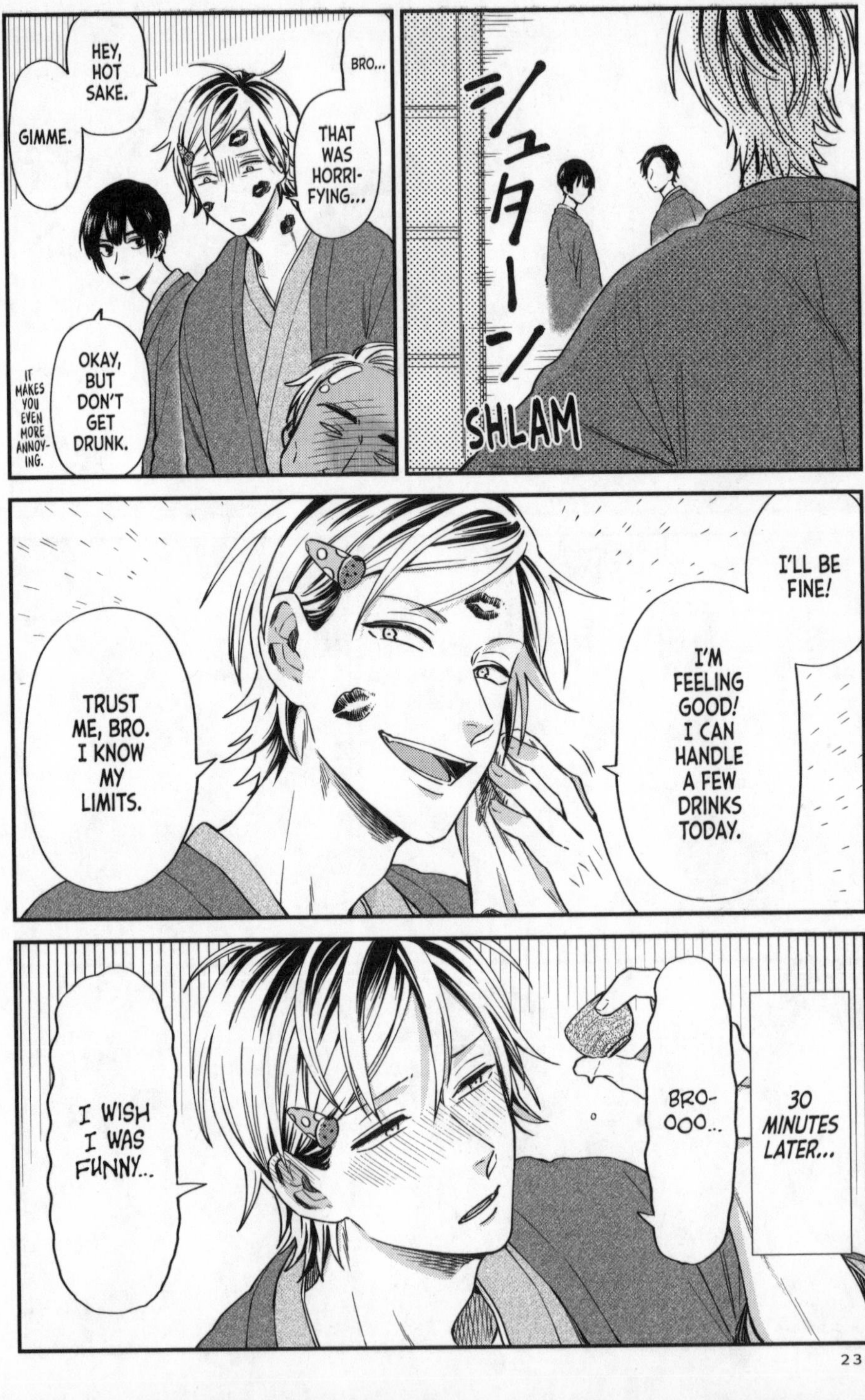
シュターン
SHLAM
BRO... THAT WAS HORRIFYING...
HEY, HOT SAKE. GIMME.
OKAY, BUT DON'T GET DRUNK.
IT MAKES YOU EVEN MORE ANNOYING.
I'LL BE FINE! I'M FEELING GOOD! I CAN HANDLE A FEW DRINKS TODAY.
TRUST ME, BRO. I KNOW MY LIMITS.
30 MINUTES LATER...
BRO-OOO...
I WISH I WAS FUNNY...

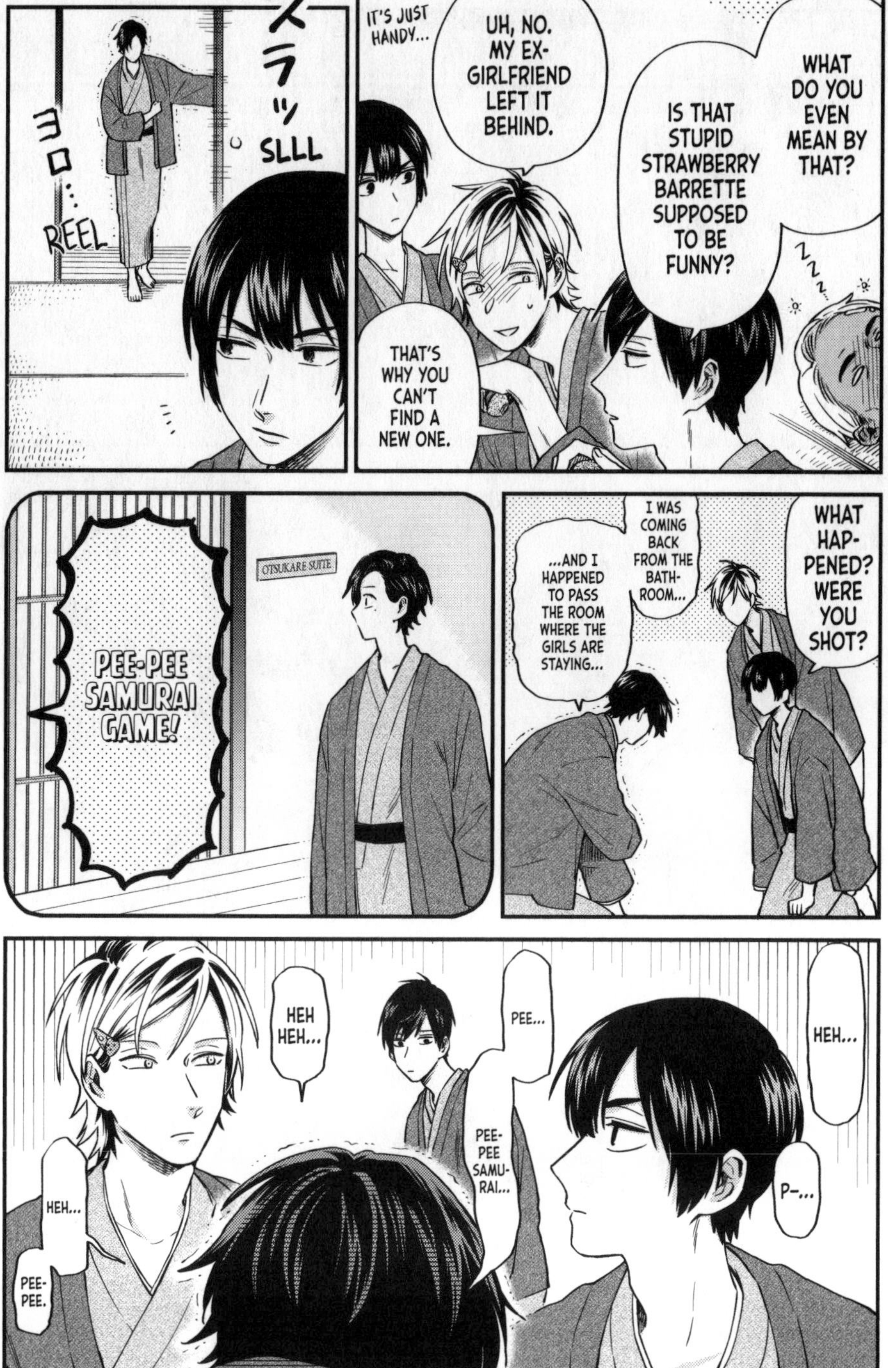
WHAT DO YOU EVEN MEAN BY THAT?
IS THAT STUPID STRAWBERRY BARRETTE SUPPOSED TO BE FUNNY?
UH, NO. MY EX-GIRLFRIEND LEFT IT BEHIND.
IT'S JUST HANDY...
THAT'S WHY YOU CAN'T FIND A NEW ONE.
ZZZ
スラッ
SLLL
ヨロ…
REEL
WHAT HAP-PENED? WERE YOU SHOT?
I WAS COMING BACK FROM THE BATH-ROOM...
...AND I HAPPENED TO PASS THE ROOM WHERE THE GIRLS ARE STAYING...
OTSUKARE SUITE
PEE-PEE SAMURAI GAME!
HEH...
P-...
PEE...
PEE-PEE SAMURAI...
HEH HEH...
HEH...
PEE-PEE.

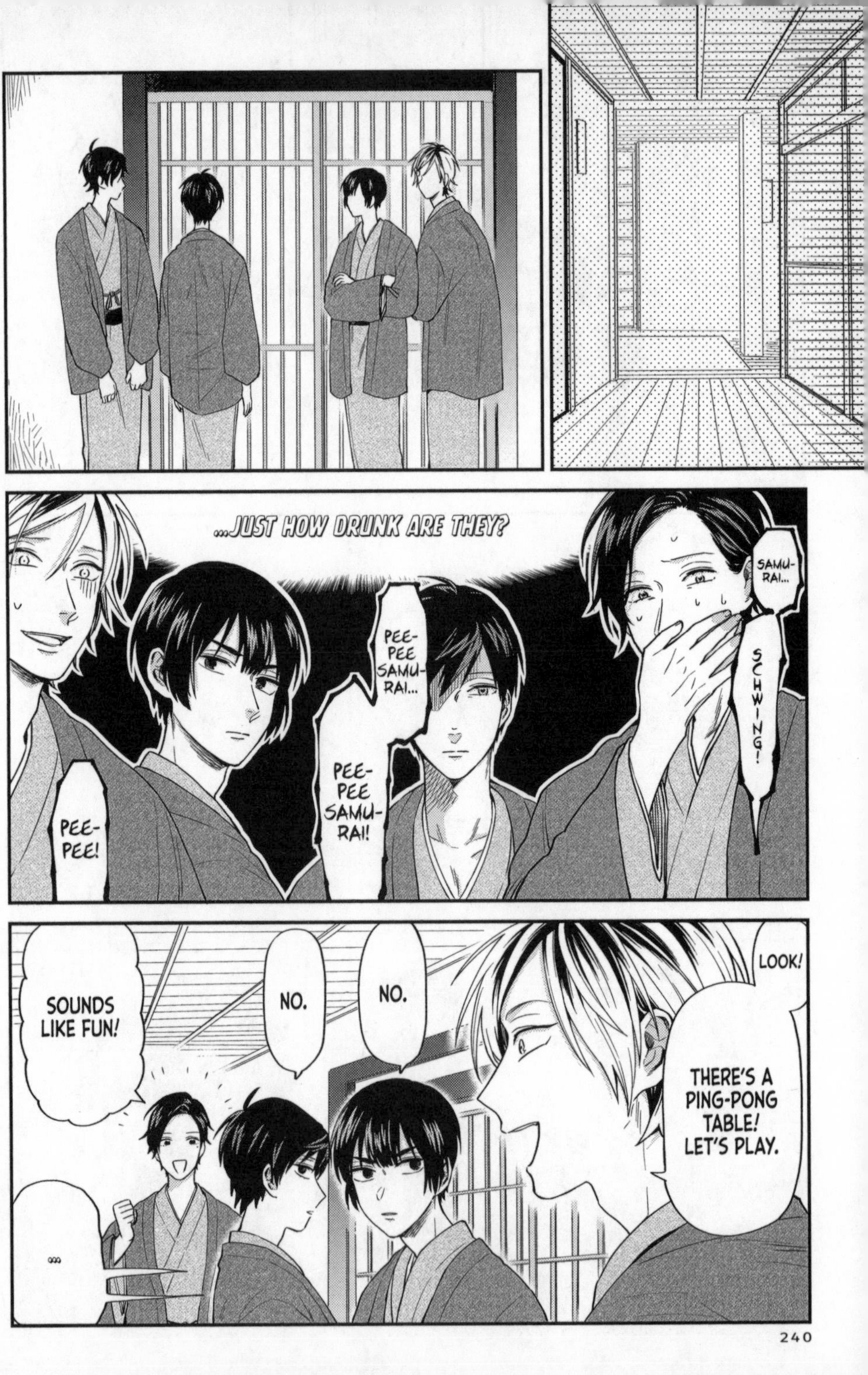
...JUST HOW DRUNK ARE THEY?
SAMURAI...
SCHWING!
PEE-PEE SAMURAI...
PEE-PEE SAMURAI!
PEE-PEE!
LOOK!
THERE'S A PING-PONG TABLE! LET'S PLAY.
NO.
NO.
SOUNDS LIKE FUN!
...

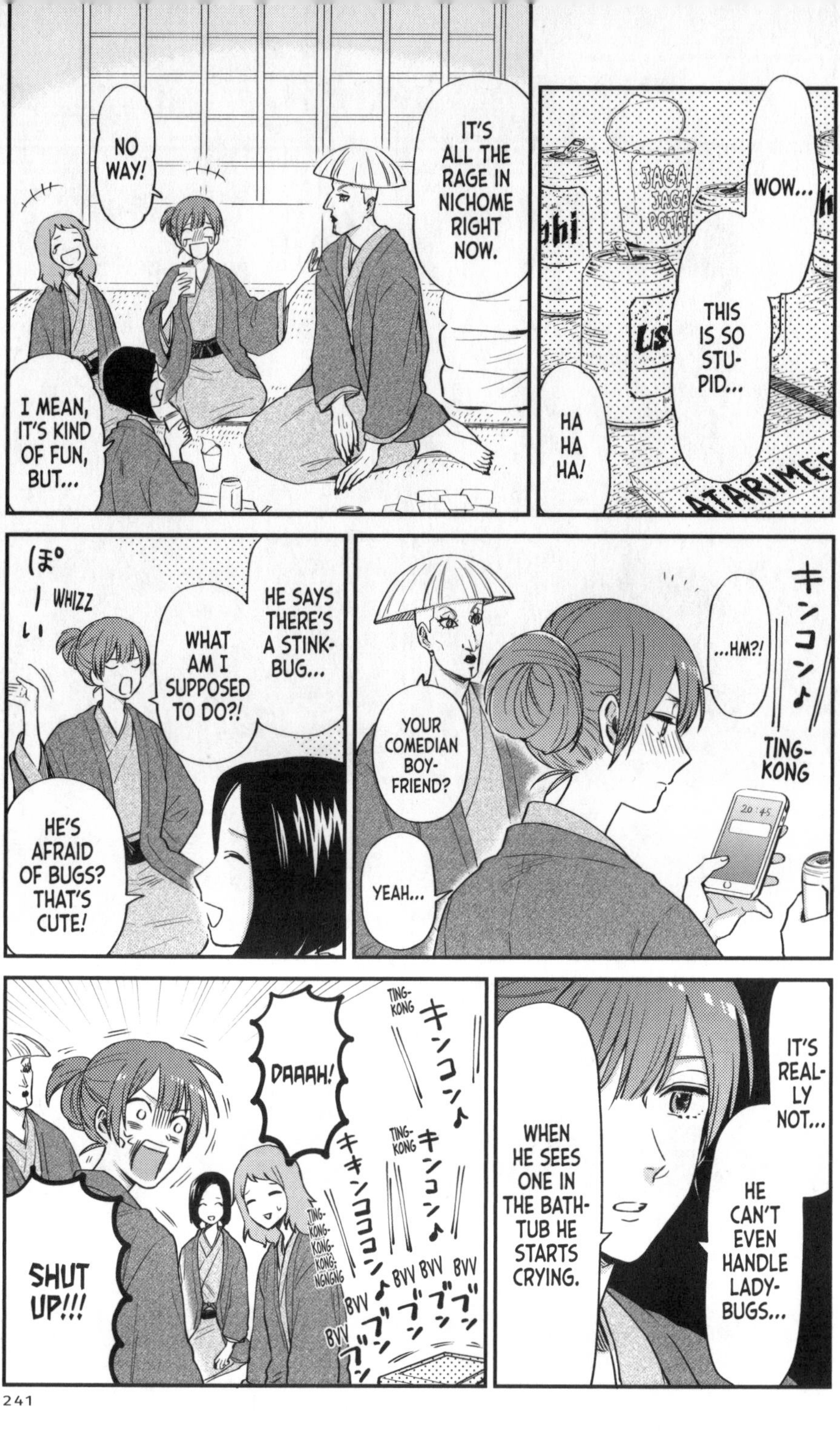
WOW...
THIS IS SO STUPID...
HA HA HA!
JAGA JAGA POTATO
ATARIME
IT'S ALL THE RAGE IN NICHOME RIGHT NOW.
NO WAY!
I MEAN, IT'S KIND OF FUN, BUT...
キンコン♪
TING-KONG
...HM?!
YOUR COMEDIAN BOYFRIEND?
YEAH...
HE SAYS THERE'S A STINK-BUG...
WHAT AM I SUPPOSED TO DO?!
ぽい
WHIZZ
HE'S AFRAID OF BUGS? THAT'S CUTE!
IT'S REALLY NOT...
HE CAN'T EVEN HANDLE LADYBUGS...
WHEN HE SEES ONE IN THE BATHTUB HE STARTS CRYING.
キンコン♪
TING-KONG
キンコン♪
TING-KONG
キンコココン♪
TING-KONG-KONG-KONG-NGNGNG
ブブブブブブン
BVV BVV BVV BVV BVV
DAAAH!
SHUT UP!!!

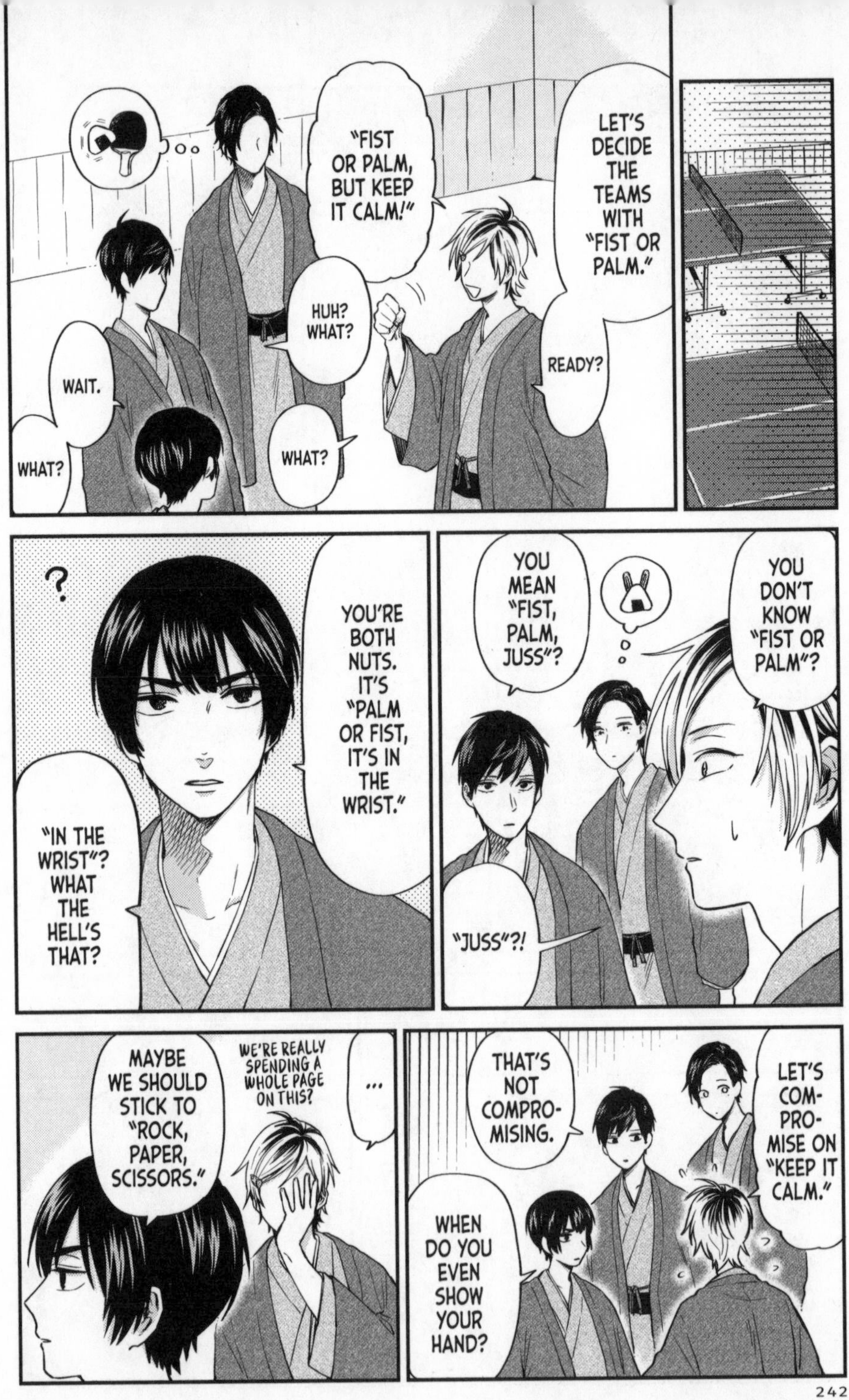
LET'S DECIDE THE TEAMS WITH "FIST OR PALM."
READY?
"FIST OR PALM, BUT KEEP IT CALM!"
HUH? WHAT?
WAIT.
WHAT?
WHAT?
YOU DON'T KNOW "FIST OR PALM"?
YOU MEAN "FIST, PALM, JUSS"?
"JUSS"?!
YOU'RE BOTH NUTS. IT'S "PALM OR FIST, IT'S IN THE WRIST."
?
"IN THE WRIST"? WHAT THE HELL'S THAT?
LET'S COMPROMISE ON "KEEP IT CALM."
THAT'S NOT COMPROMISING.
WHEN DO YOU EVEN SHOW YOUR HAND?
...
WE'RE REALLY SPENDING A WHOLE PAGE ON THIS?
MAYBE WE SHOULD STICK TO "ROCK, PAPER, SCISSORS."

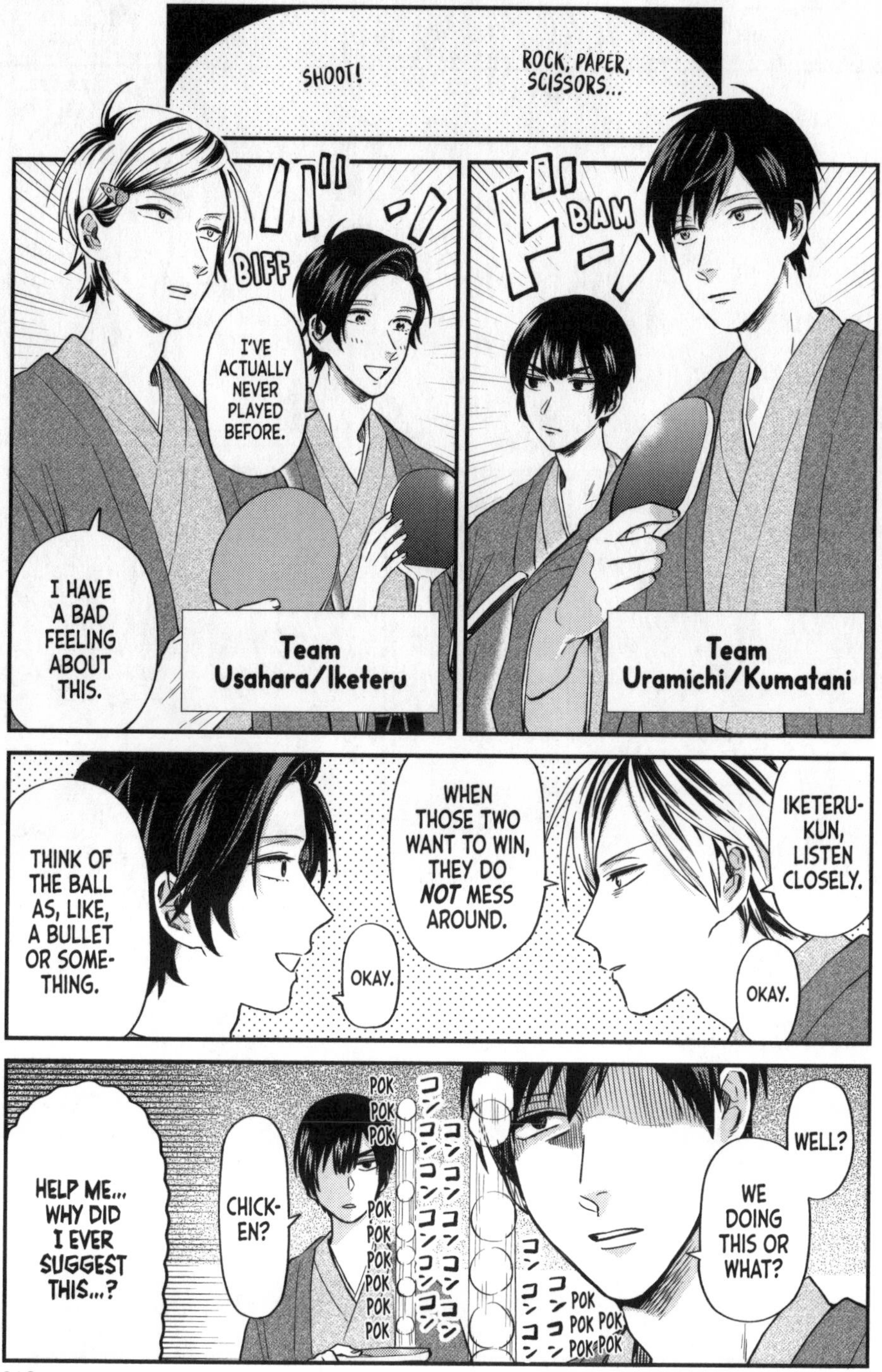
ROCK, PAPER, SCISSORS...
SHOOT!
BAM
Team Uramichi/Kumatani
BIFF
I'VE ACTUALLY NEVER PLAYED BEFORE.
Team Usahara/Iketeru
I HAVE A BAD FEELING ABOUT THIS.
IKETERU-KUN, LISTEN CLOSELY.
WHEN THOSE TWO WANT TO WIN, THEY DO *NOT* MESS AROUND.
OKAY.
THINK OF THE BALL AS, LIKE, A BULLET OR SOME-THING.
OKAY.
WELL?
WE DOING THIS OR WHAT?
POK POK POK POK POK
CHICK-EN?
HELP ME... WHY DID I EVER SUGGEST THIS...?

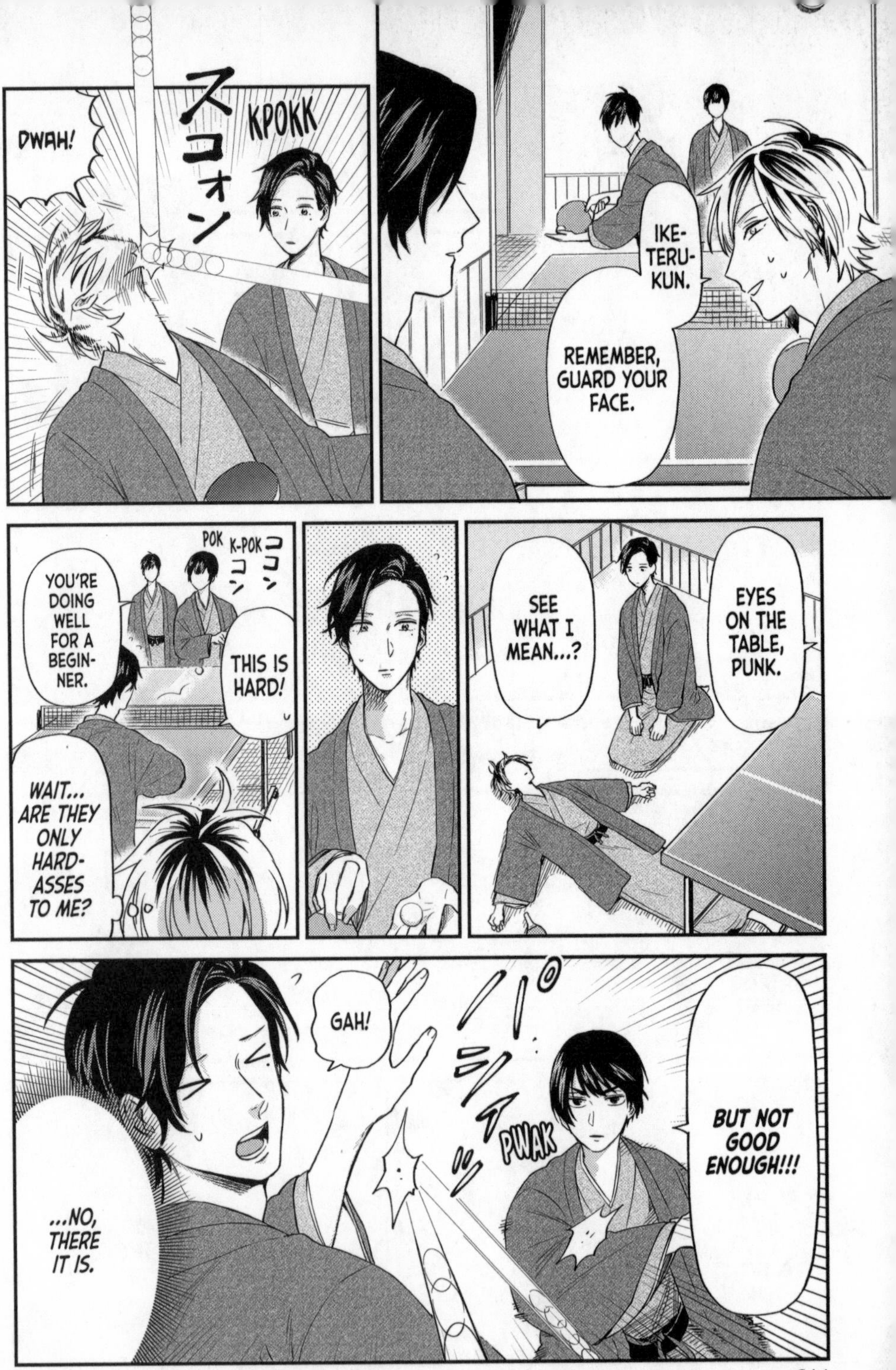
IKE-TERU-KUN.
REMEMBER, GUARD YOUR FACE.
スコォン
KPOKK
DWAH!
EYES ON THE TABLE, PUNK.
SEE WHAT I MEAN...?
ココン
K-POK
コン
POK
THIS IS HARD!
YOU'RE DOING WELL FOR A BEGINNER.
WAIT... ARE THEY ONLY HARD-ASSES TO ME?
BUT NOT GOOD ENOUGH!!!
パシィ
PWAK
GAH!
...NO, THERE IT IS.

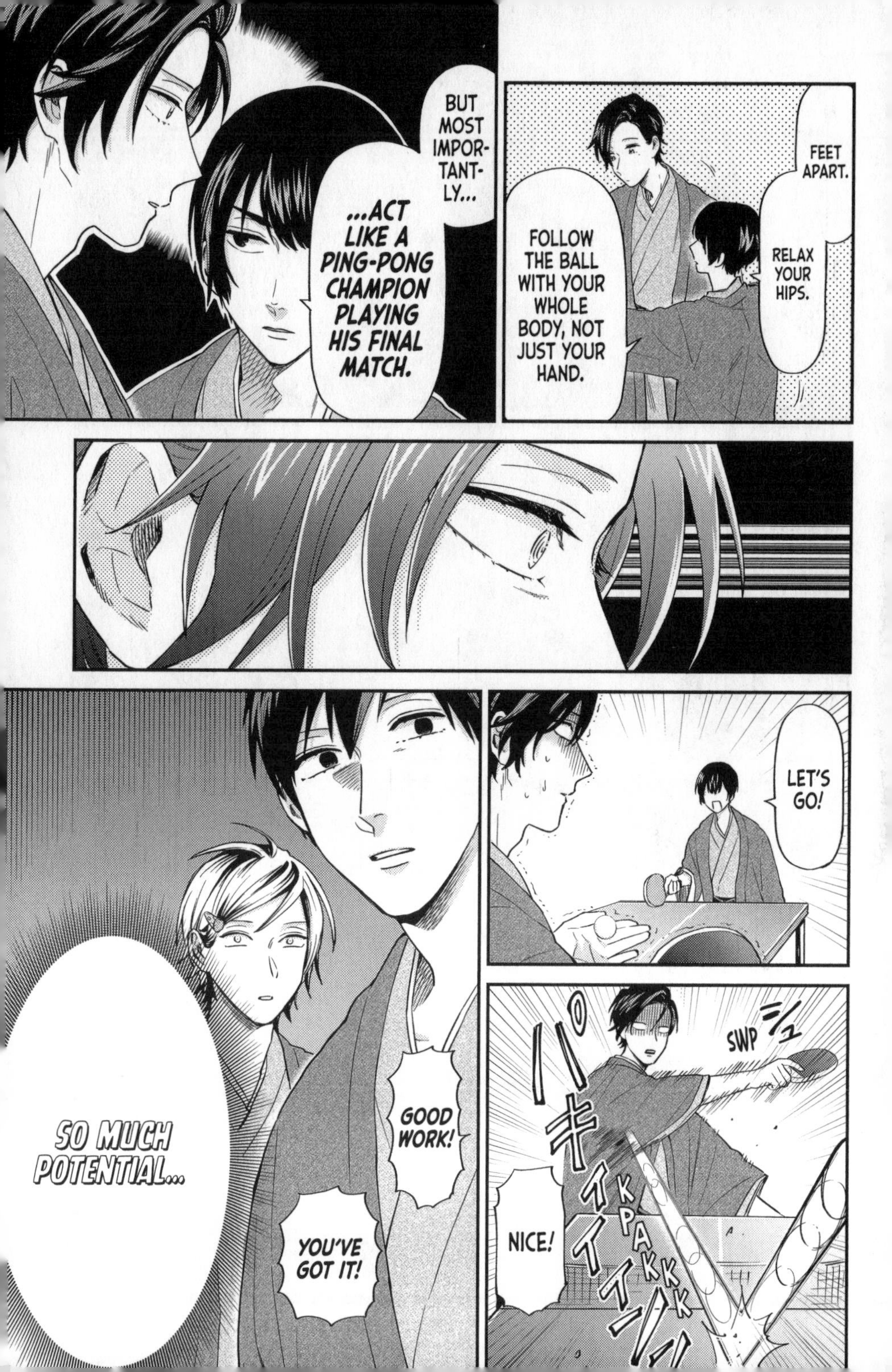
FEET APART.
RELAX YOUR HIPS.
FOLLOW THE BALL WITH YOUR WHOLE BODY, NOT JUST YOUR HAND.
BUT MOST IMPOR-TANT-LY...
...ACT LIKE A PING-PONG CHAMPION PLAYING HIS FINAL MATCH.
LET'S GO!
SWP
KPAKKK
NICE!
GOOD WORK!
YOU'VE GOT IT!
SO MUCH POTENTIAL...

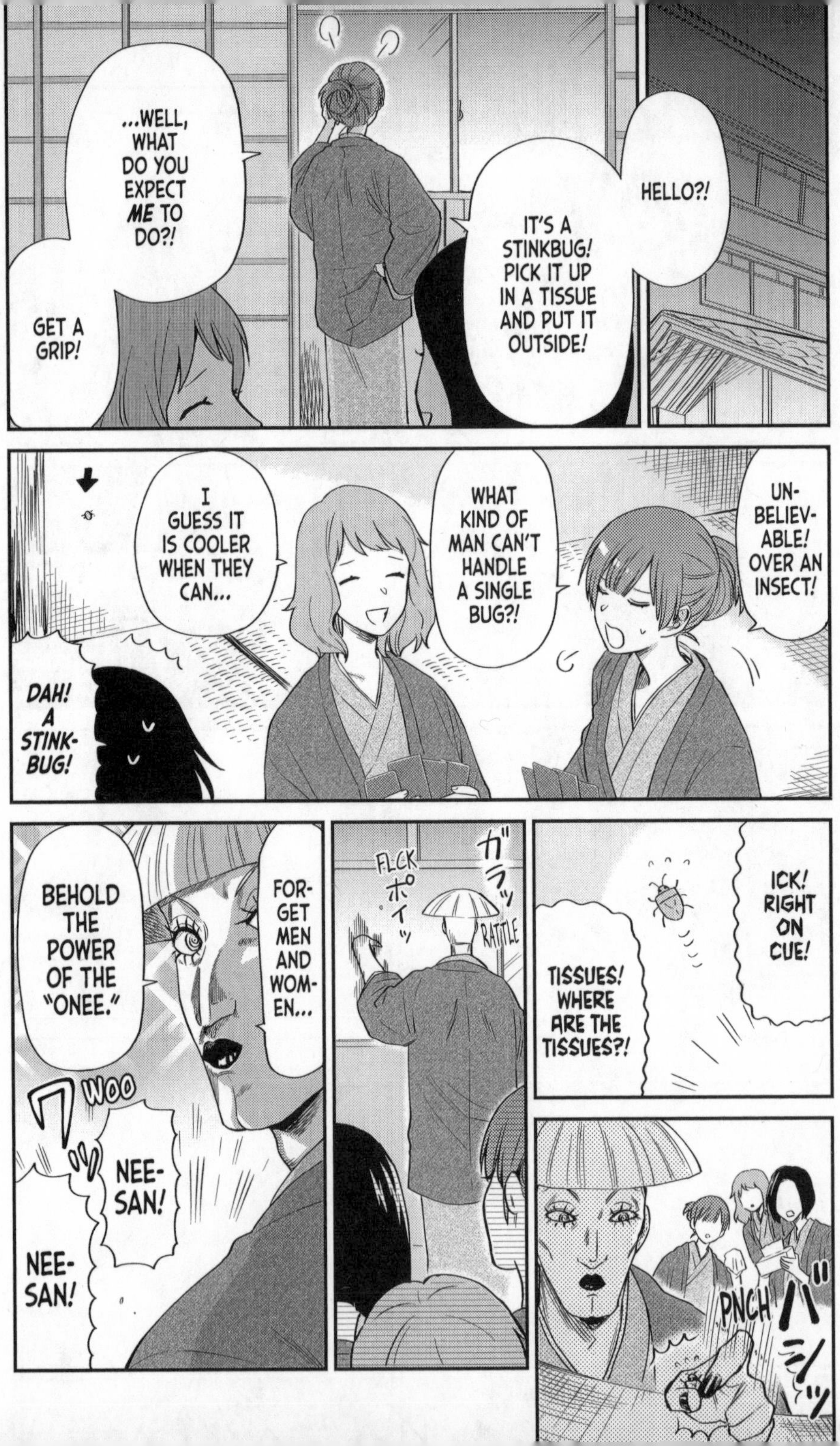
HELLO?!
IT'S A STINKBUG! PICK IT UP IN A TISSUE AND PUT IT OUTSIDE!
...WELL, WHAT DO YOU EXPECT *ME* TO DO?!
GET A GRIP!
UN-BELIEV-ABLE! OVER AN INSECT!
WHAT KIND OF MAN CAN'T HANDLE A SINGLE BUG?!
I GUESS IT IS COOLER WHEN THEY CAN...
DAH! A STINK-BUG!
ICK! RIGHT ON CUE!
TISSUES! WHERE ARE THE TISSUES?!
PNCH
RATTLE
FLCK
FOR-GET MEN AND WOM-EN...
BEHOLD THE POWER OF THE "ONEE."
WOO
NEE-SAN!
NEE-SAN!

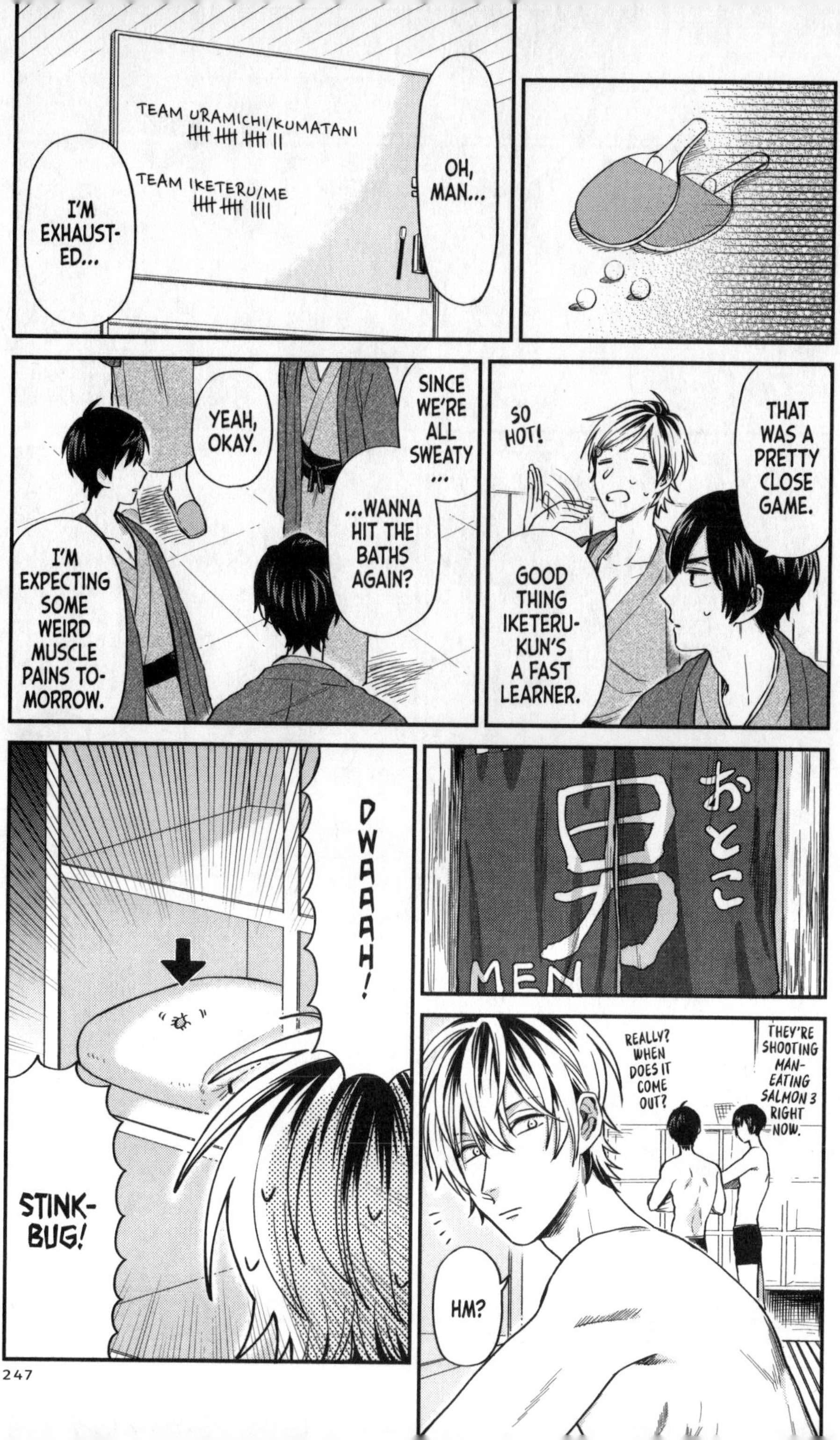
TEAM URAMICHI/KUMATANI
TEAM IKETERU/ME
OH, MAN...
I'M EXHAUST-ED...
THAT WAS A PRETTY CLOSE GAME.
SO HOT!
GOOD THING IKETERU-KUN'S A FAST LEARNER.
SINCE WE'RE ALL SWEATY...
...WANNA HIT THE BATHS AGAIN?
YEAH, OKAY.
I'M EXPECTING SOME WEIRD MUSCLE PAINS TO-MORROW.
おとこ
男
MEN
THEY'RE SHOOTING MAN-EATING SALMON 3 RIGHT NOW.
REALLY? WHEN DOES IT COME OUT?
HM?
DWAAAAH!
STINK-BUG!

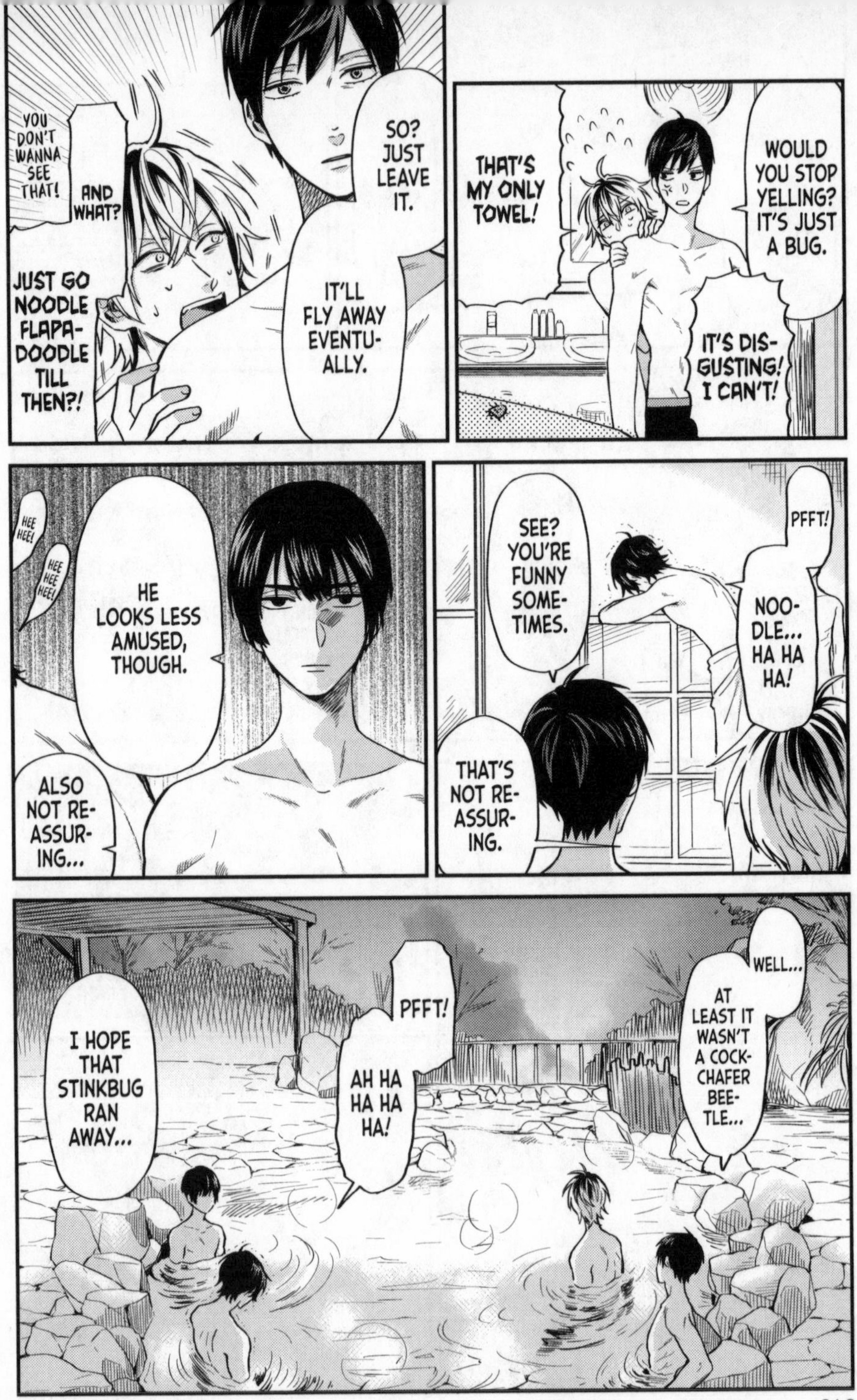
WOULD YOU STOP YELLING? IT'S JUST A BUG.
THAT'S MY ONLY TOWEL!
IT'S DISGUSTING! I CAN'T!
SO? JUST LEAVE IT.
YOU DON'T WANNA SEE THAT!
AND WHAT?
IT'LL FLY AWAY EVENTUALLY.
JUST GO NOODLE FLAPA-DOODLE TILL THEN?!
PFFT!
SEE? YOU'RE FUNNY SOMETIMES.
NOODLE... HA HA HA!
THAT'S NOT REASSURING.
HEE HEE!
HEE HEE HEE!
HE LOOKS LESS AMUSED, THOUGH.
ALSO NOT REASSURING...
WELL...
AT LEAST IT WASN'T A COCKCHAFER BEETLE...
PFFT!
AH HA HA HA HA!
I HOPE THAT STINKBUG RAN AWAY...

Life Lessons with
Uramichi Oniisan

HEY!
BOMF
ばさぁ
I'M TRYING TO LAY OUT THE BEDDING.
MOVE.
...
もく
WORKING
もく
IN
もく
SILENCE
...
HEY! LET'S TELL SCARY STORIES!
パッ
BWP
NO.
NO.
SOUNDS LIKE FUN!
...

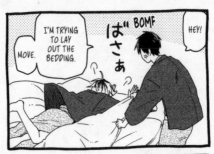

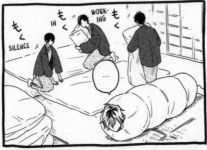

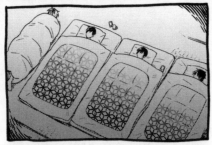

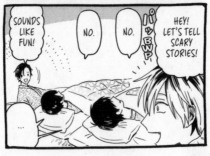

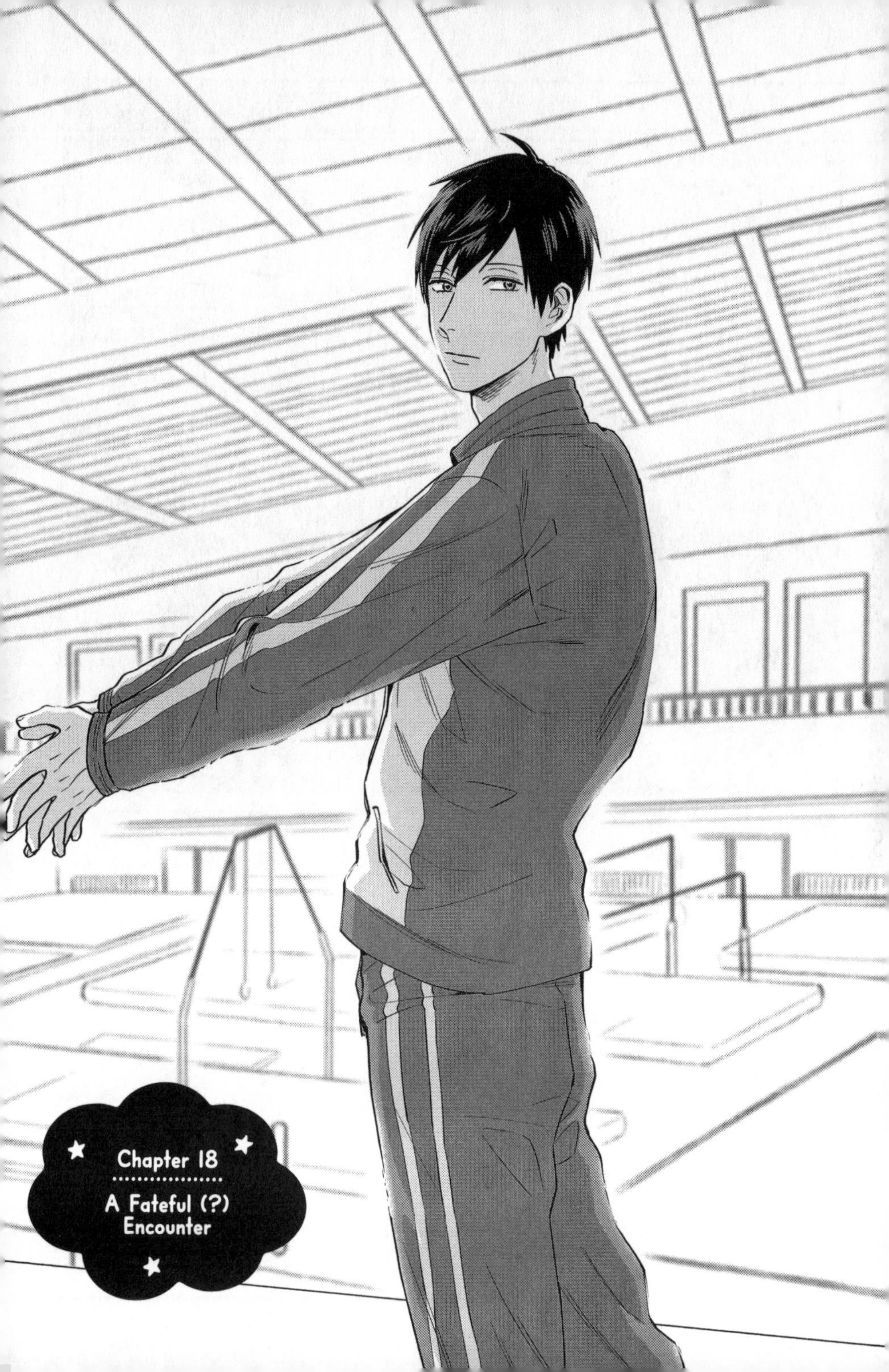
Chapter 18
A Fateful (?) Encounter

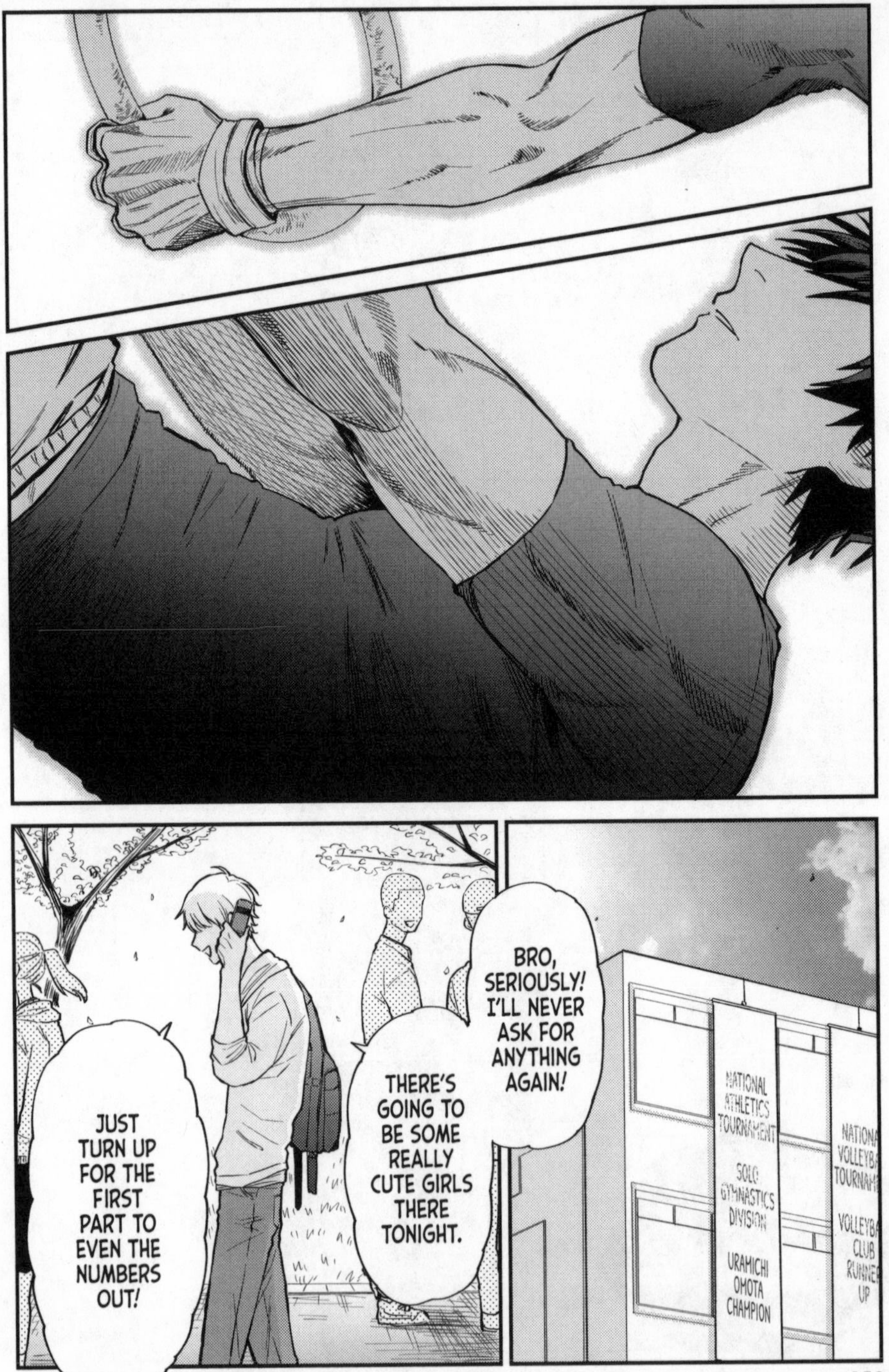
NATIONA VOLLEYBA TOURNAM
VOLLEYBA CLUB RUNNE UP
NATIONAL ATHLETICS TOURNAMENT
SOLO GYMNASTICS DIVISION
URAMICHI OMOTA CHAMPION
BRO, SERIOUSLY! I'LL NEVER ASK FOR ANYTHING AGAIN!
THERE'S GOING TO BE SOME REALLY CUTE GIRLS THERE TONIGHT.
JUST TURN UP FOR THE FIRST PART TO EVEN THE NUMBERS OUT!

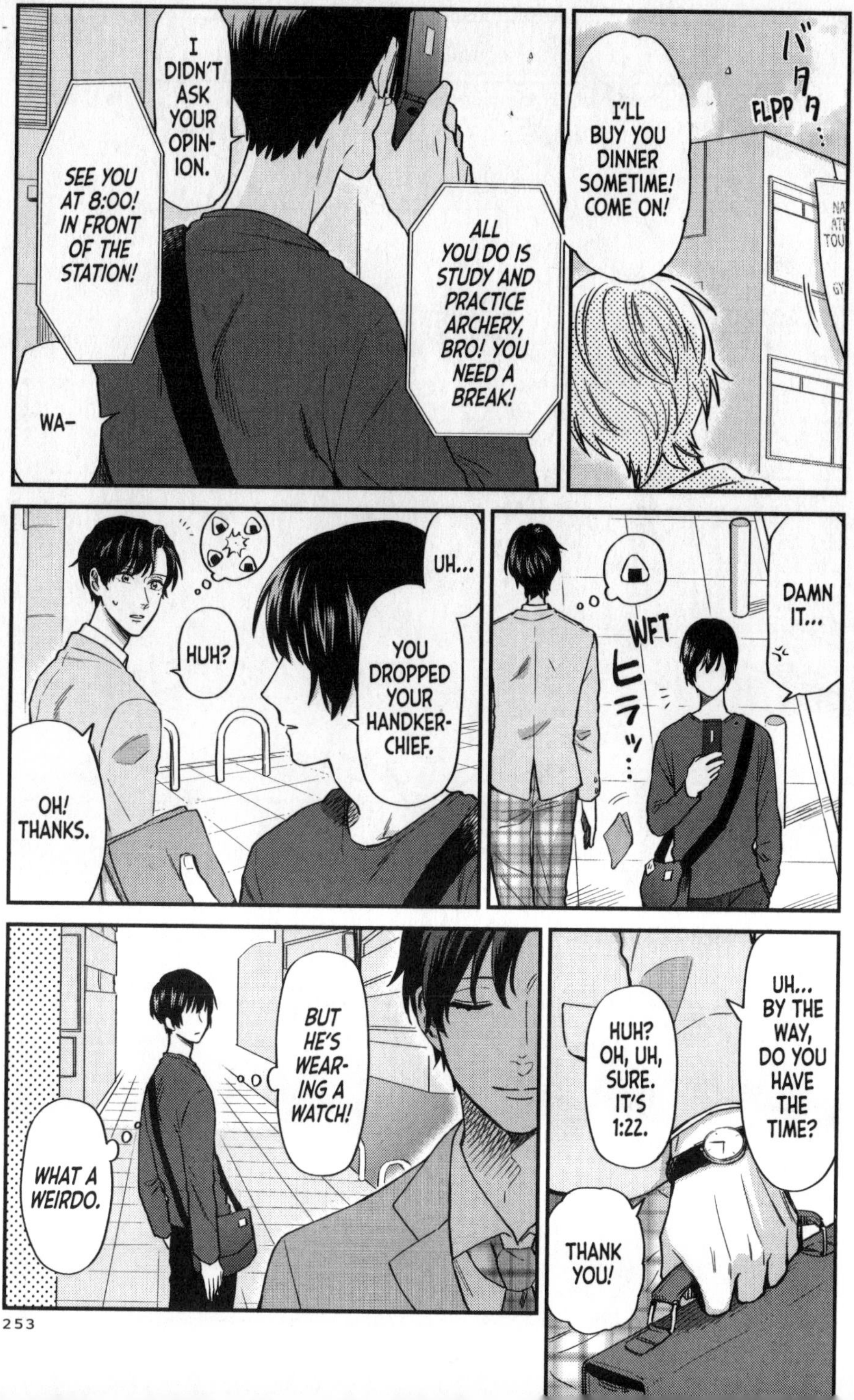
バタバタ…
FLPP
I'LL BUY YOU DINNER SOMETIME! COME ON!
ALL YOU DO IS STUDY AND PRACTICE ARCHERY, BRO! YOU NEED A BREAK!
I DIDN'T ASK YOUR OPINION.
SEE YOU AT 8:00! IN FRONT OF THE STATION!
WA-
DAMN IT...
ヒラッ…
WFT
UH...
YOU DROPPED YOUR HANDKER-CHIEF.
HUH?
OH! THANKS.
UH... BY THE WAY, DO YOU HAVE THE TIME?
HUH? OH, UH, SURE. IT'S 1:22.
THANK YOU!
BUT HE'S WEAR-ING A WATCH!
WHAT A WEIRDO.

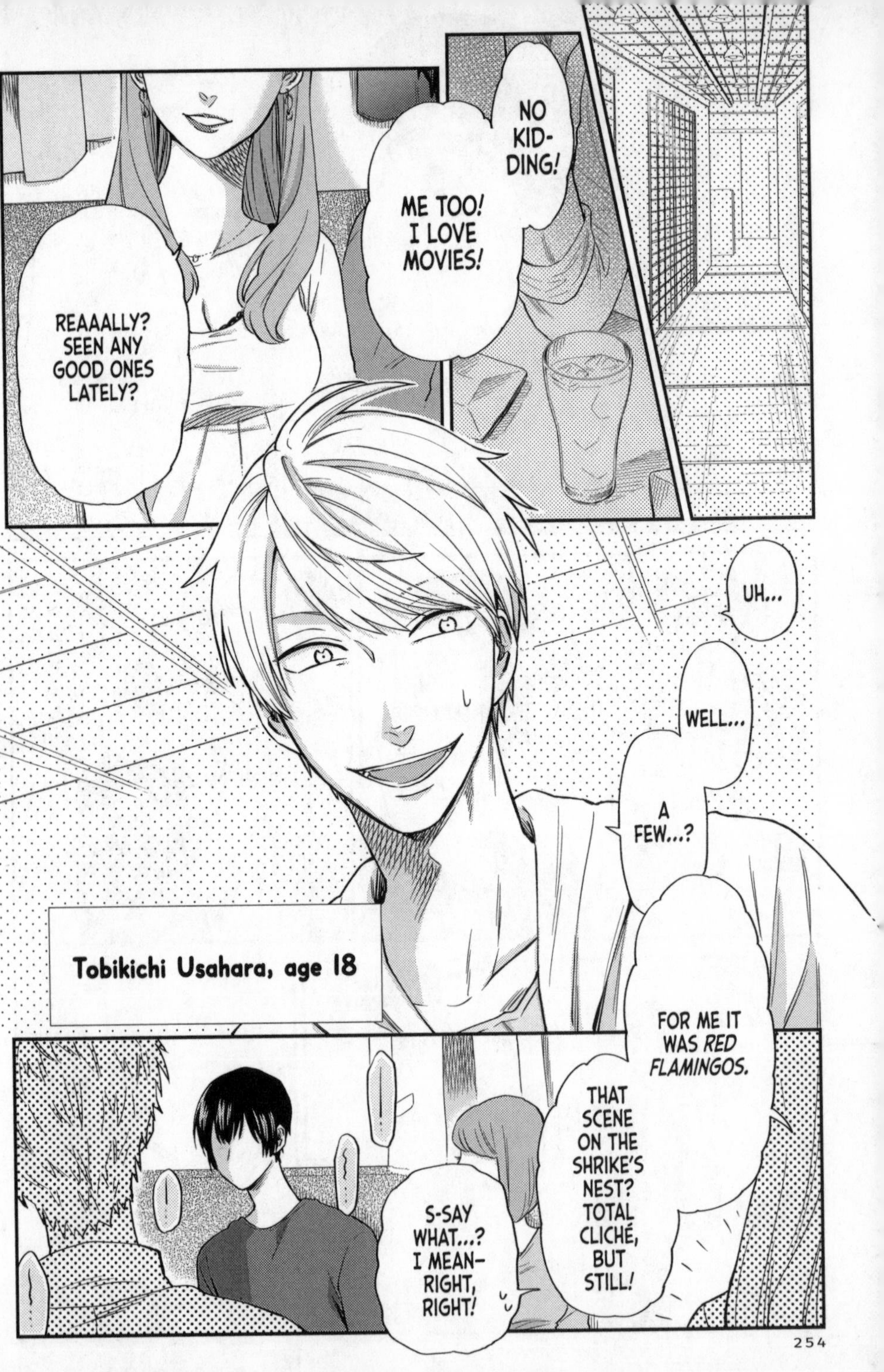
NO KIDDING!
ME TOO! I LOVE MOVIES!
REAAALLY? SEEN ANY GOOD ONES LATELY?
UH...
WELL...
A FEW...?
Tobikichi Usahara, age 18
FOR ME IT WAS *RED FLAMINGOS.*
THAT SCENE ON THE SHRIKE'S NEST? TOTAL CLICHÉ, BUT STILL!
S-SAY WHAT...? I MEAN–RIGHT, RIGHT!

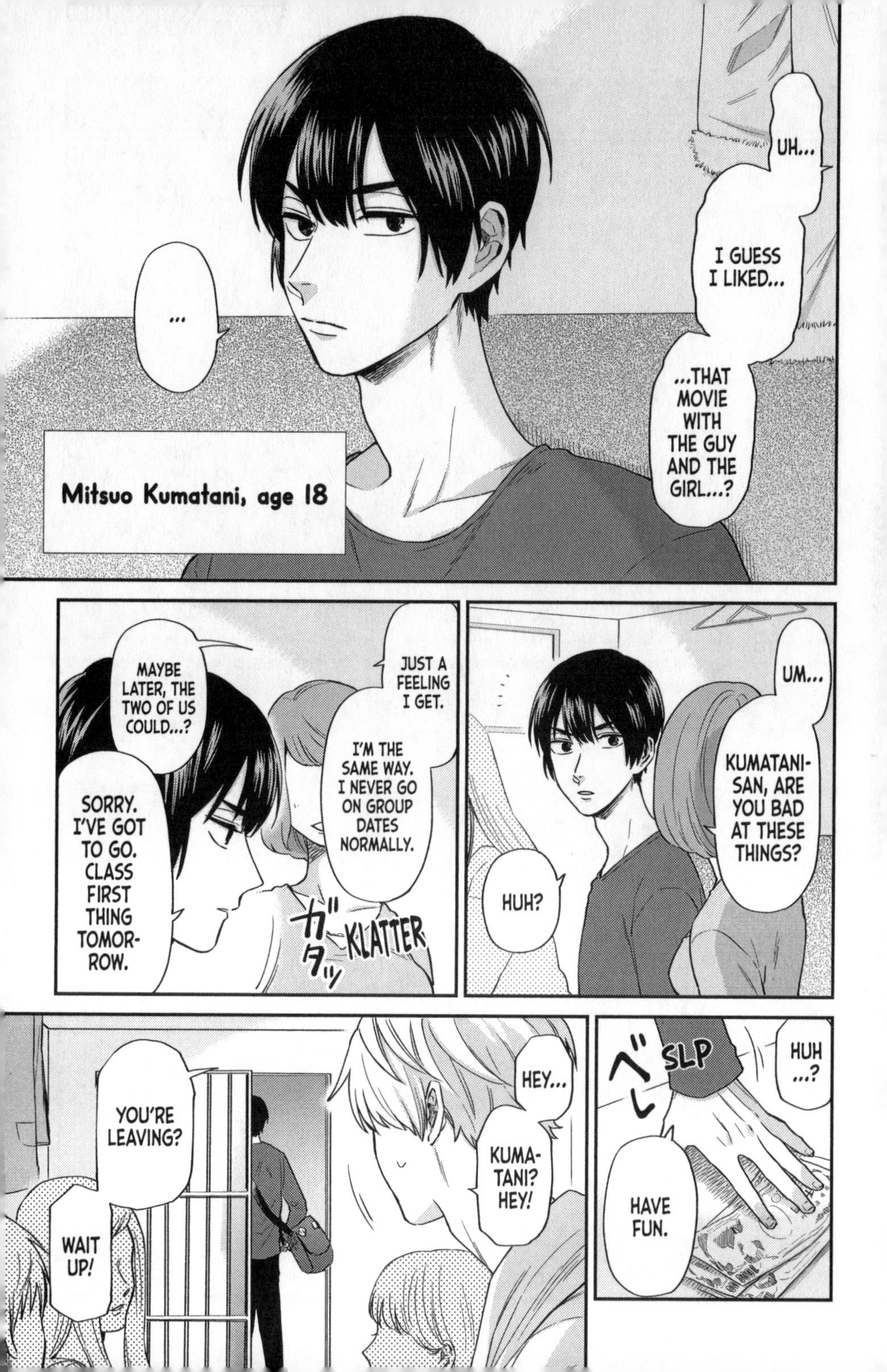
UH...
I GUESS I LIKED...
...THAT MOVIE WITH THE GUY AND THE GIRL...?
...
Mitsuo Kumatani, age 18
UM...
KUMATANI-SAN, ARE YOU BAD AT THESE THINGS?
HUH?
JUST A FEELING I GET.
I'M THE SAME WAY. I NEVER GO ON GROUP DATES NORMALLY.
MAYBE LATER, THE TWO OF US COULD...?
SORRY. I'VE GOT TO GO. CLASS FIRST THING TOMORROW.
ガタッ KLATTER
べし SLP
HUH ...?
HAVE FUN.
HEY...
KUMA-TANI? HEY!
YOU'RE LEAVING?
WAIT UP!

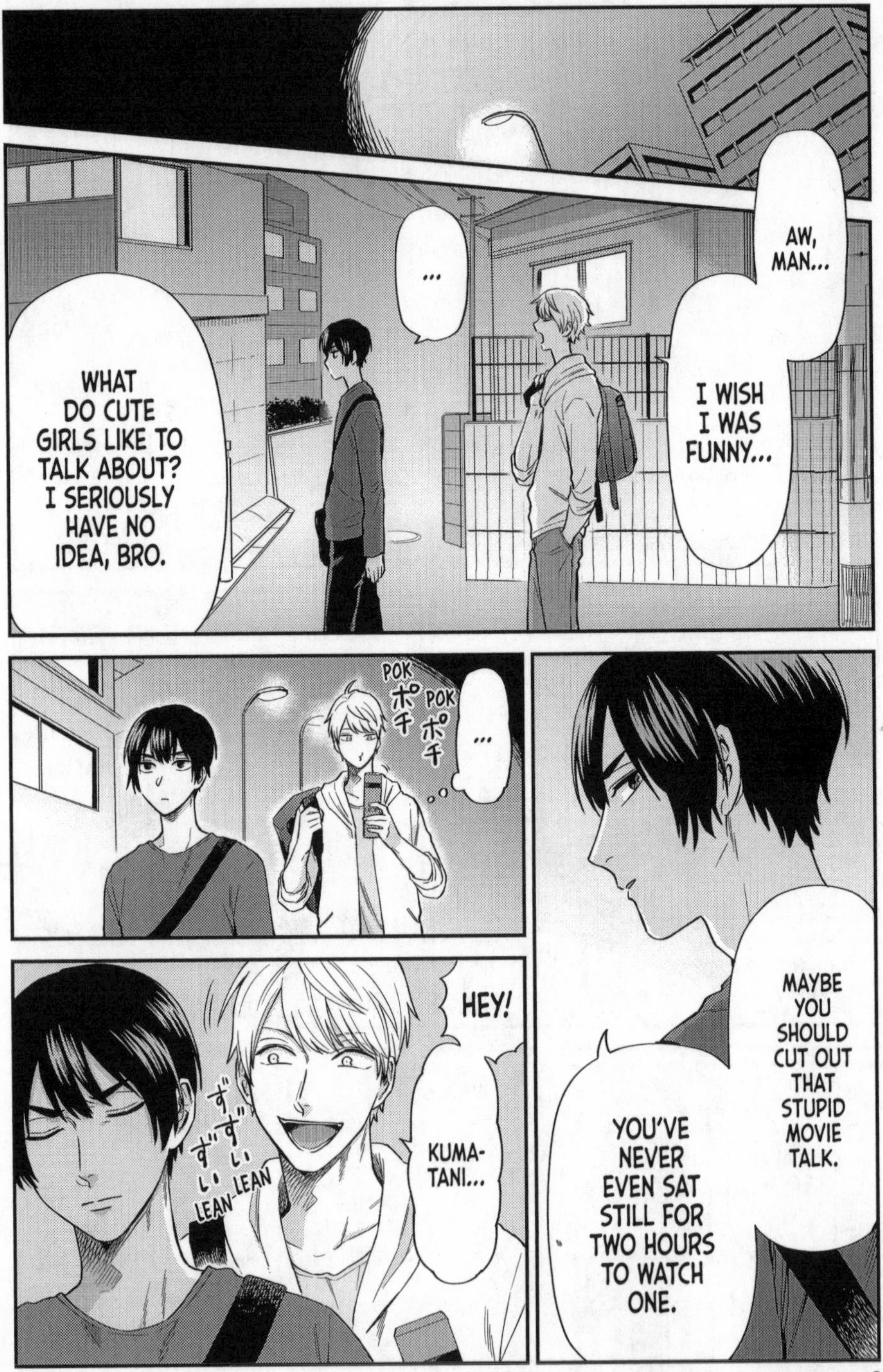
AW, MAN...
I WISH I WAS FUNNY...
...
WHAT DO CUTE GIRLS LIKE TO TALK ABOUT? I SERIOUSLY HAVE NO IDEA, BRO.
MAYBE YOU SHOULD CUT OUT THAT STUPID MOVIE TALK.
YOU'VE NEVER EVEN SAT STILL FOR TWO HOURS TO WATCH ONE.
POK ポチ POK ポチ
...
HEY!
KUMA-TANI...
ずい ずい ずい LEAN LEAN

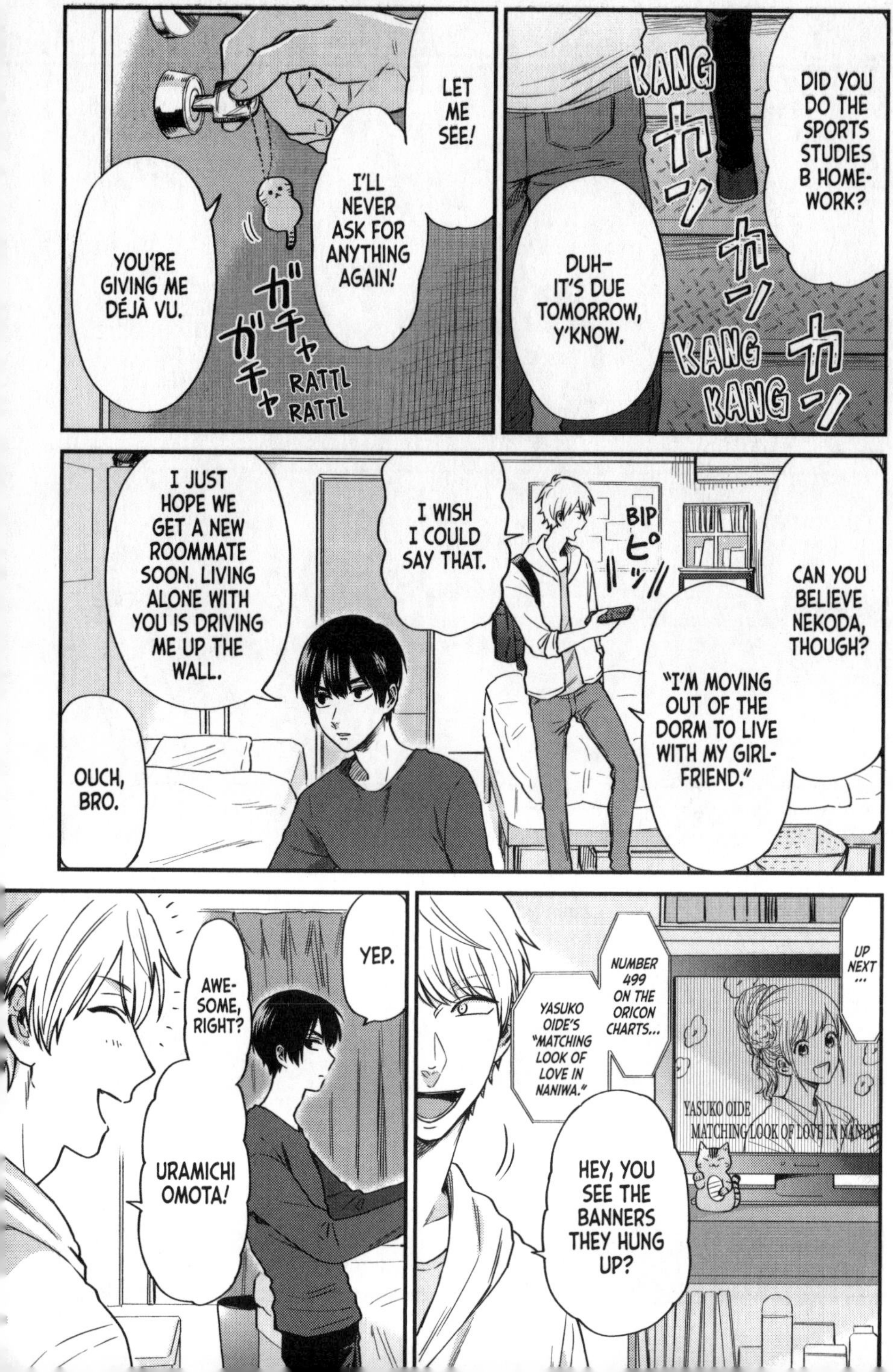
DID YOU DO THE SPORTS STUDIES B HOME-WORK?
KANG カーン
カーン KANG
カーン KANG
DUH— IT'S DUE TOMORROW, Y'KNOW.
LET ME SEE!
I'LL NEVER ASK FOR ANYTHING AGAIN!
YOU'RE GIVING ME DÉJÀ VU.
ガチャガチャ RATTL RATTL
CAN YOU BELIEVE NEKODA, THOUGH?
"I'M MOVING OUT OF THE DORM TO LIVE WITH MY GIRL-FRIEND."
BIP ピッ
I WISH I COULD SAY THAT.
I JUST HOPE WE GET A NEW ROOMMATE SOON. LIVING ALONE WITH YOU IS DRIVING ME UP THE WALL.
OUCH, BRO.
UP NEXT...
NUMBER 499 ON THE ORICON CHARTS...
YASUKO OIDE'S "MATCHING LOOK OF LOVE IN NANIWA."
YASUKO OIDE
HEY, YOU SEE THE BANNERS THEY HUNG UP?
YEP.
AWE-SOME, RIGHT?
URAMICHI OMOTA!

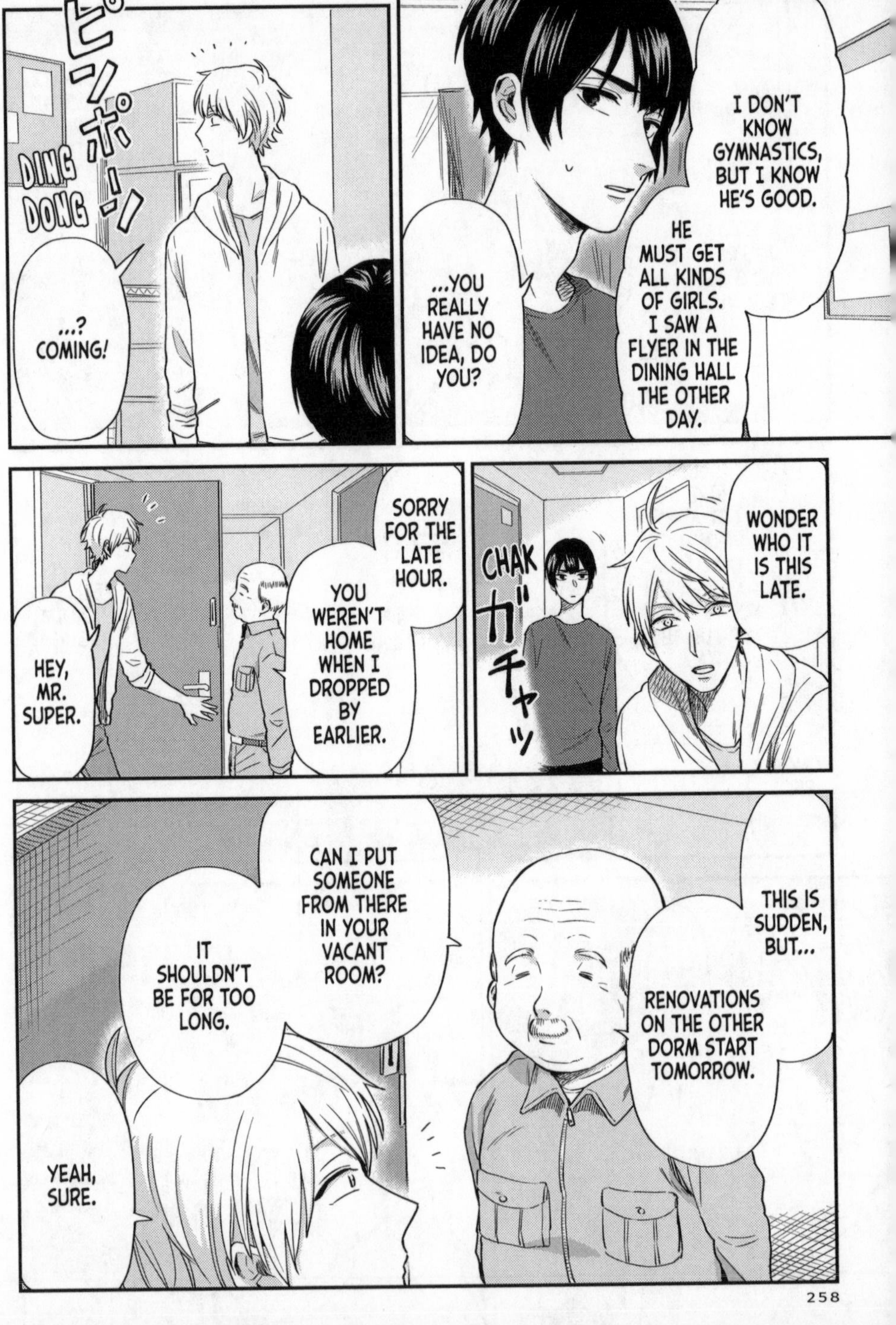
I DON'T KNOW GYMNASTICS, BUT I KNOW HE'S GOOD.
HE MUST GET ALL KINDS OF GIRLS. I SAW A FLYER IN THE DINING HALL THE OTHER DAY.
...YOU REALLY HAVE NO IDEA, DO YOU?
ピンポーン
DING DONG
...? COMING!
WONDER WHO IT IS THIS LATE.
CHAK
ガチャッ
SORRY FOR THE LATE HOUR.
YOU WEREN'T HOME WHEN I DROPPED BY EARLIER.
HEY, MR. SUPER.
THIS IS SUDDEN, BUT...
RENOVATIONS ON THE OTHER DORM START TOMORROW.
CAN I PUT SOMEONE FROM THERE IN YOUR VACANT ROOM?
IT SHOULDN'T BE FOR TOO LONG.
YEAH, SURE.

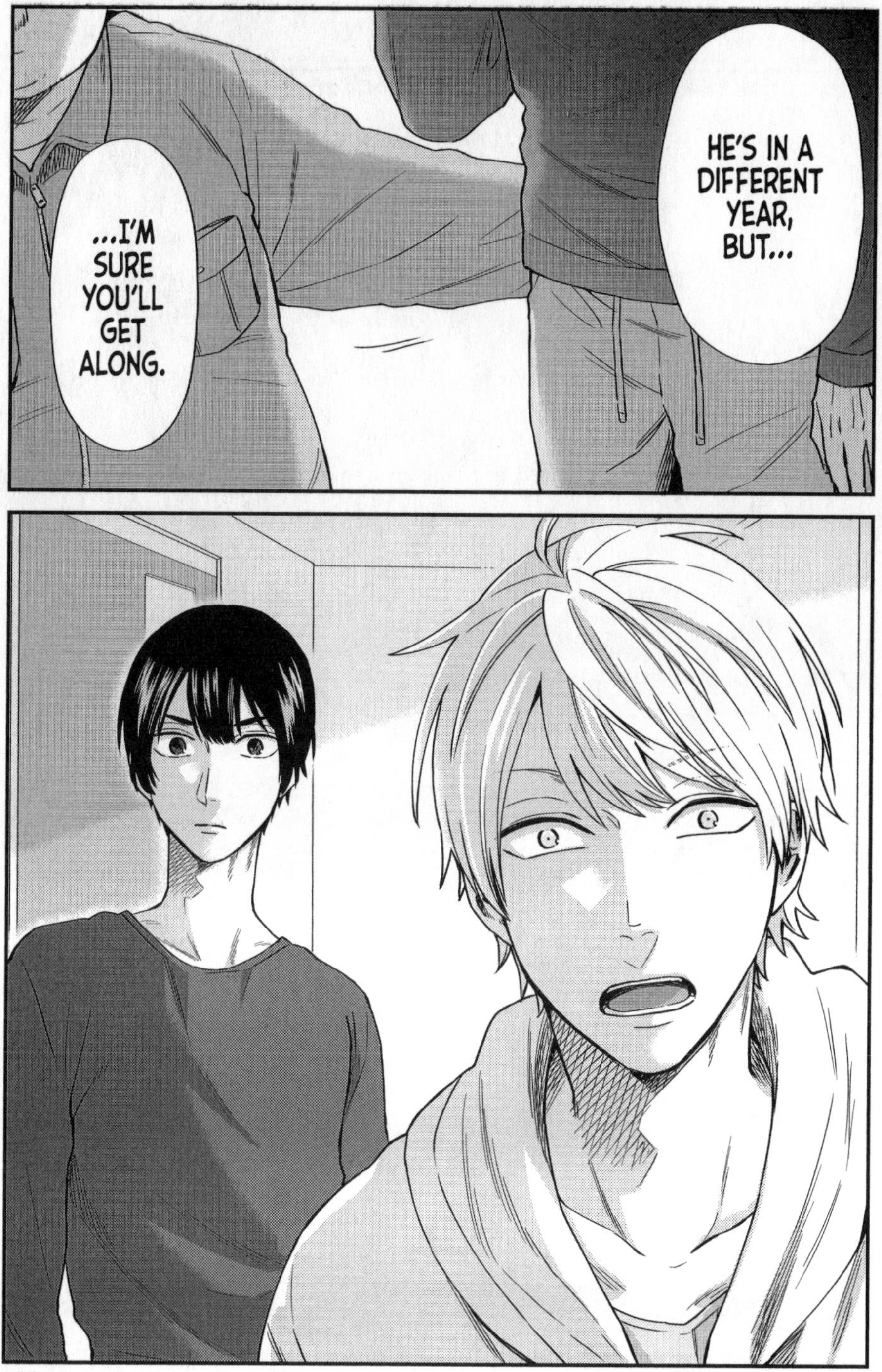
HE'S IN A DIFFERENT YEAR, BUT...
...I'M SURE YOU'LL GET ALONG.

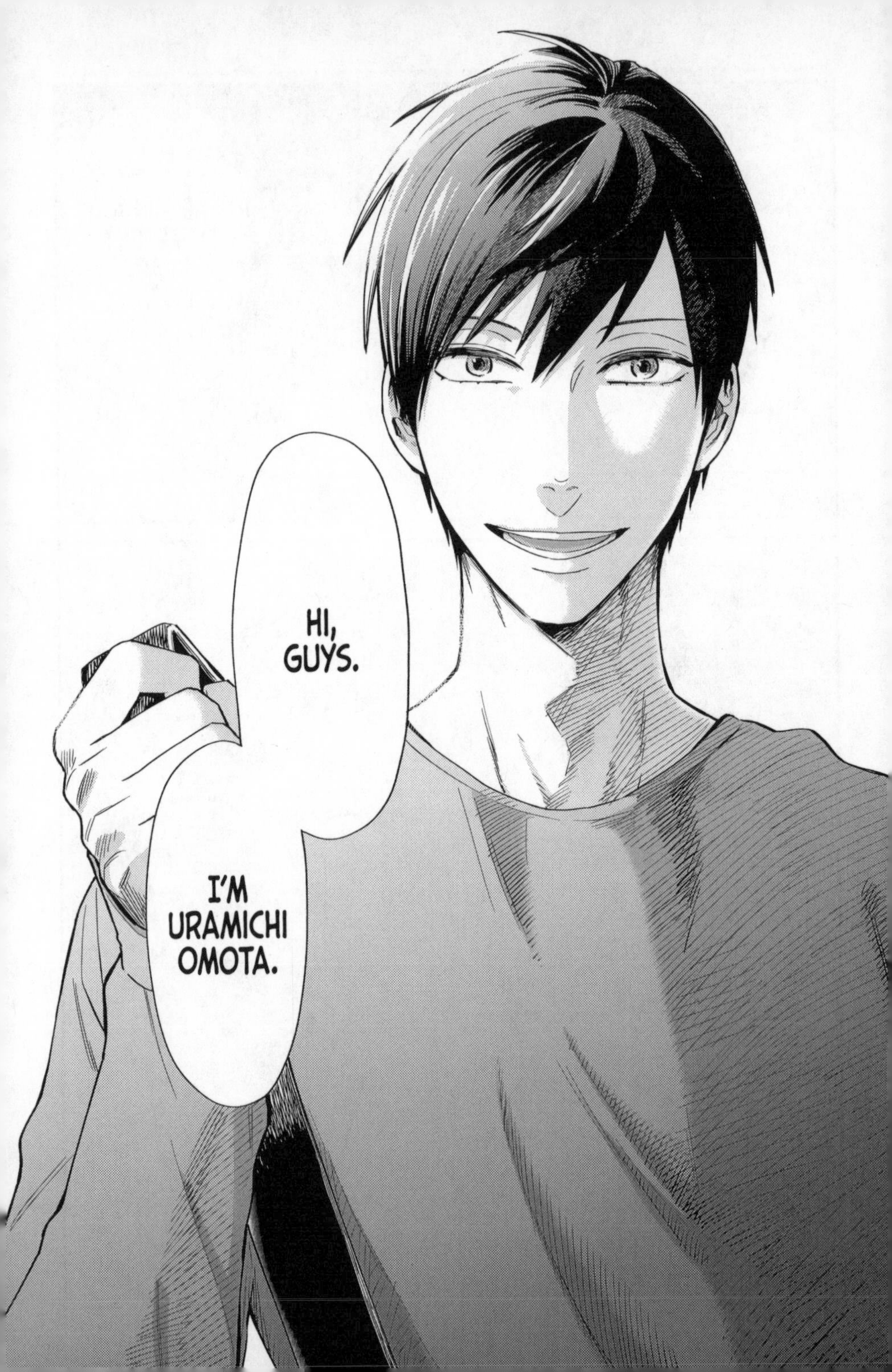
HI, GUYS.
I'M URAMICHI OMOTA.

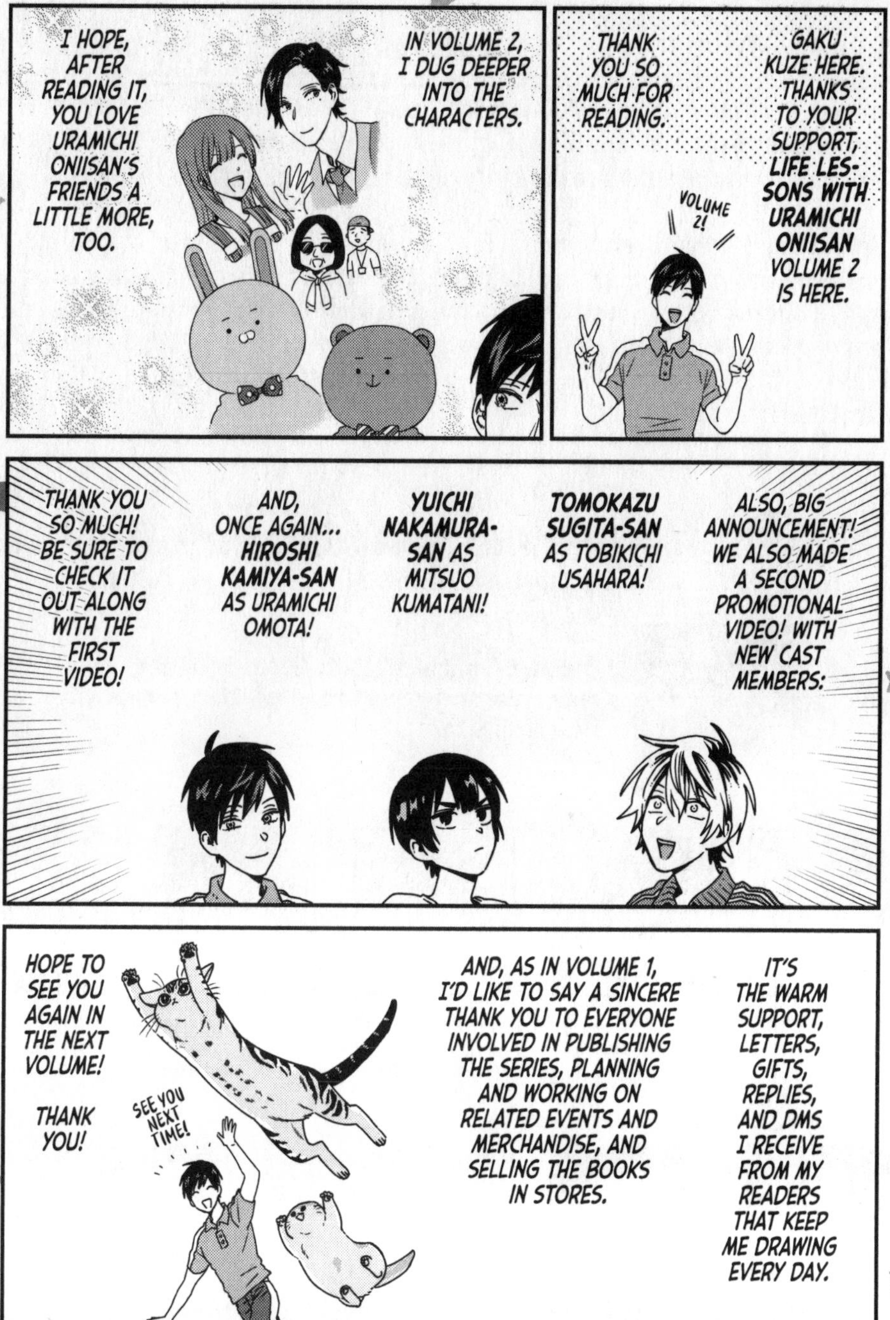
GAKU KUZE HERE. THANKS TO YOUR SUPPORT, LIFE LESSONS WITH URAMICHI ONIISAN VOLUME 2 IS HERE.
THANK YOU SO MUCH FOR READING.
VOLUME 2!
IN VOLUME 2, I DUG DEEPER INTO THE CHARACTERS.
I HOPE, AFTER READING IT, YOU LOVE URAMICHI ONIISAN'S FRIENDS A LITTLE MORE, TOO.
ALSO, BIG ANNOUNCEMENT! WE ALSO MADE A SECOND PROMOTIONAL VIDEO! WITH NEW CAST MEMBERS:
TOMOKAZU SUGITA-SAN AS TOBIKICHI USAHARA!
YUICHI NAKAMURA-SAN AS MITSUO KUMATANI!
AND, ONCE AGAIN... HIROSHI KAMIYA-SAN AS URAMICHI OMOTA!
THANK YOU SO MUCH! BE SURE TO CHECK IT OUT ALONG WITH THE FIRST VIDEO!
IT'S THE WARM SUPPORT, LETTERS, GIFTS, REPLIES, AND DMS I RECEIVE FROM MY READERS THAT KEEP ME DRAWING EVERY DAY.
AND, AS IN VOLUME 1, I'D LIKE TO SAY A SINCERE THANK YOU TO EVERYONE INVOLVED IN PUBLISHING THE SERIES, PLANNING AND WORKING ON RELATED EVENTS AND MERCHANDISE, AND SELLING THE BOOKS IN STORES.
HOPE TO SEE YOU AGAIN IN THE NEXT VOLUME!
THANK YOU!
SEE YOU NEXT TIME!

Translation Notes

Oniisan and Oneesan

In Japanese, *oniisan* and *oneesan* literally mean "older brother" and "older sister." While normally used in a family setting, they can also be used to refer to people who are older than children, but are not quite on the level of parents.

For decades now, it has been common for children's television shows in Japan to be hosted by *oniisan* and *oneesan* (alongside puppets and suited characters). Each oniisan or oneesan has a special role on the program. The classics here are *uta no oniisan/oneesan* (i.e. Iketeru and Utano), who sing songs (*uta*), and *taiso no oniisan/oneesan* (i.e. Uramichi), who leads the children in calisthenics (*taiso*)—in other words, physical exercises and games.

Names

Many of the character names in the series include some kind of joke or pun, based on how they are read or spelled in Japanese. Here are the ones in this volume.

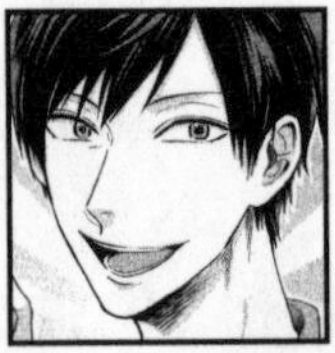

Omota Uramichi: Literally "Front-field Back-road." Also a reference to beloved *taiso no oniisan*, Hiromichi Sato.

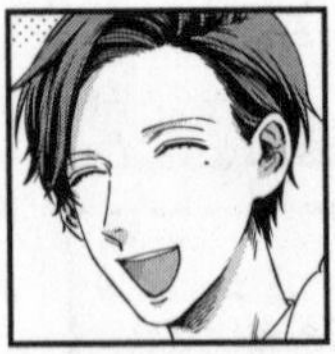

Daga Iketeru
"But he's hot."

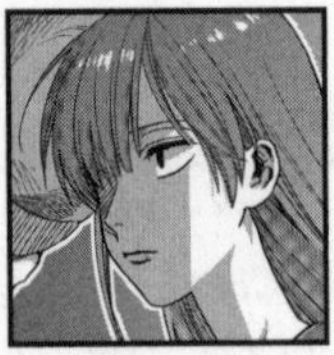

Tadano Utano
"Just an *uta no (oneesan)*."

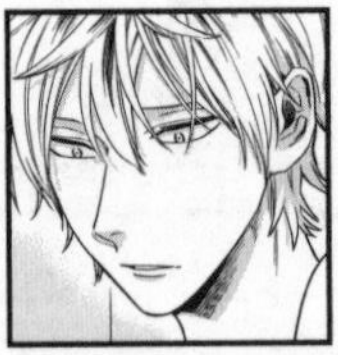

Usahara Tobikichi
Literally "Rabbit-plain Jump-luck."

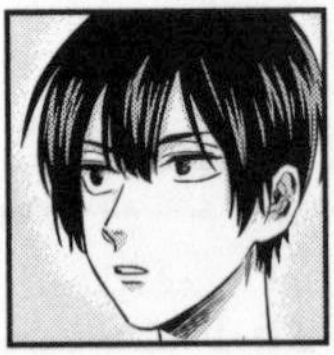

Kumatani Mitsuo
Literally "Bear-valley Honey-man."

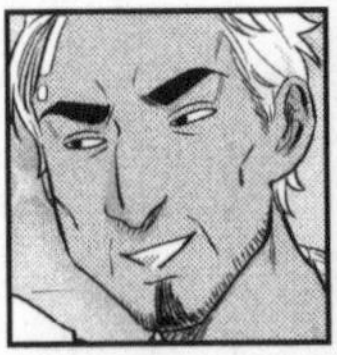

Furode Yusao
"Producer."

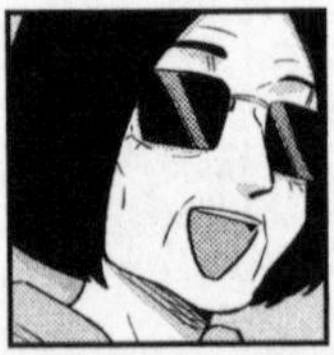

Derekida Tekito
"The director is half-assed."

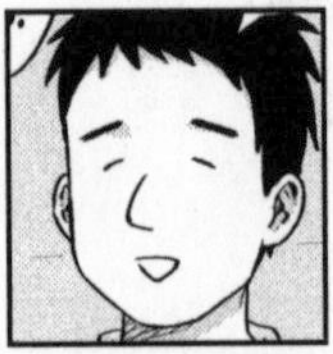

Edei Eddie
Edei = A.D. = "Assistant Director"

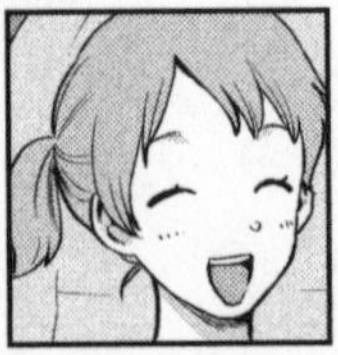

Ennoshita Kayo
"Where was she, under the porch?"

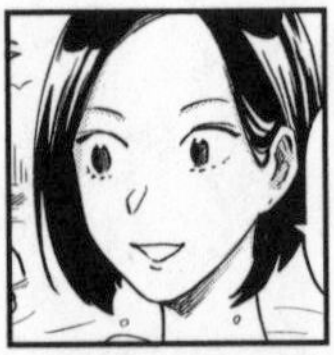

Heame Ikuko
"Hair and makeup girl."

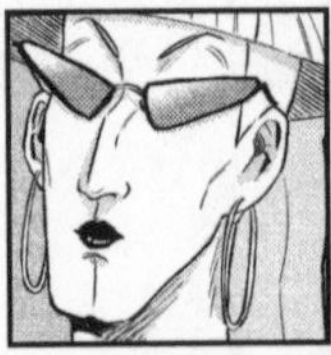

Furitsuke Capellini
Furitsuke = "Choreography"

Anzai-sensei, page 15
Although Usahara appears to be reflecting on their college days in this scene, the coach and quote he mentions are from the classic basketball manga and anime *Slam Dunk*.

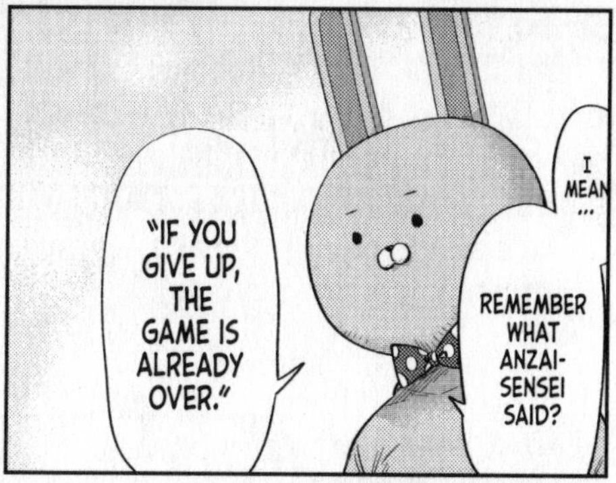
I MEAN…
REMEMBER WHAT ANZAI-SENSEI SAID?
"IF YOU GIVE UP, THE GAME IS ALREADY OVER."

***Enka*, page 36**
A genre of Japanese music associated with sentimental balladry and vaguely traditional-sounding melodies and instrumentation. As a result, it has a bit of an old-fashioned reputation.

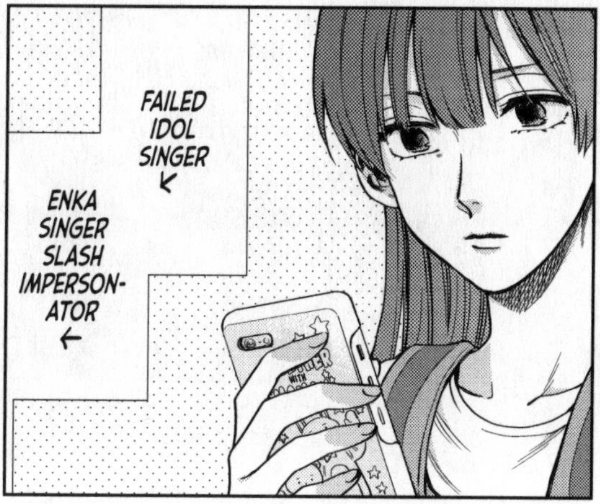
FAILED IDOL SINGER
ENKA SINGER SLASH IMPERSON-ATOR

Baseball, page 63
Iketeru Oniisan is (correctly) surmising that Utano Oneesan likes not just tigers, but the Hanshin Tigers baseball team based in Hyogo prefecture, known for their devoted fans.

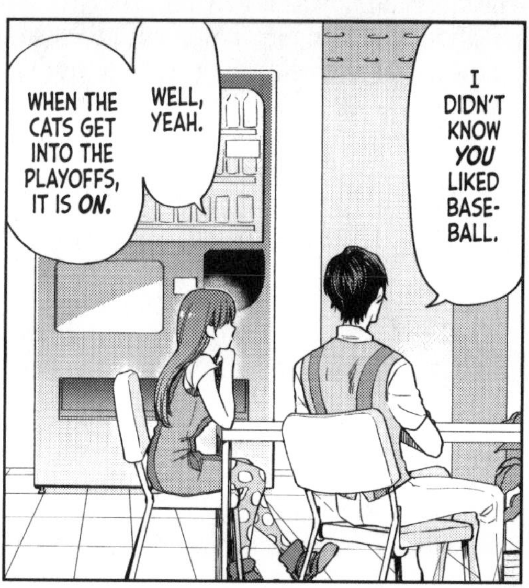
I DIDN'T KNOW *YOU* LIKED BASE-BALL.
WELL, YEAH.
WHEN THE CATS GET INTO THE PLAYOFFS, IT IS *ON*.

***Senbu,* page 118**
Uramichi's alarm clock includes a mention of the six-day *rokuyo* cycle, which offers guidance on one's fortune during the day. On *senbu,* the morning is unlucky and the afternoon lucky, and it's best to do nothing at all (which Uramichi is unfortunately unable to do).

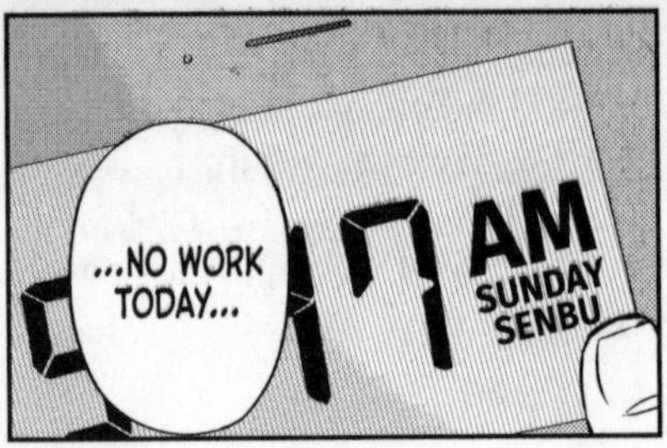
AM
SUNDAY SENBU
...NO WORK TODAY...

***Shochu,* page 126**
Shochu is a distilled alcoholic beverage that has more of an "earthy" flavor when compared with traditional *sake*.

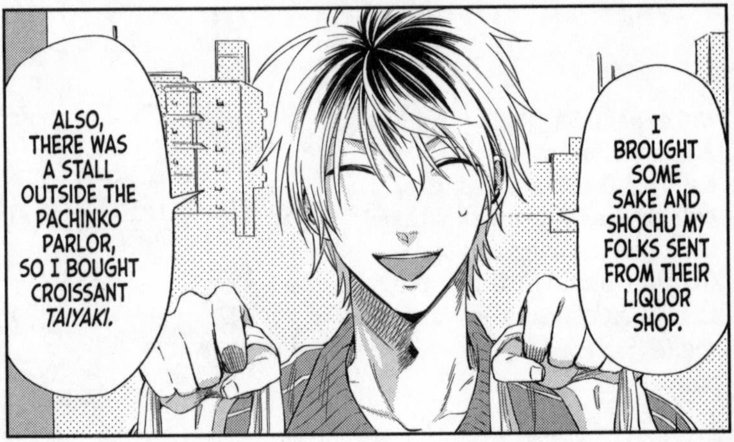
I BROUGHT SOME SAKE AND SHOCHU MY FOLKS SENT FROM THEIR LIQUOR SHOP.
ALSO, THERE WAS A STALL OUTSIDE THE PACHINKO PARLOR, SO I BOUGHT CROISSANT *TAIYAKI.*

***Taiyaki,* page 126**
A fish-shaped cake containing a filling (usually red bean paste). The croissant *taiyaki* is a hybrid pastry that uses croissant dough formed into rectangles, with the fish shape imprinted on the surface, as seen hanging from Usahara's mouth.

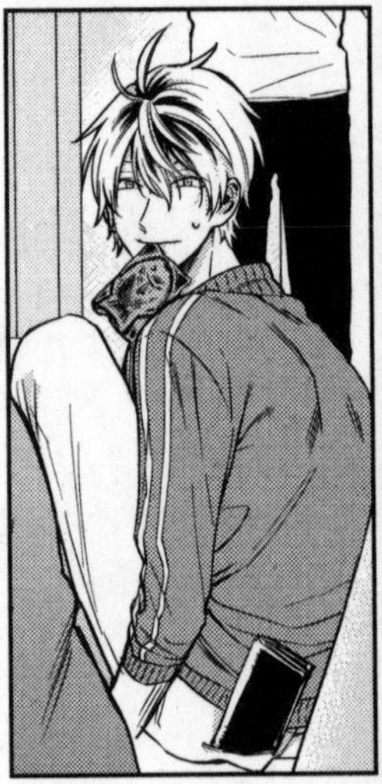

***Tsugi ni Kuru Manga Awards* and *Web Manga General Election*, page 129**
In both of these ranking competitions, thousands of manga series submitted for several genre-based categories are whittled down to a virtual handful of finalists, and the winners are determined by votes from fans.

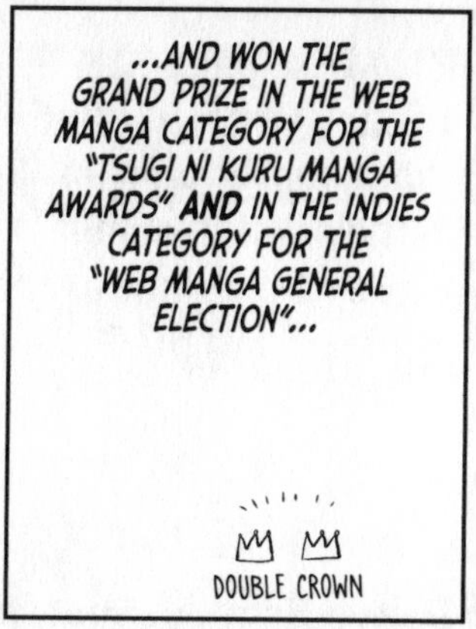
...AND WON THE GRAND PRIZE IN THE WEB MANGA CATEGORY FOR THE "TSUGI NI KURU MANGA AWARDS" AND IN THE INDIES CATEGORY FOR THE "WEB MANGA GENERAL ELECTION"...
DOUBLE CROWN

***Yakitori* and *kushiyaki*, page 187**
Both of these cuisines are skewer dishes, with *kushiyaki* being a blanket term for skewered foods either grilled or fried, meat or non-meat, whereas *yakitori* specifically refers to skewered chicken parts.

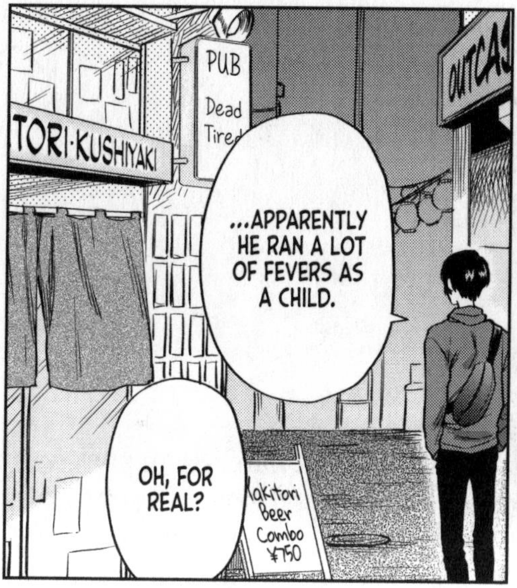
PUB
Dead
TORI·KUSHIYAKI
...APPARENTLY HE RAN A LOT OF FEVERS AS A CHILD.
OH, FOR REAL?
Yakitori Beer Combo ¥750

Lots of sake, page 216
Uramichi is seen purchasing the "super-value size" of a carton of sake. Similar to the reputation of boxed wine in the West, carton sake generally reflects one's desire to get as much liquor as possible for the lowest price, with little concern for quality.

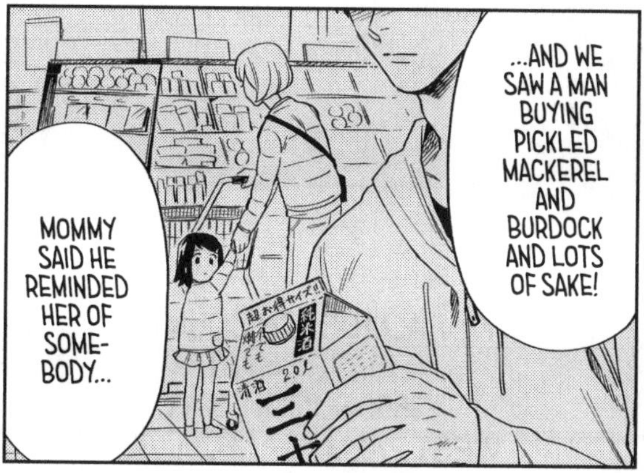
...AND WE SAW A MAN BUYING PICKLED MACKEREL AND BURDOCK AND LOTS OF SAKE!
MOMMY SAID HE REMINDED HER OF SOME-BODY...

Hiro Inn, page 228
Though written with Chinese characters that mean "Scarlet Sakura" in the original manga, *hiro* is pronounced the same as the word for "fatigue."

HOT SPRINGS
HIRO INN

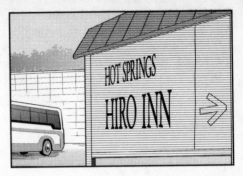

Dakyo Banquet Hall, page 233
Similar to "Hiro Inn," *dakyo* is written with characters that mean "Indolent Feast" in the original manga, but is pronounced the same as the word for "compromise."

BANQUET HALL
DAKYO

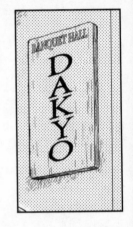

Naniwa, page 233
Naniwa was the name of an ancient capital that stood where the city of Osaka does today. Today, it is often used as a slightly poetic term for the city and area.

SHA LA LA LA LAAA
MATCHING LOOK OF
LOVE IN NANIWA
YASUKO OIDE
SHA SHA SHA
SHA- LA- LA- LA
SHA LA LA LA LA
SHWA LA LAAA

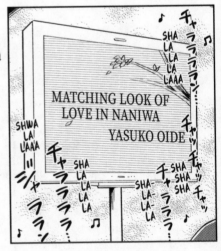

Nichome, page 240

Nichome is an area in Shinjuku, Tokyo that was historically–and is currently–known as a gay neighborhood. It is the hub for Japan's same-sex and LGBTQ+ subculture, and houses many restaurants, bars, bookstores, parks, clubs, and more.

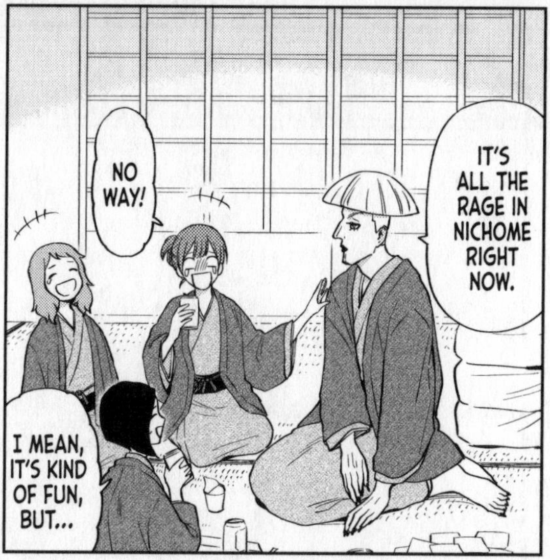
IT'S ALL THE RAGE IN NICHOME RIGHT NOW.
NO WAY!
I MEAN, IT'S KIND OF FUN, BUT...

***Onee*, page 245**

"*Onee*" (literally "older sister") is a term typically used for men who adopt distinctly feminine, and often flamboyant, mannerisms or speech patterns. In the early 2000s, the duality of femininity and crudity was iconic of the "*onee*" concept among gay men, but the term has since taken on a fluidity that can represent male-assigned persons (regardless of gender presentation and/or sexual orientation) who identify as female at heart. The term *onee* has come to be used in mass media as a digestible, albeit flexible identity.

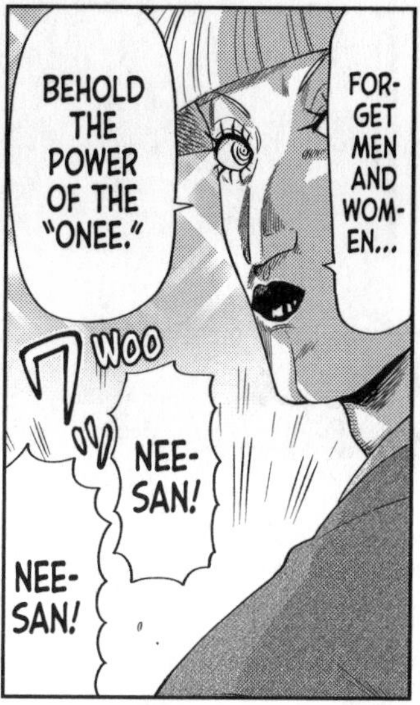
FOR-GET MEN AND WOM-EN...
BEHOLD THE POWER OF THE "ONEE."
WOO
NEE-SAN!
NEE-SAN!

Young characters and steampunk setting, like *Howl's Moving Castle* and *Battle Angel Alita*

Beyond the Clouds © 2018 Nicke / Ki-oon

A boy with a talent for machines and a mysterious girl whose wings he's fixed will take you beyond the clouds! In the tradition of the high-flying, resonant adventure stories of Studio Ghibli comes a gorgeous tale about the longing of young hearts for adventure and friendship!

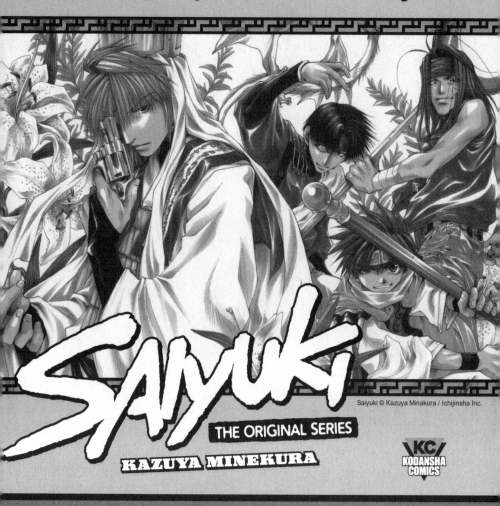

Knight of the Ice ©Yayoi Ogawa/Kodansha Ltd.

Yayoi Ogawa

SKATING THRILLS AND ICY CHILLS WITH THIS NEW TINGLY ROMANCE SERIES!

A rom-com on ice, perfect for fans of *Princess Jellyfish* and *Wotakoi*. Kokoro is the talk of the figure-skating world, winning trophies and hearts. But little do they know... he's actually a huge nerd! From the beloved creator of *You're My Pet* (*Tramps Like Us*).

Chitose is a serious young woman, working for the health magazine *SASSO*. Or at least, she would be, if she wasn't constantly getting distracted by her childhood friend, international figure skating star Kokoro Kijinami! In the public eye and on the ice, Kokoro is a gallant, flawless knight, but behind his glittery costumes and breathtaking spins lies a secret: He's actually a hopelessly romantic otaku, who can only land his quad jumps when Chitose is on hand to recite a spell from his favorite magical girl anime!

KC
KODANSHA
COMICS

PERFECT WORLD

Rie Aruga

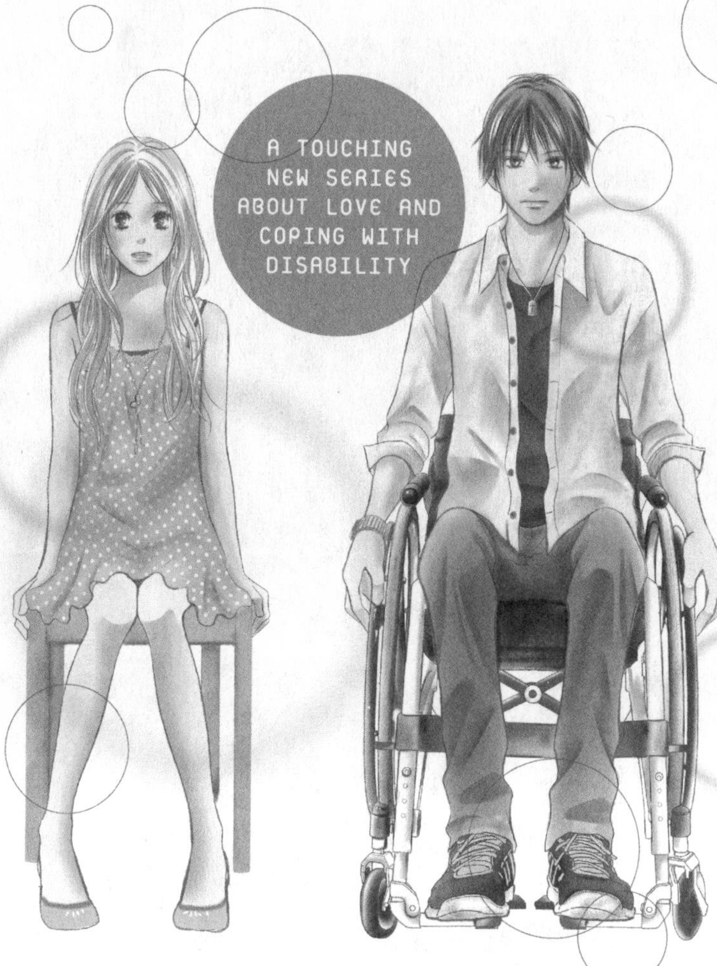
A TOUCHING NEW SERIES ABOUT LOVE AND COPING WITH DISABILITY

An office party reunites Tsugumi with her high school crush Itsuki. He's realized his dream of becoming an architect, but along the way, he experienced a spinal injury that put him in a wheelchair. Now Tsugumi's rekindled feelings will butt up against prejudices she never considered — and Itsuki will have to decide if he's ready to let someone into his heart...

"Depicts with great delicacy and courage the difficulties some with disabilities experience getting involved in romantic relationships... Rie Aruga refuses to romanticize, pushing her heroine to face the reality of disability. She invites her readers to the same tasks of empathy, knowledge and recognition."
—Slate.fr

"An important entry [in manga romance]... The emotional core of both plot and characters indicates thoughtfulness... [Aruga's] research is readily apparent in the text and artwork, making this feel like a real story."
—Anime News Network

KC KODANSHA COMICS

THE SWEET SCENT OF LOVE IS IN THE AIR! FOR FANS OF OFFBEAT ROMANCES LIKE *WOTAKOI*

Sweat and Soap © Kintetsu Yamada / Kodansha Ltd.

In an office romance, there's a fine line between sexy and awkward... and that line is where Asako — a woman who sweats copiously — meets Koutarou — a perfume developer who can't get enough of Asako's, er, scent. Don't miss a romcom manga like no other!

Something's Wrong With Us

NATSUMI ANDO

The dark, psychological, sexy shojo series readers have been waiting for!

A spine-chilling and steamy romance between a Japanese sweets maker and the man who framed her mother for murder!

Following in her mother's footsteps, Nao became a traditional Japanese sweets maker, and with unparalleled artistry and a bright attitude, she gets an offer to work at a world-class confectionary company. But when she meets the young, handsome owner, she recognizes his cold stare...

KC KODANSHA COMICS

The adorable new odd-couple cat comedy manga from the creator of the beloved *Chi's Sweet Home*, in full color!

Sue & Tai-chan

Konami Kanata

Sue is an aging housecat who's looking forward to living out her life in peace... but her plans change when the mischievous black tomcat Tai-chan enters the picture! Hey! Sue never signed up to be a catsitter! *Sue & Tai-chan* is the latest from the reigning meow-narch of cute kitty comics, Konami Kanata.

KC
KODANSHA
COMICS

CUTE ANIMALS AND LIFE LESSONS, PERFECT FOR ASPIRING PET VETS OF ALL AGES!

For an 11-year-old, Yuzu has a lot on her plate. When her mom gets sick and has to be hospitalized, Yuzu goes to live with her uncle who runs the local veterinary clinic. Yuzu's always been scared of animals, but she tries to help out. Through all the tough moments in her life, Yuzu realizes that she can help make things all right with a little help from her animal pals, peers, and kind grown-ups.

Every new patient is a furry friend in the making!

A SMART, NEW ROMANTIC COMEDY FOR FANS OF *SHORTCAKE CAKE* AND *TERRACE HOUSE*!

Date: 9/22/21

GRA 741.5 LIF V.1
Kuze, Gaku,
Life lessons with Uramichi
Oniisan.

A romance manga starring high school girl Meeko, who learns to live on her own in a boarding house whose living room is home to the odd (but handsome) Matsunaga-san. She begins to adjust to her new life away from her parents, but Meeko soon learns that no matter how far away from home she is, she's still a young girl at heart — especially when she finds herself falling for Matsunaga-san.

SAINT ☆ YOUNG MEN

A LONG AWAITED ARRIVAL IN PREMIUM 2-IN-1 HARDCOVER

After centuries of hard work, Jesus and Buddha take a break from their heavenly duties to relax among the people of Japan, and their adventures in this lighthearted buddy comedy are sure to bring mirth and merriment to all!

"Brilliant...the physical comedy and facial expressions will make you literally LOL."

—Sam Humphries
(host of *DC Daily*; writer, *Green Lanterns*, *Legendary Star-Lord*)

A Kodansha Comics Trade Paperback Original
Life Lessons with Uramichi Oniisan 1 copyright © 2017, 2018 Gaku Kuze
English translation copyright © 2020 Gaku Kuze

Published in the United States by Kodansha Comics, an imprint of
Kodansha USA Publishing, LLC, New York.

Publication rights for this English edition arranged through
Kodansha Ltd., Tokyo.

First published in Japan in 2017, 2018 by Ichijinsha Inc., Tokyo
as *Uramichi oniisan*, volumes 1 and 2.

ISBN 978-1-64651-114-3

Printed in the United States of America.

www.kodanshacomics.com

9 8 7 6 5 4 3 2 1
Translation: Matt Treyvaud
Lettering: Michael Martin
Editing: Vanessa Tenazas
Kodansha Comics edition cover design by Phil Balsman

Publisher: Kiichiro Sugawara

Director of publishing services: Ben Applegate
Associate director of operations: Stephen Pakula
Publishing services managing editor: Noelle Webster
Assistant production manager: Emi Lotto, Angela Zurlo
Logo and character art ©Kodansha USA Publishing, LLC